EASA Series

Published in association with the European Association of Social Anthropologists (EASA)
Series Editor: James G. Carrier, Senior Research Associate, Oxford Brookes University

Social anthropology in Europe is growing, and the variety of work being done is expanding. This series is intended to present the best of the work produced by members of the EASA, both in monographs and in edited collections. The studies in this series describe societies, processes and institutions around the world and are intended for both scholarly and student readership.

Being Human, Being Migrant

BEING HUMAN, BEING MIGRANT

Senses of Self and Well-Being

Edited by
Anne Sigfrid Grønseth

berghahn
NEW YORK · OXFORD
www.berghahnbooks.com

Published in 2013 by

Berghahn Books

www.berghahnbooks.com

Library of Congress Cataloging-in-Publication Data

Grønseth, Anne Sigfrid.
  Being human, being migrant: sense of self and well-being / edited by
Anne Sigfrid Gronseth.
      pages cm -- (EASA series; volume 23)
    ISBN 978-1-78238-045-0 (hardback: alk. paper) -- ISBN 978-1-78238-
046-7 (institutional ebook)
  1. Human beings--Migrations. 2. Immigrants--Psychology. 3.
Emigration and immigration--Psychological aspects. I. Title.
  GN370.G76 2013
    304.8--dc23
                                                                    2013020233

British Library Cataloguing in Publication Data
A catalogue record for this book is available from the British Library

Printed in the United States on acid-free paper

ISBN 978-1-78238-045-0 (hardback)
ISBN 978-1-78238-046-7 (institutional ebook)

Contents

Acknowledgements

In shaping this volume I have come to owe a debt to many people. I owe gratitude to all the authors of the volume for contributing their research and their insights. I express my sincere thanks to Nigel Rapport, Karen Fog Olwig, Pamela Stewart, Andrew Strathern, and Hogne Øian who have enhanced the publication by reading drafts and engaging in discussion. I also thank the EASA series editor James Carrier and the anonymous reviewers for their thoughtful and constructive comments that have helped to sharpen the focus of this volume. My thanks also go to the staff at Berghahn Books who have supplied kind and professional assistance throughout the publication process, and Lillehammer University College which has provided a research allowance permitting me to pursue this publication. Not least, I wish to express a heartfelt and humble thankfulness and respect to all the individuals who have allowed their stories and everyday lives to be displayed for publication. I hope that they consider the exposure and engagement in this research to have been worthwhile.

Anne Sigfrid Grønseth
Lillehammer, October 2012

Introduction

Being Human, Being Migrant

Senses of Self and Well-Being

Anne Sigfrid Grønseth

Introduction: Exploring Migrants' Life-Worlds

This volume is as much about being human as it is about being a migrant. It takes as its starting point the proposition that migrant experiences tell us about the human condition, on the basis that our multi-sensorial perceptions and experiences of well-being, self, other and humanity are challenged when people move between shifting social and cultural contexts. Our contemporary world is characterized by an increasing degree of movement that highlights how societies and cultural units are never separate but overlapping, rapidly changing and engaged in repeated processes of fission and fusion (Gellner 1994). Migrants, being people who move between places, times and conditions, can be seen as an archetypical example. This book underscores how migrant experiences accentuate some general aspects of the human condition by exploring migrants' movements not only as geographical movements from here to there, but also as movements that constitute an embodied, cognitive and existential experience of living 'in between' or on the 'borderlands' between differently figured life-worlds.

Current issues regarding multiculturalism have developed into some of the most heated debates between both politicians and academics. These debates tend to focus on relations between distinct groups of migrants and majority populations. This volume does not aim to engage in this important and pressing debate as such, but rather draws attention to an easily overlooked perspective, namely that of the migrants' individual narratives and experiences in everyday life. By exploring individuals' stories and life experiences, we can recognize how migrants' engagement in cultural practices, meanings and values are related to their pasts, while highlighting the human disposition to create and become involved in new cultural, social and climatic contexts. The following chapters present migrant narratives and ethnography from European countries. While not stressing the politically derived social structures of inclusion and exclusion as such, the volume presents the experiences of alienation and discrimination as they are perceived by individual migrants to and within Europe. The aim in including narratives that discuss the experiences of both voluntary middle-class and forced refugee migrants is to highlight how, beyond the significant differences, there are similarities that illuminate their shared and equivalent experiences as humans as much as migrants.

Migrants carry a unique and vital experience of habituated and familiar life-worlds that are constituted, shaped and figured socially and culturally (Holland et al. 2001; Bourdieu 1989; Husserl 1970), while also being challenged by crossing over to other life-worlds that are both similar and different. Inspired by phenomenological perspectives, a life-world is a horizon of all our experiences that creates a background against which identity and meaning emerge and are decided upon. Such life-worlds are not static and unchangeable, but are the dynamic horizons in which we live, and which 'live with us' (Husserl 1970). This implies that nothing can enter or appear in our life-world except what is lived. As such, the life-world is always intimately linked to the individual person's historicity, though not to such an extent that it is purely individual. Rather, the life-world is inherently intersubjective in terms of the possibility of communicating and sharing meaning, while also necessarily being personal and individual. This perspective emerges in all the volume's chapters as in their different ways they all highlight individual migrants' experiences as they are shaped in the intersection of individual historicity and social environmental structures.

Furthermore, examining migrants' life-worlds confronts us with a tension between what we can conceive as differently constituted life-worlds and single human life-worlds. Instead of taking a fixed position, this volume explores the land in between, recognizing differences both among individuals and groups, while also acknowledging aspects that are common and mutual based on an understanding of a shared humanity. This position is reflected in the concern with how migrants carry with them fragments of the familiar and known, while simultaneously being confronted with new and unknown life-worlds. Thus, migrants can be seen to live their everyday lives on the borderlands in between differently constituted, though mutually human, life-worlds.

Being Migrant: A Human Capacity for Agency and Creativity

Before focusing on migrants' reasons for leaving and on what happens when they arrive, this book highlights the condition in between as it is embodied in people's senses of self, well-being, emotions and consciousness in everyday living. It underscores how studies of migrants can open up 'zones in between' places, times, life-worlds, moralities and identities, and suggests how such a journey may bring peoples and individuals into existential experiences of being in their own right as human beings. Moreover, studying the daily lives of migrants requires knowledge that can help to stimulate peaceful coexistence in a world characterized by crises of migration, globalization, war and conflict. Thus, by relating to anthropological literature on migration and refugee issues, this volume adopts a perspective that explores the potential of mutual human solidarity. This view is seen to be in line with the volume's appreciation of a life-world, as it is how 'we, each "I-the-man" and all of us together, belong to the world as living with one another in the world; and the world is our world, valid for our consciousness as existing precisely through this "living together"' (Husserl 1970: 108).

Individually the chapters draw attention to the here and now, to memories and nostalgia, to future dreams and visions. As a whole, the volume aims to demonstrate how the past, present and future in migrants' experience, imagination and improvization interact and offer zones of ambivalence and ambiguity between the (often nostalgic) remembrance of the past and hope for new beginnings (see also Rapport in this volume). In this dialectic lies, I suggest, an opportunity for a complex and subtle agency that appears in the mundane day-to-day negotiations and dealings. This is an agency that stems from the vulnerability, pain, fantasy and hope, that can allow migrants to transcend what they have left, the boundaries they newly encounter, and the ways in which they creatively craft lives of their own. It should be stressed that this 'everyday agency' does not always or necessarily enable such transcendence, fulfilment and achievement, but may instead turn to self-denial and self-destruction, as well as upheaval and longstanding resistance to perceived structural injustice and discrimination. However, by adopting an approach to migration that addresses the human condition, the human capacity to expand and transform experiences within everyday life become of crucial concern.

The migration narratives presented in the individual chapters contribute to migration studies as they tend to be stories of suffering, though they are also followed by longer-term collective, familial or individual success. Stories such as those told in this volume carry messages of agency as this relates to individuals' creativity, imagination, improvization and humanity. The chapters tell stories of how, within often restrictive and oppressive circumstances, migrants and refugees negotiate and improvise in their daily lives to create a better life for themselves and their families. In this exploration of migrants' experiences and narratives, the human capacity to create appears in everyday habituated behaviour, in familiar and traditional practices, as the individual needs to respond actively to shifting possibilities and constraints produced by the actual time, context and environment. Thus, the volume discusses how, in the realm of everyday life, the habituated and repetitive alleviate pain and fear while alternating and being supplied with moments of transcendence and creativity that transform the self and the world (see Lefebvre 2002). Through the migrant experience of moving to a new place and environment, the habituated and familiar self and body are sensed in new ways, and thus the person's practices and perceptions of the old and new environments also shift, even when a familiar form of practice is being repeated. While practice and performance may be repetitive and (almost) the same in form, the individual, positioned in a new context, actively searches for new and different ways to achieve the desired sensations and experiences that are attached to such practices.

This view recognizes how people negotiate, perform and improvise creatively while engaging with the different realities that exist in different locations and at different times. Thus, creativity is not seen as equal to innovation and originality. Indeed, the view I am suggesting is in line with Tim Ingold and Elizabeth Hallam's point that creative power is seen as an effect of the 'freedom of the human imagination ... to transcend the determinations of both nature and society' (Ingold and Hallam 2007: 3). Thus, the chapters illustrate how creativity and newness reach beyond the search for the exceptional individual as it stands out and against the collectivity, or the novelty in the present as it is distinct from the traditions of the past, or the active mind as it differs from what is passive or unwilling (see Ingold and Hallam 2007: 3). Rather, agency and creativity are seen as embodied human capacities that respond and adjust to day-to-day living in shifting times, circumstances and environments, and as such transform senses of self and well-being as highlighted in the experience of migration. It should also be underlined that while individuals are creatively involved in migration processes, the cultural and social changes in turn enrich or impoverish the conditions in which creativity can emerge.

Migrancy: A Quest for Human Recognition

Migrancy is a concept that encompasses a variety of different people and individuals who all move for different reasons (Chambers 1994). The present volume suggests how movement is not only 'the quintessential experience' of our age (Berger 1984: 55), but suggests that migration, as it involves distinct kinds of movement, is a 'quintessential experience of being human'. This appears in how migrancy is seen to include the geographical, sensuous, emotional and cognitive movement of migrants. Furthermore, the ethnographic cases presented below discuss various individual migrant experiences rather than teasing out any categories such as labour or forced migration. The case studies present both men and women, although with an emphasis on female experiences and narratives. While this volume does not have gender and woman studies as its focus, I suggest that it may modestly contribute to our understanding of the experiences of contemporary gendered migration, as it demonstrates how female migrants meet shifting challenges due not only to how distinct societies view women as a social category, but also to how social structures and cultural ideologies shape women's lives and affect their sense of self and subjective identity (e.g. Moore 1988, 1994;

Lewin and Leap 2002; Behar 2003; Mahler and Pessar 2001, 2006; Geller and Stockett 2006). The feminist attention to variability, issues of power and forces of social and cultural change is addressed in this volume by narrating women migrants' stories that display experiences of relative isolation (see in particular Svašek and Maehara), powerlessness (see in particular Pinelli and Grønseth), and poverty (see in particular Pinelli). Simultaneously, the chapters discuss the individual women's and men's (see Georgiadou and Mikola) everyday agency and creativity in performing, negotiating, and dealing with her/his new environment and conditions as they are perceived and embodied as social experiences framed by being refugees, immigrants and minority groups, stigmatized and alienated. However, the volume's concern with both genders' senses of self and well-being takes it beyond women studies as such; it addresses issues of identity and difference as they intersect with social positions such as minority groups, ethnicity, race, class and age.

Moreover, by addressing the human capacities for agency and creativity, it is demonstrated that gender and other social and cultural distinctions are not innate biological differences or essentials;. instead the emphasis is on the creation of subjects through the exercise of power (Foucault 1977, 1980) and on the ongoing performative nature of creating differences between human beings. Thus, recognizing the difference in gendered experience, the volume seeks to transcend issues of gender and to highlight the human condition, encompassing a mutuality of differences, such as male and female experiences, as these are displayed in the different studies of being gendered, being a migrant and being human in these chapters.

Whatever the particular reasons for migration, the practice of migration in itself, the volume argues, instantiates a set of experiences and capacities that are intrinsic to our humanity. It is part of a human ontology to transcend particular life-worlds, as Nigel Rapport puts it (Epilogue in this volume); migration is often precipitated by a lack of being recognized as a fully human being in a 'home' milieu and a political desire to achieve recognition and expression elsewhere. Migration illustrates a capacity for expression and a desire which can be said to call for a human (global) moral response. Acknowledging both moral and ontological perspectives, the volume addresses the connection between being a migrant and being human as it understands the migrant's constituting of self, identity and well-being as a universal human quest undertaken by an agent.

When examining various forms of migrancy, the collection uses both traditional and more recent concepts such as 'labour migrants', 'exiles', 'refugees', 'asylum seekers', 'diasporas', 'creoles', 'hybrids' and 'transnationals'; but these are also transcended, as each author seeks to go beyond these categories to seek what is understood as a mutual humanness. Accordingly, terms which are closely associated with these various traditions of migrant studies – such as assimilation, integration, class, ethnicity and rootedness – are less frequently used, as the volume highlights concepts that recognize the commonalities and mutuality of being human, rather than classifications and distinctions.

This approach of mutual humanity rests in a view in which identity and belonging are created in the course of social life, rather than in an 'ethnos' that is often designated as an indisputable 'biological fact' (see Baumann 1997: 213). Furthermore, it is recognized that identity is individually created and defined in interaction and performance, rather than being pre-ascribed (see also Amit-Talai 1995: 131). While agreeing with these views, the volume focuses on the bodily, cognitive and emotional experiences of migration, stressing the way in which assertions of fixed and closed identities, communities and categories are, as Nigel Rapport argues, ontologically and morally illicit (Epilogue in this volume).

In the following, I will address briefly how this volume is situated within anthropological studies of migration and how it offers a new perspective. I will also reflect on how the migrants' engagement with and experience of everyday life captures a human disposition of movement and change, and position of living "in between" or on the borderlands of differently figured life-worlds. The third section addresses the way in which the contributors to this volume emphasize migrants' sense of well-being, belonging and self as this appears in a complex existential agency while moving between and dealing with the past, the here and now, and their hopes for the future. The fourth section discusses how migrants' experiences offer a keyhole into a shared and reciprocal existential humanness that bespeaks a cosmopolitan morality of responsibility and solidarity with all human beings. Finally, an overview of the individual chapters shows how the distinct theoretical approaches nevertheless share a common bottom-up and face-to-face focus on migrants' movements, which impress themselves on the ethnographer and provide insights into self and agency that are as concerned with 'being human' as 'being a migrant'.

Studies of Migration: Towards Everyday Life Agency and Well-Being

As this book is as much about being human as being a migrant, the aim of this section is not to present a complete overview or thorough discussion of the anthropology of migration (see rather Malkki 1995a; Brettell 2000; Foner 2000). However, I will briefly point out some facets and features that can help to identify this volume's position as it examines migrant experiences with the intention of imparting something about what it is to be human. Thus, the following is not meant to assess the theoretical shifts and empirical concerns of migration studies as such, but to sketch out how studies of migration can be seen to have progressed and thus highlight this volume's overall concern with individual agency and the human condition.

The early migration studies of the 1940s and 1950s generally addressed the fundamental socio-economic changes or rapid urbanization and shifts from agricultural subsistence to industrial labour (e.g. Epstein 1958; Gluckman

1965; Mitchell 1969 and others). As anthropologists began to focus on peasants and 'tribesmen' living in the cities, the concern with migration increased (e.g. Mayer 1961; Mangin 1970 and others). Many of these studies felt a need to develop analytical concepts that could grasp social processes better than the earlier emphasis on structures. Thus, studies of migration saw a shift of interest in anthropology from principles and patterns of social and cultural order towards a focus on continuous processes of change and movement.

With an emphasis on case studies developed by Max Gluckman and the Manchester School, the concepts of the social network and group identity became vital in anthropology and the social sciences and still run through much work in contemporary anthropology (Roger and Vertovec 1995; Banks 1996; Harbottle 2000; Schiller and Faist 2010; Schiller and Çağlar 2011). Generally, anthropological research on migration pays attention to the places that migrants originate from and the places they go, including how people locally respond to global processes. Brettell (2000: 98) points out how issues of adaptation and cultural change, forms of social organization, identity and ethnicity all became of central concern. The theme of ethnicity was hotly debated following Barth's (1998 [1969]) influential conceptualization highlighting the fluent, contextual negotiation of boundaries for ethnicity and identity. An appreciation of the fluency and contextual perspective of new concepts such as hybridity (e.g. Çağlar 1997), creolization (e.g. Palmie 2006) and cosmopolitanism (e.g. Wardle 2000; Wardle and Rapport 2010; Breckenridge et al. 2002; Werbner 2008; Nowicka and Rovisco 2009; Schiller et al. 2011) came to the forefront of analysis.

While studies of identity remain of great interest for anthropology, the concept of transnationalism has become vital to our understanding of the agency and practices of today's migrants (Schiller et al. 1992; Basch et al. 1994; Portes et al. 1999; Levitt et al. 2003; Vertovec 2009). The interest in transnationalism continues and runs parallel with a growing concern with globalization, which together make up a framework that has provided an opportunity to rethink notions of culture in light of global flows and forms of deterritorialization (Appadurai 1996; Hannerz 1996; Olwig and Hastrup 1997; Gupta and Ferguson 1997), which are crucial in shaping the migrant experience and human conditions. The combined concern for global flows and fluent identities has also led to an interest in multi-ethnic settings and multiculturalism (Grillo 1998), while underscoring the need for a non-reifying understanding of culture (Baumann 1999; Watson 2000). While recognizing and including a concern for the transnational and multicultural, this volume aims to reach beyond the substance of relations and cultures in themselves by attending to migrants' sense of self and well-being as constituted in experiences of the moving dynamics that take place in the areas in between places, times, relations, cultures and life-worlds.

In the literature on migration and transnationalism, one also finds an increasing attention being paid to second- and third-generation migrants and the way in which their relations with or images of past origins might affect their lives today (Schiller et al. 1992; Basch et al. 1994; Hinnels 2007; Kibria 2002; Roosens 1989). In the aftermath of the Second World War and the era of (post-)colonialism, migration studies have included the global situation of increased forced international migration related to conflict and war. In this context one finds that refugees have become a vital object for anthropological and other social science studies. Much of this research has been conducted close to the war zones and refugee camps (Malkki 1995b; Daniel and Knudsen 1995; Agier 2005; Hammond 2004; Zmegac 2007).

Forced migration and refugee studies have not only focused on ethnicity and conflict. The war experiences of the refugees have had overwhelming humanitarian costs, including losses and reduced social and economic security, as well as social status. Many studies have focused on questions relating to social suffering, cultural continuity, illness and health (Schulz and Hammer 2003; Sideris 2003; Coker 2004; Migliorino 2008; Bradby and Hundt 2010; Oakley and Grønseth 2007; Grønseth 2010). The present volume is situated within migration and refugee research, with well-being, agency and creativity as core issues. Questions of health, well-being, and migration are complex because of the linkage between social forces and ill health. Research suggests that mental health concerns frequently relate to more general issues, such as economic welfare, environmental living conditions and the kinds of resources available to a person, family or community (Desjarlais et al. 1995: 15). The reasons for dislocation, the escape journeys and the living conditions where a person or family resettles create threats and challenges for personal and social well-being. However, this book looks at the more mundane experiences that migrants and refugees face in a variety of contexts such as negotiating work and education opportunities, making asylum applications, and striving to achieve a sense of belonging within family and kin relations, as well as within larger social networks.

Within studies of multiculturalism (Lamphere 1992; Modood and Werbner 1997; Sanjek 1998; Baumann 1996; Werbner 2002; Wise and Velayutham 2009), there has also been a shift of interest towards the roles of individual agency and consciousness. In many studies of globalization, multiculturalism and migration, questions of individual and group identity, together with concepts of diaspora, network, authenticity, belonging, relatedness, place making, home and origin, all became topics for discussion (e.g. Rapport and Dawson 1998; Brettell 2003; Manuh 2005; Delanty et al. 2008; Olwig 2007; Vertovec 2010 and others). However, in more recent studies these questions have been downplayed as concepts such as urban diversity, super-diversity and conviviality have come to the fore (Schiffauer et al. 2004; Vertovec 2007; Hylland Eriksen 2007; Vertovec and Wessendorf 2010).

The notion of super-diversity is meant to underline a level and complexity that transcend multiculturality, as it tends to focus on distinct groups and individuals within these, and more so highlight the dynamic interplay of variables such as multiple origins, transnational connections, socio-economic differentiation and legal stratification among immigrants who have arrived in

Europe during the last decade (Vertovec 2007). Through this volume's inclusion of chapters that narrate migrant experiences as they relate to different legal statuses, socio-economic positions and transnational connections, and from distinct places of origin, while all currently living in Europe, I suggest that the volume as a whole casts light on the super-diverse complex dynamics at play that shape the migrant experience and human circumstances. Furthermore, the volume's concern with both refugee and middle-class migrant narratives demonstrates the diversity and complexity of migrant experiences, while exposing a shared human sense of self and a shared quest for well-being.

Being Human: Experiences of Everyday Life in the Borderlands of the 'In between'

To capture the experience of living in the borderlands – bodily, existentially, emotionally and cognitively – the volume refers to a phenomenological zone which is experienced as being inbetween distinct though overlapping life-worlds. Living in such a zone involves habituated and familiar relations, events, practices, meanings and values no longer being as clearly distinct, determined or full as they were (see Jackson 2009: xii). Entering the border zones between different places and life-worlds implies realizing that things are not necessarily what we conceive them to be: they have no fixed and distinct essence, and are open to new interpretations, meanings and connections. This is reflected in how Svašek, in this volume, suggests how Anna, a migrant woman from the Netherlands who settled in Northern Ireland and more than a decade later is preparing to return to the Netherlands, makes sense of her life as she is confronted with distinct though mutual notions of personhood, family ties and personal fears, dreams and hopes. As such, the chapter offers a personalized migrant tale of the challenges of loss, love and hopes, while also being a human tale at the heart of everyday life on the borderlands of the inbetween.

Focusing the investigations on migrants' senses of self and well-being, the volume addresses how transformations, creativity and agency appear in the improvizations, negotiations and narrated stories of the less attended experiences of ordinary day-to-day living (see also Sandywell 2004). Everyday life, I suggest, can be seen to link social and institutional structures with individual performance, subjective experience and social practices (Lefebvre 2002). The different chapters demonstrate and discuss how moments and locations of everyday life bring together structures, activities, emotions, sensations and meanings that make up a wholeness of the individual self and of social reality. By exploring narratives and narrations from the realm of everyday life, the volume offers an insight into how routine and tradition alternate with dynamic improvization, negotiation, performance and creative transformations as the migrants and refugees are exposed to new structures, environments and conditions. This relates to the way in which the volume understands narrations as more than a mere list of events on a timeline since they convey the significance and meaning of events by situating interactions with an influence on other events and actions in a single, interrelated account. As such, narration is a form of communication that arranges human actions and events by specifying their interactive or cause-and-effect relations to the whole. Thus, narratives are always about the explanation and meaning of events and actions in human life, however simple these may be (Smith 2003: 65–66). In this view the close link between narration and everyday life is suggested to highlight the migrant experience as it shaped in the borderland between individual subjectivity and structural conditions, which together tell us about the human condition in which we sense our own selves and our well-being.

As Michael Jackson points out, 'Border situations not only imply a radical break from the known; they presage new possibilities of relatedness that often transcend specifically interpersonal ties' (2009: xiii). Thus, living on the borders actualizes the human capacity to form bonds and connect to any Other whatever without limits. In this context, we address how the study of migrants, as they are conceived to live on the borders and inbetween, illuminates the becoming and nature of human beings. As Wittgenstein observes (see Monk 1990: 302–3), exploring statements in themselves does not convey the existential and immediate depth of nature. Rather, the nature of things appears when the 'shifting spaces between statements, descriptions, and persons, and in the course of events' (Jackson 2009: xiv) are explored. The human self is therefore recognized as creative, moving and flexible, open and ready to connect with new others and new environments.

This agentive force in the migrant experience is explored in Barbara Pinelli's chapter about Rolanda, a Togolese woman who sought asylum in Italy. Exploring Rolanda's subjectivity in terms of vulnerability and fantasy, Pinelli shows us how Rolanda is confronted by power dynamics, yet managed to regain a sense of independence, desire for motherhood and experiences of well-being. This flexibility and movement of the self is illuminated by exploring the experience of migrants living in between the spaces of the here and there, and the shifting sense of time between memories of the past, the here and now, and the imagery of the future. The individual migrant narratives of the volume suggest how the migrant experiences the tenses – the past, present and the future – as differently located spatially. It appears that the past and the future are perceived as located somewhere other than where the migrants are placed in the here and now, while the spatiality of the present is perceived as temporary, as not meant to be or not meant to be continued (Ricoeur 1980). Furthermore, I suggest, it is from the sense of self, as it improvises, moves and connects with others, that we experience (new) wholeness, identity, well-being and success. Thus, living on the borders not only engenders suffering from endings, losses and uncertainty, but also supplies an existential and agentive force in creating new beginnings, selves and well-being.

The study of migrants is seen to illustrate how people's and the self's movements are always and above all bodily experiences. This view relies on the phenomenology of Merleau-Ponty (1962 [1945]), in which the self and consciousness do not come from a disembodied thought, but from the bodily disposition and intention to act. The body is always intentionally positioned in a particular place in the world, from which it perceives and embodies its surroundings. This perspective emphasizes how individuals, on an existential level, perceive, position and figure themselves in everyday life experiences and in wider social and cultural environments. Recognizing bodily perceptions as pre-objective, they create the existential ground for consciousness and knowledge (see Csordas 1994).

The existential and emotional power in changing bodily position in the world is illustrated in Naoko Maehara's chapter, in which she explores the narrative of Naomi, a Japanese woman who migrated to Ireland. Maehara addresses how Naomi's bodily attunement and subjectivity are formed by her relationships with the physical and social environment, as well as through the intrapersonal processes of bodily memory and symbolic formation. Thus the chapter demonstrates how Naomi experiences a movement in her embodied self and creates a sense of belonging in the new place of Ireland that links her current experiences and embodied past.

This relates to the volume's suggestion that it is not migrants' consciousness or a thought alone that brings the body from one place to another. Rather, I argue that exploring migrants' everyday lives in the borderlands illuminates how consciousness expresses interrelationships between self and other, subject and object, which are pre-conditioned through the intermediary of the body (Jackson 1995: 169). As such, a phenomenology of 'being-in-the-world' and embodiment stresses social and cultural processes like migration as part of perception, existential experiences and human capacities (see also Grønseth 2010).

The bodily perceptive experience implies a sense of home, of being in the world, as a mobile habitat (Chambers 1994: 4). Thus, living and dwelling are conceived as a mobile habitation of time and space, not as fixed and closed structures, but as supplying an opening and movement in what constitutes our sense of identity, place, belonging and well-being. There is no one place, time, language or tradition that can claim this role. It emerges that the migrant self is challenged by the differences of other life-worlds and discovers that its living is sustained beyond encounters and confrontations with other places, histories and other peoples. This implies, as is evident in Anna's return home (Svašek, this volume), that there is no return to home other than to the existential experience of the initial self-in-the-world. Moreover, being in between or in movement does not necessarily imply geographical movement or travel. Migrancy involves a movement in which point of departure and point of arrival are uncertain and mutable.

Metaphorically speaking, migrants can be seen to live in a zone that is characterized by 'the limit, as happening between the two deaths, as the point in which death is engaged with life' (Das 1995: 161; see also Lacan 1992: 270–83, which includes Lacan's discussion of the Greek tragedy *Antigone* by Sophocles). As migrants leave something behind, embody and engage with life anew, they demonstrate what is seen as a human natural disposition. From this I suggest that intrinsically the experience of living in between – neither here nor there – involves the uniqueness of being human (see Lacan 1992). Fundamentally, it refers to a human need to be able actively to extend and involve oneself, to be recognized and mirrored by the others, which together provide a space for reflection and the creation of self, well-being and life-projects (Rapport 2003). When migrants experience alienation, exclusion, repression and pain, this volume suggests they suffer an embodied (often unspeakable) acknowledgement of social circumstances (Lacan 1992; Nussbaum 1986; Grønseth 2010) related to power inequalities, legal status and relations between migrants and states, bureaucrats, officials and others. Moreover, such a view is seen to contribute to an acknowledgement of the limits of the body and self and a recognition of the humanness of voices, bodies and worlds on the other side, beyond one's self. Seeking to cross borders, the self is paradoxically forced to confront its own confines and by effort (and often pain) engage in relations across them. Therefore, bringing one's self into the borderlands potentially (and hopefully) opens a space for recognition and responsibility for other human and mutual life-worlds, places, histories and futures. As such, engaging in everyday life with others brings one's self in between and offers a human experience of movement and migrancy in mind and body. Thus, I suggest that the migrant experience captures vital aspects of what it is to be human, while also recognizing that the human position is to inhabit and explore this passage. As such, being human means being a migrant.

Migrants' Sense of Self and Well-Being: Existential Agency and Temporality

Studies of migrants and refugees tend to focus on the suffering, the pain, the losses, the splintering of kin and family, the broken bounds, the nostalgia, the homesickness, illness and disease. Illness, pain and well-being always need to be understood as part of the systems of power relations and resistance within social structures (see e.g. Farmer 2005; Scheper-Hughes 1992; Das 1990; Kleinman 1988). The present volume suggests that the migrant experience comes from in between these, in a way within but also transcending such structures and powers. Although highlighting individual migrants' everyday experiences, the chapters recognize how these experiences are perceived and conceived from a position in between that calls for a critical assessment of distinct and overlapping life-worlds, social structures, moralities and identities. Such critical assessment is vital in all chapters, though it appears via different approaches. Naoko Mahera's chapter about Naomi explores images of identity and well-being, and discusses how cognitive, emotional and bodily experiences of home, belonging and self interplay with experiences of local inclusion and family membership in Ireland. Thus, the chapter draws attention to how, by investigating migrants' everyday experiences, one can grasp the multifaceted agency that emerges from the contradictions and tensions of living in between, not only between places and times, but as a cognitive, bodily, emotional and existential human experience.

Experiences of pain and well-being are embedded in social relations and constitute a crucial part of the individual's constitution of herself or himself, as self is seen as an embodied relation (Grønseth 2010). When recognizing how the distribution of infectious diseases and pathologies reflects social inequalities (Farmer 2001: 5), and how education, employment and health are unevenly shared, the meanings and explanations of a person's level of welfare can easily be reduced to external circumstances or some inner core essence. Instead, this volume looks at the zone in between, in which the struggle for being is not a pre-set and fixed course, but a dynamic relational process of self-reflection and dialogue between the environment and a person's capacities (see Jackson 1998, 2005; Sartre 1956). Studies of well-being do not necessarily imply the investigation of the actual (or a static) condition of well-being in its various empirical forms. Indeed, I suggest seeing them as explorations of a quest for different experiences, sensations and feelings of comfort, contentment, security, joy, pleasure, achievement and success, which may occur in various degrees along a continuum between illness and health as it shifts in different everyday moments and phases of a life-span. Thus, well-being is understood as something to be experienced not as a static condition of comfort, but rather as a dynamic and shifting experience that comes from the border zone in which the self is realized, not independently, but as a mutual part of the other.

Recognizing that knowledge and the meaning of suffering and well-being are attained and embodied by living in an everyday world on the limits and borders, between fractions and portions of social life and meaning, I suggest that an existential agency emerges. It is understood as a bodily experience of intersubjectivity, made up of paradoxes, contradictions and ambivalences. It is an agency that gains force not from an individual will towards self-realization or authenticity, but from the everyday struggle to create continuous intuitive, idealistic and opportunistic changes of course that suggest more or less satisfactory solutions to the events that form the life lived. Such complex and existential agency is discussed in all of the chapters, and strikingly so in the stories of Rolanda who opposes victimization (Pinelli, this volume), the two young Russian asylum seekers in Slovenia who by means of silence create a space for dialogue (Mikola, this volume), and Ismat and Zhia who make efforts to be resilient by intertwining habit and creativity in everyday life (Georgiadou, this volume).

It is in border situations and critical junctures – such as migrancy and exile – that we stretch ourselves between a sense of being actively engaged in the familiar and being passively acted upon in a foreign world (Jackson 2009: 37) and that we most fully experience our human nature. Being in movement and migrancy, which implies living in between, provides a feeling of being torn and thrown away, while paradoxically also being thrown open to new possibilities and connections. However, from living in between, or living in ambivalence, one does not always succeed in creating a new life of one's own. In the case of Rolanda, living so to speak between Togo and Italy, it is exposed as subject to changing and contradictory emotions and understandings of herself and the world around her (Pinelli, this volume). Taken together, the stories demonstrate how (inter-)relations of the past, present and future constitute senses of self and well-being as part of being both migrant and human.

Pinelli's chapter reminds us that when the self is stretched to the limits of its endurance by suffering, not all persons find ways in which to carve out a new life. As Jackson (2009) observes, some persons find it enough to survive, having lived through the rupture and the night to see the dawn (Jaspers 2000: 535, 543), while others surrender. Others again may 'migrate inwards', struggling with anxieties of separation, a lack of continuity and the sense of self connected to the present life. Recognizing that all that is new requires a kind of ending (like falling behind, forgetting or sometimes death), this volume addresses migrancy as the human disposition and potential to create anew and connect to others, in which the sense of self emerges.

As in Pinelli's chapter, Mahera's highlights how the self is seen to occur in the transfiguration between relationships, rather than in any pre-defined and distinct essence or identity. This fits in with my suggestion that it is in the space of the intersubjective as experienced in the interplay between self and other – being other persons, gods, objects, institutions, ideologies, cosmologies, ideas or imagery – that the sense of self, pain and well-being emerge. Dealing with and negotiating between memories of what used to be, the here and now, and hopes and dreams for the future not only brings about a sense of loss and longing, but also the motivation and direction to actions in the present that can provide experiences of pleasure and success in retrieving a life of one's own in the new settlement and surroundings.

This view also appears in Georgiadou's chapter, in which the everyday life of two young Afghan refugee men in Athens, Zhia and Ismat, illustrates how self and subjectivity emerge from experiences, emotions, motivations and dreams challenged by the socio-political and cultural environment. Thus the lives of Zhia and Ismat demonstrate how the subjective self carries the relations between memories of the past, experiences of the present and aspirations for the future. Many migrant studies have explored how nostalgia and memories of the past interact in migrants' experience and practices of the here and now (e.g. Schneider 2001). This volume introduces a novel perspective by recognizing that interests, visions, dreams and hopes for the future also play a significant role in promoting a sense of self, meaning, motivation and direction for the practices of the everyday life of today. Grønseth's chapter introduces us to Malar, a Tamil refugee woman resettled in Norway, and discusses how her pain is linked to breaches between past, present and future. While Malar experiences being squeezed between the Norwegian and Tamil life-worlds, she re-creates and negotiates embodied practices and opens up a space in which to create a life of her own in the present, motivated by visions for the future.

This view relates to how, by not simply passively living and reproducing our life-world, but by actively producing and transforming, we create a sense of life as worth living and a sense of well-being (encapsulated in Bourdieu's concept of 'conatus'; Jackson 2005: xxii). If a person's habitus (Bourdieu 1989) is no longer efficient, the capacity for action is challenged and may lead to a loss of confidence, contentment and joy, and eventually to a feeling that life has lost its meaning and is no longer worth living. Such an experience deeply affects our sense of time (Jackson 2005: xxii). Time is no longer experienced as forthcoming (Bourdieu 2000) but as an empty and threatening absence of a future, mixed with a diffuse longing for the past. As embodied history, or habitus, implies the presence of the past in the present and conditions the possibilities of the future, living on the borders – as migrant, refugee, asylum seeker, culturally torn so-called 'halfies' or second-class citizens – profoundly challenges the sense of self as it is associated to what is forthcoming. If there is no hope for the future, one may seek a sort of recognition through violence toward oneself or others. This is illustrated in Maša Mikola's chapter, in which she discloses how two young Russian men encounter the Ljubljana Asylum Home in Slovenia, and enter an existential struggle to retain a sense of self and of the future by stretching communication and engagement beyond particular social structures, places and languages. It appears that migrants' challenges in creating self and well-being are linked to an existential need to be recognized as mutual human beings beyond distinctions and diversity.

Being a Migrant, Being Human: Calling for a Cosmopolitan Morality and Solidarity

Our contemporary world is characterized by increased migration and a global politics that offers the promise of a shared human identity and human rights, while presenting a Janus face of Othering and stigma leading to discrimination, exploitation, war and genocide. In this light the present volume explores how the study of migrants' everyday lives can contribute insights in a shared humanity across difference that inspires a cosmopolitan ethics of solidarity and peaceful co-existence. It is a cosmopolitan approach that appreciates group identities, while also recognizing the individual freedom and human rights in encounters with actual social contexts of structures, practices, meanings and values (see Rapport 2010). A cosmopolitan appreciation of a human singularity – as all humans are equally human – holds out an invitation to a mutual and imparted and as such – a single human life-world, though not denying difference and variation, as these are seen as a crucial aspect of humanity. Searching for knowledge about the human condition, a cosmopolitan and phenomenological perspective of an 'embodied being in the world' fits in with the volume's ethnographic endeavour as created in the borderlands between ethnographer and informant, as between self and other, and us and them (see also Grønseth and Davis 2010). As the chapters of this volume demonstrate, it is by employing the methods of participant observation, often demanding painful engagement in face-to-face relations while sharing and embodying events in the everyday life of the Other, that anthropology attains its characteristic and distinct mode of knowledge. While the chapters present narratives of migrants' movements, both voluntarily and forced, it is through anthropologists' willingness to move to the limits and enter the borderlands between distinctly figured life-worlds that we learn not only about migrant experiences, but also what it is like to be human.

Taking this insight to be at the heart of anthropology and the ethnographer's effort requires us to recognize that knowledge exchanged and created at the borders entails not only contractually agreed bonds but an ethical responsibility to the people and persons with whom one has lived and worked. Such a perspective recognizes how anthropological knowledge is created through relations (Strathern 1993) as the ethnographer engages in the life-worlds of others and senses connections not from above or from an objective stance, but relying instead on a subjective stance within (Hastrup 2005). This view is iterated in Georgiadou's chapter as she explores Ismat and Zhia's intimate 'moral worlds' (Kleinman et al. 1997: 95). Georgiadou argues that it is only profound involvement, commitment and concern that enable an ethnography of the Other as human beings, rather than as representing categories of differentiation, such as in this case 'victims of forced migration'. Thus, by engaging in everyday life not only by 'being with' but by 'being for' the Other (Bauman 1995: 51), Georgiadou points out how the anthropologist is confronted with moral responsibility for the Other with whom he/she has worked; this also includes a duty to assess what needs to be done – and to act.

Engaging in responsible relations is an emotional, cognitive and embodied approach of cosmopolitanism that comes from intersubjective moments which recognize a mutual humanity. Following the thoughts of Ulrich Beck (2006), this is also a 'cosmopolitan realism' in that it has entered the reality of the human condition in terms of global risks and threats of terror, as well as individuals' everyday lives. As such it is a concept that features the era of reflexive modernity in which national borders and differences are dissolving and simultaneously must be negotiated from a new perspective: being the cosmopolitan (Beck 2006: 2). Furthermore, cosmopolitanism challenges and transcends the distinctions between universalism and relativism as well as nationalism and ethnicity, as it is meant to affirm the Other as different and yet the same (see also Josephides 2010).

While recognizing cosmopolitanism as departing from a politics of otherness, social inequality, modernity, nation states and globalization, this volume highlights the ethical responsibility for the Other that arises in intersubjective moments. These are moments in which the self arises and is shaped by continuously changing modes of embodied social practices, from the interplay between object and subject, self and other. As intersubjectivity arises in the space between self and other, it is seen as a shared experience which can include both empathy and conflict and affirms sameness and difference along a continuum (Jackson 1989: 4; Grønseth and Davis 2010). Achieving a between-ness in the encounter between self and Other lies at the heart of intersubjectivity, where we can (hopefully) experience a mutual humanity and dependency, as well as a responsibility for the Other (Grønseth 2014; Jackson 1998; Rorty 1989; Levinas 2003 [1972]). The contributions in this collection share this approach; it is strongly iterated in Mikola's chapter, as she invokes the moral responsibility of acknowledging asylum-seekers as human beings who cannot be detained in asylum centres that keep them apart and beyond dialogue and social space. However, all the chapters take us beyond the losses and traumas associated with migrant and refugee categories and bring us to individual persons' everyday struggles for a meaningful life of their own as distinct but also equal human beings.

Exploring migrancy and intersubjectivity in the borderlands, I propose to highlight the empirical person by drawing attention to the relationship between singular persons, but also between persons and a world of ideas and objects held in common. Otherness and selfhood are not something that is given through merely existing. Rather, they are both an outcome of intersubjective engagement. When entering 'in between', as in intersubjective spaces and moments, it emerges that across great social inequality between self and Other, each being is essentially dependent, obliged and indebted to the Other. It is an approach that recognizes how sensing and recognizing the vulnerability and sensitivity of the Other as part of oneself stimulates a heartfelt responsibility (see also Grønseth and Davis 2010; Grønseth forthcoming). From such a phenomenological perspective cosmopolitanism calls one to take ethical responsibility for the Other. Thus, I suggest that the study of migrants in engaged face-to-face relations not only offers ethical rules and solutions, but also generates an ethical source (Levinas 2003 [1972]) that offers hope and potentiality. This is a humanism not based on the self, but on the fellow human being's humanity.

Exploring Migrant Bodies: An Anthropological Approach to Humanity

Together and individually, the chapters illustrate and discuss the migrant experience and struggle for senses of self, identity, well-being and agency. Each author demonstrates how migrant experiences of illness, losses, exclusion and inclusion, together with memories of the past and hopes for the future, interact in the daily task of creating a life of their own. By examining such experiences as they are seen to take place on the borderlands in between self and Other, the chapters constitute a volume that explores how migrancy carries a particular uniqueness of being human.

As a whole, the collection demonstrates not only how the everyday migrant life takes place in situations of flux, but also how the individual self is in constant flux as it lives at the intersections of time – past, present and future. While the individual migrants' lives are explored, their fears and hopes for love and social relatedness are displayed as poignant for migrants as much as for all human beings. The volume thus highlights how hopes and dreams for the future, together with memories of the past, are literally at the heart of migrants' everyday lives and as such constitute their sense of self and well-being, as well as their fear of losing both. This brings the volume to the interesting paradox that moments of wellness often occur through their closeness to the biting force of pain, as if the one was caused by the other (Jackson 2009: 94).

Barbara Pinelli's chapter discusses subjectivity and agency by exploring how the Togolese woman Rolanda, by applying for asylum in Italy, experiences vulnerability and suffering that are socially structured by asylum reception and assistance policy. A vital element of Rolanda's accounts, actions and experiences in everyday life is how memories of the past are crossed by the present, together with desires, fantasies and hopes for retrieving identities and well-being in the future. As Pinelli points out, highlighting fantasies and desires for the future makes possible a vital dimension in migrant and refugee studies which acknowledges that migration is a process with no end. Rather, it is the processes of becoming and of being human that continue across space and time.

Visions and hopes for the future are also seen as crucial in Anne Sigfrid Grønseth's chapter, in which she explores the illness and pain of Tamil refugees in Norway as embodied experiences of living in between distinct lifeworlds. Exploring the case of Malar, a Tamil refugee woman, the chapter discusses how her painful experience of living in between, or of 'living in a tunnel' gave her the opportunity to recognize that what appears to be distinct can connect and change. Striving towards her future goals, Malar involved herself in the here and now and connected with others, and transferred her sense of being lost and alone to include an experience of mutuality and belonging with the Other as fellow human beings. While exploring links between senses of time and tenses, spatiality and localities, Grønseth's chapter highlights how migrants' experiences of living in between and on the borderlands activate a human disposition to connect in everyday life and to create future visions that include new senses of identity and well-being which embrace the Other as part of the self.

In a more autobiographical narrative, Maruška Svašek draws attention to how the story of the migrant and re-migrant Anna from the Netherlands is enveloped by desires, hopes and fears, and how she changes her perceptions of past and future. By Svašek's interpretive analysis we come close to Anna's emotional dynamics and sense of freedom, belonging and alienation, which are all central to her awareness of self and well-being. Anna's narrative is analysed as part of a discourse, practice and embodied experience of emotions and highlights how subjectivity and the self emerge in transits and transformations in a world of movement. Paying attention to the shifts and movements in Anna's narration, Svašek observes how Anna experiences emotional stimulus and awareness of herself in flux when her narration enters zones of ambiguity and being in between times and spaces. As such the chapter offers decisive insights into the complex interplay of changing perceptions of time and space together with emotional dynamics in human senses of self, agency and well-being.

In a similar vein, Naoko Maehara explores how interactions in embodied memories, perceptions and emotions, in Naomi's narrative of her migration from Japan to Ireland, affect her sense of (non-)belonging, loss and quest for well-being. With reference to Edward Casey's concept of 'place memory' (Casey 2000), Maehara analyses Naomi's suffering as not being able to engage in the activity of re-emplacing or re-experiencing past places, the disruption of embodied knowledge and the lack of future visions. However, Naomi's narrative and photographic diary display how, with the aid of imagination, she is gradually able to appropriate her new surroundings as part of her own ongoing life while she 'attunes her body' to the new place and achieves a sense of continuity from the past into the present and future possibilities. Thus, the chapter demonstrates the human disposition towards and also the fluid contingency of subjectivity, self and well-being.

Staying with the study of individual life stories, Christina Georgiadou studies the everyday life of Zhia and Ismat, two young men from Afghan seeking refuge in Athens, Greece. Exploring the everyday lives of these two men, Georgiadou transgresses the politics of classification and Othering that would reduce Zhia and Ismat to refugees and offers instead a morally engaged ethnographic approach that highlights a mutual and shared humanity. Her exploration offers a view of Zhia and Ismat that goes beyond the problematic and passive victims whom the media and politicians tend to display, and rather recognize their existential efforts towards resistance, resilience and creativity in reconstructing a new life in exile. Georgiadou's chapter highlights how creativity and subjectivity constitutes a part of everyday human life, as it is directed towards individual fulfilment and well-being negotiated and challenged by institutional structures and disciplinary technologies constructed and effectuated by the politics of asylum-seekers' reception and thus sets the boundaries between legality and illegality.

Adding to the theme of Othering, Maša Mikola investigates how the spatial relocation of the Ljubljana Asylum Home in Slovenia stems from an economy of fear and fosters a certain kind of resistance within the Home. Mikola describes how, in the struggle to maintain and restate their sense of self, two young men from Russia living in the Home opposed the structural and spatial boundaries between 'us' and the 'others' by cutting their veins, and by this bodily communication creating a zone for possible dialogue. Surviving the attempted suicide, they embarked on a hunger strike which became part of a public debate on asylum in Slovenia. Mikola points out how the two young men communicated a sense of self and being by means of silence, as silence is seen as a 'speaking of the threshold' (Irigaray 2008) in encounters between different subjectivities, such that a dialogue can begin. As the chapter points out, it is not from a shared common meaning, but from the thresholds – in this case the embodied silence – that self and Other can meet and humanity speak.

Calling for studies of migrants that move between memories, dreams and hopes in the here and now, I argue that this volume will contribute to an anthropology that illuminates the diversity and mutuality of the human experiences of self, well-being, emotions and consciousness in everyday life. The volume sheds light on social and existential conditions relating to the migrant experience as it is uniquely human. In investigating both social and existential conditions, together and individually the chapters illuminate the complex relationships between migration, self and well-being which acknowledge how experiences of illness and health are embedded in structures and power relations, while also transgressing these by acknowledging that migrants' positions are both within and in between. By emphasizing the position in between, the volume addresses a crucial embodied agency that acknowledges that migrants, however they may be categorized, are intentional agents who create lives for themselves within day-to-day living.

I therefore suggest that the volume demonstrates how illness, health and senses of self and well-being are closely interwoven with experiences of being recognized – or in various degrees not recognized – as fully and equal human beings. All chapters illustrate self and well-being as emerging in embodied, intersubjective and agentive moments and spaces. In adopting this perspective, I argue that senses of self and well-being are inter-related to experiences of intersubjectivity and agency. As intersubjectivity arises in the borderlands between self and Other in a broad sense, the study of migrants provides a vital occasion for the investigation of self and well-being. Thus, this volume suggests that the migrant condition is a human condition.

Exploring the migrant embodied experience provides access to the life in between and reveals implicit, embodied and intersubjective data on what it is to be human. As such, exploring migrant bodies as they live their lives in the borderlands – between places, times, moralities, identities and life-worlds – calls for an anthropology that underscores the need for the ethnographer to stretch herself or himself into the borderlands between self and Other. Thus, the ethnographer's effort to engage and move the self may serve as an anthropological approach that gains access to migrant/human bodies in movement. Thus, movement makes us humans as much as it makes us migrants.

Acknowledgement

I owe grateful thanks to anonymous referees and to EASA series editor James Carrier for their encouraging, thoughtful and precise comments.

References

Agier, M. 2005. *On the Margins of the World: The Refugee Experience Today.* Cambridge: Politi Press.

Amit-Talai, V. 1995. 'Anthropology, Multiculturalism and the Concept of Culture', *Folk* 37: 135–44.

Appadurai, A. 1996. *Modernity at Large: Cultural Dimensions of Globalization.* Minneapolis: University of Minnesota Press.

Banks, M. 1996. *Ethnicity: Anthropological Constructions.* London: Routledge.

Barth, F. (ed.). 1998. *Ethnic Groups and Boundaries: The Social Organisation of Cultural Difference.* Prospect Heights, IL: Waveland Press (Original, Oslo: University Press, 1969).

Basch, L., N.G. Schiller, and C. Szanton Blanc. 1994. *Nations Unbound: Transnational Projects, Postcolonial Predicaments and Deterritorialized Nation-States.* Langhorne, PA: Gordon and Breach.

Bauman, Z. 1995. *Life in Fragments: Essays in Postmodern Morality.* Cambridge, MA: Basil Blackwell.

Baumann, G. 1996. *Contesting Culture: Discourses of Identity in Multi-ethnic London.* Cambridge: Cambridge University Press.

_____. 1997. 'Dominant and Demotic Discourses of Culture: Their Relevance to Multi-ethnic Alliances', in P. Werber and T. Modood (eds), *Debating Cultural Hybridity: Multi-Cultural Identities and the Politics of Anti-Racism.* London: Zed Books, pp. 209–25.

_____. 1999. *The Multicultural Riddle: Rethinking National, Ethnic and Religious Identities.* London: Routledge.

Beck, U. 2006. *The Cosmopolitan Vision.* Cambridge: Polity Press.

Behar, R. 2003. *Translated Woman: Crossing the Border with Esperanza's Story.* Boston, MA: Beacon Press.

Berger, J. 1984. *And our Faces, My Heart, Brief as Photos.* London: Writers & Readers.

Bourdieu, P. 1989. *Outline of a Theory of Practice.* Cambridge: Cambridge University Press.

_____. 2000. *Pascalian Meditations*, trans. Richard Nice. Cambridge: Polity Press.

Bradby, H. and G. Lewando Hundt (eds). 2010. *Global Perspectives on War, Gender and Health. The Sociology and Anthropology of Suffering: Global Connections.* Farnham: Ashgate.

Breckenridge, C.A., S. Pollock, H.K. Bhabha and D. Chakrabarty. 2002. *Cosmopolitanism.* Durham, NC: Duke University Press.

Brettell, C.B. 2000. 'Theorizing Migration in Anthropology: the Social Construction of Networks, Identities, Communities and Globalscapes', in C.B. Brettell and J.F. Hollifield (eds), *Migration Theory.* New York: Routledge, pp. 97–135.

_____. 2003. *Anthropology and Migration: Essays on Transnationalism, Ethnicity, and Identity.* Walnut Creek, CA: AltaMira Press.

Cağlar, A.S. 1997. 'Hyphenated Identities and the Limits of "Culture"', in T. Modood and P. Werbner (eds), *The Politics of Multiculturalism in the New Europe: Racism, Identity and Community*. London: Allen & Unwin, pp. 169–86.

Casey, E.S. 2000. *Remembering: A Phenomenological Study. Studies in Phenomenology and Existential Philosophy*. 2nd edition. Bloomington: Indiana University Press.

Chambers, I. 1994. *Migrancy, Culture, Identity*. London: A Comedia book, Routledge.

Coker, E.M. 2004. '"Traveling Pains": Embodied Metaphors of Suffering among Southern Sudanese Refugees in Cairo', *Culture, Medicine and Psychiatry* 28(1): 15–39.

Csordas, T. (ed.). 1994. *Embodiment and Experience: The Existential Ground of Culture and Self*. Cambridge: Cambridge University Press.

Daniel, V. and J. Chr. Knudsen (eds). 1995. *Mistrusting Refugees*. Berkeley: University of California Press.

Das, V. 1990. 'What do we Mean by Health?', in J.C. Caldwell (ed.), *What we Know about the Health Transition: The Cultural, Social and Behavioural Determinants of Health*. Vol 1, Health Transitions Series No. 2, pp. 27–46.

_____. 1995. 'Voice as Birth of Culture', *Ethnos* 60(3–4): 159–79.

Delanty, G., R. Wodak and P. Jones (eds). 2008. *Identity, Belonging, and Migration*. Liverpool: Liverpool University Press.

Desjarlais, R., L. Eisenberg, B. Good and A. Kleinman. 1995. *World Mental Health: Problems and Priorities in Low-Income Countries*. Oxford: Oxford University Press.

Epstein, A.L. 1958. *Politics in an Urban African Community*. Manchester: Manchester University Press.

Farmer, P. 2001. *Infections and Inequalities: The Modern Plagues*. Updated edition. Berkeley: University of California Press.

_____. 2005. *Pathologies of Power: Health, Human Rights, and the New War on the Poor*. Berkeley: University of California Press.

Foner, N. 2000. 'Anthropology and the Study of Immigration', in N. Foner et al. (eds), *Immigration Research for a New Century*. New York: Russell Sage Foundation, pp. 49–53.

Foucault, M. 1977. *Discipline and Punish: The Birth of the Prison*. New York: Random House.

_____. 1980. *Power/Knowledge: Selected Interviews and Other Writings*, ed. C. Gordon. New York: Pantheon Books.

Geller, P.L. and M.K. Stockett. 2006. *Feminist Anthropology: Past, Present and Future*. Philadelphia: University of Pennsylvania Press.

Gellner, E. 1994. *Encounters with Nationalism*. Oxford: Blackwell Publishers.

Gluckman, M. 1965. *Politics, Law and Ritual in Tribal Society*. Oxford: Blackwell.

Grillo. R. 1998. *Pluralism and the Politics of Difference: State, Culture, and Ethnicity in Comparative Perspective*. Oxford: Clarendon Press.

Grønseth, A.S. 2010. *Lost Selves and Lonely Persons: Experiences of Illness and Well-Being among Tamil Refugees in Norway*. Carolina: Carolina Academic Press.

_____. 2014. 'Experiences of Pain: A Gateway to Cosmopolitan Subjectivity', in L. Josephides and A. Hall (eds), *We the Cosmopolitans: Moral and Existential Conditions of Being Human*. Oxford: Berghahn Books.

Grønseth, A.S. and D.L. Davis (eds). 2010. *Mutuality and Empathy: Self and Other in the Ethnographic Encounter*. Wantage: Sean Kingston Publishing.

Gupta, A. and J. Ferguson (eds). 1997. *Culture, Power and Place: Explorations in Critical Anthropology.* Durham, NC: Duke University Press.

Hammond, L. 2004. *This Place Will Become Home: Refugee Repatriation To Ethiopia.* Cornell: Cornell University Press.

Hannerz, U. 1996. *Transnational Complexity: Studies in the Social Organization or Meaning.* New York: Columbia University Press.

Harbottle, L. 2000. *Food for Health, Food for Wealth: The Performance of Ethnic and Gender Identities by Iranian Settlers in Britain.* New York and Oxford: Berghahn Books.

Hastrup, K. 2005. 'Social Anthropology: Towards a Pragmatic Enlightenment?', *Social Anthropology* 13(2): 133–49.

Hinnels, J. 2007. *Religious Reconstruction in the South Asian Diasporas: From One Generation to Another.* London: Palgrave Macmillan.

Holland, D., D. Skinner, W. Lachicotte Jr. and C. Cain. 2001. *Identity and Agency in Cultural Worlds.* Cambridge, MA: Harvard University Press.

Husserl, E. 1970. *The Crisis of European Sciences and Transcendental Phenomenology: An Introduction to Phenomenological Philosophy, 1859–1938.* Evanston, IL: Northwestern University Press.

Hylland Eriksen, T. 2007. 'Complexity in Social and Cultural Integration: Some Analytical Dimensions', *Ethnic and Racial Studies* 30(6): 1055–69.

Ingold, T. and Elizabeth Hallam (eds). 2007. 'Creativity and Cultural Improvisation: An Introduction', in *Creativity and Cultural Improvisation.* Oxford: Berg, pp. 1–24.

Irigaray, L. 2008. *Sharing the World.* London: Continuum.

Jackson, M. 1989. *Paths toward a Clearing: Radical Empiricism and Ethnographic Inquiry.* Bloomington: Indiana University Press.

_____. 1995. *At Home in the World.* Durham, NC: Duke University Press.

_____. 1998. *Minima Ethnographica: Intersubjectivity and the Anthropological Project.* Chicago: University for Chicago Press.

_____. 2005. *Existential Anthropology: Events, Exigencies and Effects.* New York and Oxford: Berghahn Books.

_____. 2009. *The Palm at the End of the Mind: Relatedness, Religiosity, and the Real.* Durham, NC and London: Duke University Press.

Jasper, K. 2000. 'Journal Entries 1939-1942', in *Karl Jaspers: Basic Philosophical Writings,* ed and trans. E. Ehrlich, L.H. Ehrlich and G.B. Pepper. New York: Humanity Books.

Josephides, L. 2010. 'Cosmopolitanism as the Existential Condition of Humanity', *Social Anthropology* 18(4): 389–95.

Kibria, N. 2002. *Becoming Asian American: Second-Generation Chinese and Korean American Identities.* Baltimore, MD: Johns Hopkins University Press.

Kleinman, A. 1988. *The Illness Narratives: Suffering, Healing and the Human Condition.* New York: Basic Books.

Kleinman, A., V. Das and M. Lock (eds). 1997. *Social Suffering.* Berkeley: University of California Press.

Lacan, J. 1992. *The Seminar of Jacques Lacan: Book VII, The Ethics of Psychoanalysis, 1959–1960,* ed. J.A. Miller. New York: Morton.

Lamphere, L. 1992. *Structuring Diversity: Ethnographic Perspectives on the New Immigration.* Chicago: The University of Chicago Press.

Lefebvre, H. 2002. *Critique of Everyday Life.* London and New York: Verso.

Levinas, E. 2003 [1972]. *Humanism of the Other*. Illinois: University of Illinois Press.

Levitt, P., J. Dewind and S. Vertovec. 2003. 'International Perspectives on Transnational Migration: An Introduction', *International Migration Review* 37(3, Special Issue): 565–75.

Lewin, E. and W. Leap. 2002. *Out in Theory: The Emergence of Lesbian and Gay Anthropology*. Urbana: University of Illinois Press.

Mahler, S. and P. Pessar. 2001. 'Gendered Geographies of Power: Analysing Gender across Transnational Spaces', *Identities: Global Studies in Culture and Power* 7(4): 441–59.

_____. 2006. 'Gender Matters: Ethnographers Bring Gender from the Periphery toward the Core of Migration Studies', *International Migration Review* 40(1): 27–63.

Malkki, L. 1995a. 'Refugees and Exile: from "Refugee Studies" to the National Order of Things', *Annual Review of Anthropology* 24: 495–523.

_____. 1995b. *Purity and Exile: Violence, Memory and National Cosmology among Hutu Refugees in Tanzania*. Chicago: The University of Chicago Press.

Mangin, W. (ed.). 1970. *Peasants in Cities: Readings in the Anthropology of Urbanization*. Boston, MA: Houghton Mifflin.

Manuh, T. (ed.). 2005. *At Home in the World? International Migration and Development in Contemporary Ghana and West Africa*. Accra: Sub-Saharan Publishers.

Mayer, P. 1961. *Townsmen or Tribesmen: Conservatism and the Process of Urbanization in a South African City*. Cape Town: Oxford University Press.

Merleau-Ponty, M. 1962 [1945]. *Phenomenology of Perception*. London: Routledge & Kegan Paul.

Migliorino, N. 2008. *(Re)constructing Armenia in Lebanon and Syria: Ethno-cultural Diversity and the State in the Aftermath of a Refugee Crisis*. New York and Oxford: Berghahn Books.

Mitchell, J.C. 1969. *Social Networks in Urban Situations: Analysis of Personal Relationships in Central African Towns*. Manchester: Manchester University Press.

Modood, T. and P. Werbner (eds). 1997. *The Politics of Multiculturalism in the New Europe: Racism, Identity and Community*. London: Zed Books.

Monk, R. 1990. *Ludwig Wittgenstein: The Duty of Genius*. New York: Free Press.

Moore, H. 1988. *Feminism and Anthropology*. Cambridge: Polity Press.

_____. 1994. *A Passion for Difference: Essays in Anthropology and Gender*. Bloomington: Indiana University Press.

Nowicka, M. and M. Rovisco (eds). 2009. *Cosmopolitanism in Practice*. Burlington, VA: Ashgate.

Nussbaum, M. 1986. *The Fragility of Goodness: Luck and Ethics in Greek Tragedy and Philosophy*. London: Cambridge University Press.

Oakley, R. and A.S. Grønseth (eds). 2007. Special Issue: 'Ethnographic Humanism: Migrant Experiences in the Quest for Well-being', *Anthropology in Action* 14 (1&2).

Olwig, K.F. 2007. *Caribbean Journeys: An Ethnography of Migration and Home in Three Family Networks*. Durham, NC: Duke University Press.

Olwig, K.F. and K. Hastrup (eds). 1997. *Siting Culture: The Shifting Anthropological Object*. London: Routledge.

Palmie, S. 2006. 'Creolization and its Discontents', *Annual Review of Anthropology* 35: 433–35.

Portes, A., L.E. Guarnizo and P. Landolt. 1999. 'The Study of Transnationalism: Pitfalls and Promise of an Emergent Research Field', *Ethnic and Racial Studies* 22(2, Special Issue): 217–37.

Rapport, N. 2003. *I'm Dynamite: An Alternative Anthropology of Power.* London and New York: Routledge.

_____. 2010. 'Cosmopolitanism and Liberty', *Social Anthropology* 18(4): 464–70.

Rapport, N. and A. Dawson (eds). 1998. *Migrants of Identity: Perceptions of Home in a World of Movement.* Oxford: Berg.

Ricoeur, P. 1980. 'Narrative and Time', *Critical Inquiry* 7(1): 169–90.

Rogers, A. and S. Vertovec (eds). 1995. *The Urban Context: Ethnicity, Social Networks and Situational Analysis.* Oxford: Berg.

Roosens, E. 1989. *Creating Ethnicity: The Process of Ethnogenesis.* California: Sage.

Rorty, R. 1989. *Contingency, Irony and Solidarity.* Cambridge: Cambridge University Press.

Sandywell, B. 2004. 'The Myth of Everyday Life: Toward a Heterology of the Ordinary', *Cultural Studies* 18(2/3): 160–80.

Sanjek, R. 1998. *The Future of Us All: Race and Neighborhood Politics in New York City.* Ithaca: Cornell University Press.

Sartre, P. 1956. *Being and Nothingness: An Essay on Phenomenological Ontology,* trans. Hazel Barnes. New York: Philosophical Library.

Scheper-Hughes, N. 1992. *Death without Weeping: The Violence of Everyday Life in Brazil.* Berkeley: University of California Press.

Schiffauer, W., G. Baumann, R. Kastoryanoi and S. Vertovec (eds). 2004. *Civil Enculturation. Nation-state, School and Ethnic Difference in the Netherlands, Britain, Germany and France.* Oxford: Berghahn Books.

Schiller, N.G., L. Basch and C. Blanc-Szanton (eds). 1992. *Towards a Transnational Perspective on Migration.* New York: The New York Academy of Sciences.

Schiller, N.G. and A. Cağlar (eds). 2011. *Locating Migration: Rescaling Cities and Migrants.* Cornell: Cornell University Press.

Schiller, N.G., T. Darieva and S. Gruner-Domic. 2011. 'Defining Cosmopolitan Sociability in a Transnational Age: An Introduction', *Ethnic and Racial Studies* 34(3): 399–418.

Schiller, N.G. and T. Faist (eds). 2010. *Migration, Development and Transnationalization: A Critical Stance.* Oxford: Berghahn Books.

Schiller, N.G., L. Basch and C. Blanc-Szanton (eds). 1992. *Towards a Transnational Perspective on Migration: Race, Class, Ethnicity, and Nationalism Reconsidered.* New York: New York Academy of Sciences.

Schneider, A. 2001. *Futures Lost: Nostalgia and Identity among Italian Immigrants in Argentina.* Oxford and Berne: Peter Lang.

Schulz, H.L. and J. Hammer. 2003. *The Palestinian Diaspora: Formation of Identities and Politics of Homeland.* Global Diasporas. London: Routledge.

Sideris, T. 2003. 'War, Gender and Culture: Mozambican Women Refugees', *Social Science & Medicine* 56(4): 713–24.

Smith, Chr. 2003. *Moral, Believing Animals.* Oxford: Oxford University Press.

Strathern, M. 1993. *The Relation. Issues in Complexity and Scale.* [Inaugural lecture]. Cambridge: Cambridge University Press.

Vertovec, S. 2007. 'Super-diversity and its Implications', *Ethnic and Racial Studies* 30(6): 1024–54.

_____. 2009. *Transnationalism.* London: Routledge.

_____(ed.). 2010. *Anthropology of Migration and Multiculturalism: New Directions*. London: Routledge.

Vertovec, S. and S. Wessendorf (eds). 2010. *The Multiculturalism Backlash: European Discourses, Policies and Practices*. London and New York: Routledge.

Wardle, H. 2000. *An Ethnography of Cosmopolitanism in Kingston, Jamaica*. Lampeter: Mellen.

Wardle, H. and N. Rapport. 2010. Special Issue: 'A Cosmopolitan Anthropology?', *Social Anthropology* 18(4).

Watson, C.W. 2000. *Multiculturalism*. Buckingham: Open University Press.

Werbner, P. (ed.). 2002. *Imagined Diasporas among Manchester Muslims: The Public Performance of Pakistani Transnational Identity Politics*. Oxford: James Currey.

_____. 2008. *Anthropology and the New Cosmopolitanism: Rooted, Feminist and Vernacular Perspectives*. Oxford and New York: Berg.

Wise, A. and S. Velyutham (eds). 2009. *Everyday Multiculturalism*. London: Palgrave Macmillan.

Zmegac, J.C. 2007. *Strangers Either Way: The Lives of Croatian Refugees in Their New Home*. Oxford: Berghahn Books.

Chapter 1

Fantasy, Subjectivity and Vulnerability through the Story of a Woman Asylum Seeker in Italy

Barbara Pinelli

In 2006 when I first met Rolanda, a Togolese woman who arrived in Italy in 2002 seeking political asylum, she had just been denied asylum and granted instead a humanitarian residence permit after four long years of waiting. She reached Italy alone; her husband, a political opponent of the Togolese government, had escaped to France one year before and their three-year old daughter had been left in the care of her mother. At the time of our meeting, after having spent nearly three years in four reception centres for asylum seekers, Rolanda had left Milan assistance circuits and was sharing a small flat with another Togolese woman. Descriptions of her life in Togo and her experiences in Milan overlapped in our conversations with the expression of her strong desire to rejoin her daughter. The way in which Rolanda described her exile included both her memories of the past and her hopes of reconstructing those parts of her subjectivity, which the flight from Togo had broken into pieces.

In these pages, I tackle the issue of political refuge through the experiences of this woman, exploring the ways in which life after the flight and after the breaking down of important systems of relationship and belonging is reconstructed in the host cities. In particular, and through the vicissitudes of Rolanda, I will try to show how the drama of the flight is not the only factor defining the level of suffering and vulnerability experienced by female asylum seekers. Forms of social exclusions encountered in the arrival country expose these women to further experiences of suffering and impose on them a long and systematic 'process of subjection' (Butler 1997; Mohanty 1993). By bringing together anthropological reflections on vulnerability and approaches on subjectivity, fantasy and subjection developed in gender theories, I will focus on the formation and reconstruction of subjectivity in suffering and vulnerable conditions. In other words, I will explore the relation between agency and process of subjection. In Italy, such dynamics of social exclusion are reinforced and worsened both by the long waiting for permits and by the strong ambiguities inherent in assistance policies that consider female asylum seekers only as subjects in need of help and emancipation.[1] I have chosen to narrate Rolanda's story because she spent an initial period within reception centres for asylum seekers and later lived outside these centres. Indeed, during this second phase, her hope and desire to reconstruct her life after the flight, as well as the resources found in the informal networks, were important elements allowing the analysis of the relationship between marginality and agency.

In particular, the reception centres where Rolanda has lived over the years pursue a strong pedagogic intention, which consists in preparing female asylum seekers for the 'modernity' of the context in which they had arrived. Assistance culture, bureaucratic and administrative procedures, notably the wait for papers, reinforce a sense of time suspension and lead to a perception of life as being stuck in a stagnant present. In the following pages, I will explain this point by succinctly illustrating the dynamics of daily life in some of Milan centres for female asylum seekers I had the chance to visit during my research.[2] First, however, I will provide details both on Rolanda's flight and on Italian legislation on asylum. Rolanda's case, as I will show, illustrates the role that social networks beyond the circuits of public welfare play in providing asylum seeking women with opportunities to maintain a certain degree of control over their own lives. My description of Rolanda's subjectivity takes into account the 'relation between private experiences and macro-structural forces' (Bourgois 2008: 114), in order to highlight those social forces that socially exclude women already living in vulnerable conditions. The point I mean to stress is that in spite of her vulnerability, Rolanda never became a victim. The difference between being vulnerable, on the one hand, and being a victim, on the other one, will become clearer as I illustrate the details of her migration story (as narrated by Rolanda herself) and the theoretical framework I use to analyse her case. The themes of fantasy (Moore 1994),[3] intended as the desire and the hope to give to own future life a different form from the present time, and of vulnerability (Bourgois 2008; Das 2000), intended as a means to move beyond the representation of the female asylum seeker as the passive and silent subject, allow us to understand the drama of the flight, the marginality produced by the status of immigrant requesting asylum and the ways in which women like Rolanda try to create a breach in their marginality and to recompose their daily life. The concept of fantasy helped me to look at Rolanda's present in light of her future aspirations. In spite of the vulnerability associated with her condition of asylum seeker, Rolanda tried to manage her daily life so as to achieve what really mattered in her eyes. So, whereas the notions of vulnerability and marginality focus on the power structures which restrain the lives of asylum seeking women, those of subjectivity and fantasy cast light on the hidden side of forced migrations, i.e., the multiple practices and strategies by which asylum seekers rebuild their lives on a daily basis.

Rolanda's Life before Arrival

Rolanda was one of the women I met in the course of an ethnographic research on the experiences of female asylum seekers in Italy, which I began in 2006 thanks to a post-doctoral grant from Milan-Bicocca University. This research, involving around twenty female asylum seekers in Italy, focused on the multiple forms of violence and abuse experienced by women along the whole trajectory of forced migration: from the flight, through the transit, to the dynamics which occur at the point of arrival, in particular when female asylum seekers are forced to live in the reception centres. Part of my research was concerned with an analysis of the bureaucratic process involved in obtaining an asylum permit and the social and assistance policies associated with this. In particular, I visited some reception centres for asylum seekers, where I could observe the dynamics of relations between social workers and hosted women and the flow of daily life within these institutions. The bulk of my work has been focused on the collection of biographies and narratives of female asylum seekers.[4]

I have paid particular attention to the memory of forced migration, the experiences of these women in the arrival contexts, both within and beyond the assistance circuits, and their desires for the future. By giving voice to their experiences, I have tried to describe the process of becoming an asylum seeker from their own point of view, shedding light on what lies beneath the subjectivity of female asylum seekers and the multiple structures of social exclusion they encountered. In the years between 2006 and 2009, I met Rolanda several times. When we first met, she lived outside the reception centres and shared a small room with a friend. Our meetings took place mainly at her house, and I often accompanied Rolanda around the city of Milan, when she was looking for a new job, meeting women or men who belonged to her networks, or visiting the relevant institutions in order to obtain information on how to accelerate the process of being reunited with her daughter. During these meetings and these moments spent together, I learned her story.

Rolanda arrived in Italy on a flight from Benin in 2002. When I first met her in 2006 she had just obtained a humanitarian residence permit. She was twenty-nine and her daughter Sandra, who lived in Benin with Rolanda's mother, was five. Rolanda's husband had left Togo in 2001, following a long period of persecution.[5] Rolanda had no detailed information about her husband's flight. She only knew that he was living somewhere in France. Sporadic news had reached her through mutual acquaintances. During our conversations, she liked to describe their beautiful apartment in Togo. Large, comfortable and elegantly furnished, it was located on the top floor of a building facing the sea. In Togo, Rolanda was in charge of a tailor's workshop, with several apprentice girls under her supervision. 'I felt good', she used to tell me when recollecting her comfortable life before exile.

The decision to emigrate did not come immediately after her husband's flight but following a demonstration against the Togolese government. On that occasion, the police beat several demonstrators and one of Rolanda's legs was almost broken. Before the demonstration, and after her husband's flight, she had often been threatened by the army. Soldiers used to knock at her door and tried to get information about her husband. Scared about her future and that of her daughter Sandra, she decided to move to Benin with Sandra and her mother. Having arrived there in a poor condition, she was treated in a hospital managed by a group of Italian doctors. A couple of months later, thanks to an Italian family she met in the same hospital, she decided to migrate to Italy. Rolanda did not plan the details of her flight, mainly because she thought it as a temporary solution: fleeing represented virtually the only way to survive. Rolanda discussed her plans with her mother in the belief that, once in Italy, it would have been easier to reunite with her daughter and to reconstruct her life. Immediately after her arrival, she realized the burden of her displacement.

It was December 2002. Rolanda had no acquaintances in Milan, neither did she know the city. She was completely lost in terms of what to do and how to behave in order to cope with her new situation. At the airport information desk, she asked where she could find the police headquarters. The office staff sent her to Milan Central Railway Station. Here, Rolanda sought assistance from the Migrants' Help Centre which was then located on the ground floor. Following their directions, she spent her first night in a reception centre for asylum seeking women. So began her experience with Milan structures of assistance on which she felt heavily dependent until mid-2005, when the opportunity to share a flat with her friend Perpetua materialized.

Italian Policies for Asylum Seekers

The Juridical Framework

The Italian Law on Asylum and the procedures for applying for refugee status have been modified since 2002, through Law n. 189[6] and subsequently through Decree n. 140/2005, which has introduced new measures for the welfare of asylum seekers, and Decree n. 25/2008.[7] Although fraught with contradictions, these rules have reduced the waiting time needed to obtain a permit. The women I met during my research project arrived in or after 2002, and few of them benefitted from the new procedures or from the speeding up of the application process. These Decrees created seven Territorial Commissions intended to deal with asylum requests.[8] Before, these processes were carried out at the national level and waiting times were particularly long. The lack of proper regulations on asylum deeply affected the lives of asylum seekers, who remained entangled in a suspended time dimension.[9]

When Rolanda made her request, Italian law stated that the Commission had to reach a decision within six months. This period, however, could easily be protracted to one or two years: indeed, Rolanda waited for almost two years.

Eventually, her application was refused. One year later, after having appealed the decision, she was granted a humanitarian residence permit. This was only the first step, as the humanitarian residence permit, even if it is renewed, lasts only one year. Moreover, according to the criteria set out by the law, the permit for family reunion is far more difficult to obtain than a job permit.

In order to convert the humanitarian residence permit into a job permit, Rolanda needed a regular job and a house which met the criteria of 'proper housing' established by the law. While waiting to give a final response to an asylum request, police headquarters keep renewing temporary permits, each time for the duration of three or four months. Before she received a humanitarian residence permit, Rolanda had her permits renewed in this way. Potential employers, either from temporary recruitment or private agencies, used to tell her: 'I cannot give you a job if your permit expires in a few months and there is no guarantee on the possibility for you to stay'.

In spite of the individual resources that asylum seekers can rely on, and in spite of their longing for a better future, the gap between the formal aspects of the law and its concrete applications,[10] together with the concomitant difficulty of finding a job, force them to depend on assistance structures in order to carve out a living.

In Italy, local government, network assistance, NGOs, voluntary organizations and other local actors dealing with immigration all play a fundamental role in the implementation of national immigration policies.[11] The city of Milan offers a wide network of services and residential centres which are mostly managed by Catholic voluntary groups and by organizations such as the Red Cross. In line with local political discourse, these organizations represent immigrants as human beings in need, devoid of any autonomy and agency. Milan is the 'capital' of Northern Italy, the centre par excellence of the national economy and of employment opportunities, where those who have neither a job nor an income, and hence are dependent on the welfare system and assistance relationships, are even more excluded from regular employment and society as a whole. Yet, these people are able to access the irregular and lowly-qualified labour market, which not only develops in parallel with, but is also intimately connected to, the regular labour sector and even sustains it.

Women's Lives in Milan Reception Centres for Asylum Seekers

Milan assistance centres are divided according to gender. As I anticipated, centres for female asylum seekers embody a specific imaginary of the female subject. Assistance policies are supported by the idea that women constitute the weaker side of forced migrations, and as a result need safe places to live. Providing accommodation and food, these centres are open all day long, unlike the dormitories for men which offer shelter only at night. Besides catering to the women's primary needs, the organization of female centres manifests the explicit will to inculcate a sense of responsibility and autonomy in their beneficiaries, who are seen as subjects to be emancipated from their previous condition of female subjection and to be integrated into the new urban context. This rhetoric – which is a constitutive part of the way in which the staff represents its duty – translates into a set of daily educative practices aimed at producing a female subjectivity conceived of as modern, emancipated and self-reliant. The centres belong to the Municipality of Milan but they are managed by the Red Cross or by other catholic NGOs. Usually, the staff comprises a director, a number of social and educational workers, and at times also lawyers, psychologists and cultural mediators. All these professionals set out to help female asylum seekers to rebuild their stories for presentation at the Commission and provide care, support and assistance in relation to their traumatic experiences. Furthermore, social workers are always present in the reception centres, ensuring the control of the behaviour of hosted women and compliance with the rules. In this chapter, I pay attention to the ways in which the system of relations built up by social workers with female asylum seekers puts into action the imaginary on women asylum seekers, which describes them as subject to be emancipated and controlled. At the same time, it is necessary to stress the extent to which the work carried out by social workers is often precious and frustrating because of the structural conditions under which it is undertaken and because of the lack of economic resources. In spite of my presence sometimes being perceived as 'invading' by some of the operators – and the managers of reception centres have requested an account of my observations – other operators nevertheless had a collaborative attitude and have been helpful as I have gathered stories and carried out my research.

Each structure has its own spatial organization. As a general rule, two or three women share the same room. Common spaces include the kitchen, the living room, the bathrooms, the garden, and the children's playroom. These spaces must remain impersonal and women are not allowed to leave any personal belongings, such as photographs, in the bedrooms. Directors often describe these centres as places where women can feel at home, relate to other women and get acquainted with the social rules of the host country. In reality, however, the very organization of internal spaces reminds women of their condition as temporary guests who are not supposed to get attached to the place.

The daily rules of reception centres are very strict and the guests' movements are closely controlled by staff.[12] For example, women have to leave their employer's phone number. The request to declare their movements even when the women are outside the centres is justified by the operators as a way of instilling a sense of responsibility in the women. In addition, the order and cleanliness of both the rooms and the person are considered of great importance and closely monitored by the staff. These rules of cohabitation, together with the control of the women's daily movements, are thought to be a way of teaching the guests about the living standards of the new society. During my fieldwork, the director of the centres where Rolanda had lived and his staff remarked on their awareness of the different cultural backgrounds of asylum seeking women, as well as of the different conceptions of personhood their guests brought with them. Such differences, however, were represented in culturally hierarchical terms. Italian culture and way of living was conceived of as superior to the values and norms of the society that the asylum seeking women hailed from. Some of the staff felt a responsibility to teach the women about proper ways of living, such as how to take care of themselves and their children or how to behave correctly while at work. Reception centres have been described by their staff as a 'magna mater and an incubator',[13] as a necessary step to prepare women for life outside the centre. This is a crucial point: these women are not only seen as individuals that need to be helped, but as bodies to be educated, as female subjectivities that must be integrated, emancipated.

As many of the women I met maintained, they often had conversations with social workers or psychologists about how to handle maternity. Rolanda looked at this public management of intimacy in an ironic and stunned way. She considered discourses on maternity (how to handle it, how to wean a child, how to rescind the mother-son bond) as a form of intrusive violence which clearly exposed the social workers' ignorance of her personal background. Nobody ever considered the suffering that such discussions imposed on women like Rolanda, who had been forced by circumstances to leave their children behind in the care of relatives or acquaintances.

Encouraged by operators, Rolanda attended some of training courses organized by the reception structures she lived in. The social workers she met over the years saw this kind of educational training as an important step towards emancipation, Rolanda explained to me. But what was their purpose? Only a job, indeed a good job, could ensure the independence she aspired to. She had the feeling of being forced to start from scratch, as if her previous experiences no longer mattered and her existence only began the moment she reached Italy. The courses organized at the centres trained her for female immigrant jobs,[14] such as maid, cleaner, nurse, seamstress, without taking into account her previous competence and expertise. My conversations with the centre directors and staff brought to light a completely different point of view. In their eyes, asylum seeking women had been given the chance to live in a privileged place, i.e., Milan, and this opportunity had to be clearly explained to them.

The institutional logic implicit in this kind of assertion reflects a hierarchy of values, where the cultural models of the new social context are considered 'more modern' when compared to the female immigrants' culture of origin. The discipline that women encounter while at the centres has the specific pedagogic intention of making them develop a sense of responsibility and autonomy as if they lacked such a sense before entering into contact with the assistance circuits of the Milan municipality. The staff I met often talked of the centres as incubators where women were socialized in the cultural values and norms of the host society. Care and assistance were the explicit objectives of these structures, which nonetheless interfered with the deeper and more intimate aspects of biographical time and subjectivity.

Vulnerability, Fantasy, Time

Compassion towards asylum seekers, as Aiwa Ong (2003) explains, carries with it an expectation that the women should become emancipated, but with no consideration of their social and cultural horizons, their life experiences and the very meaning they attach to the emancipation process. The women who live in Milan reception centres, or rely on the welfare system for their livelihood, carry with them stories of suffering and, often, of violence and desperation. Furthermore, as is frequently the case for forced migrants or asylum seekers, they lack well-structured social networks. Compared to other types of migration, where family or social networks in the place of destination support the mobility of newcomers, in the case of asylum seeking women, isolation is more likely to be the norm. Sometimes they have distant relatives whom they can contact, but more often these contacts live in other cities and hardly constitute a solid network capable of supporting them at least during their initial period in Italy. Suffering, misery and solitude characterize the situation of asylum seeking women during this period, to which must be added the lack of mastery of the Italian language, a poignant economic precariousness, as they find themselves often at the limits of survival, and the juridical insecurity of their position.

Taken all together, these conditions make women's recourse to assistance structures unavoidable. Bureaucratic processes, time suspension and strongly asymmetric helping relations are part of the complex process of being an asylum seeker. The long waiting for permits and the dependence on assistance structures have important repercussions on the subjectivity of women asylum seekers. Becoming a refugee appears as 'the political effect of institutional processes deeply imbued in sociocultural values' (Ong 2003: 79) and as a long and systematic process of subjection. Writing on the construction of subjectivity and on the forms of power that shape it, Judith Butler asserts that 'subjection is paradoxical' (Butler 1997: 1): it indicates at the same time 'the process of becoming subordinated by power as well as the process of becoming subject' (Butler 1997: 2). If power plays a role in 'forming the subject as well as providing the very condition of its existence and the trajectory of its desire, then power is not simply what we oppose but also, in a strong sense, what we depend on for our existence' (Butler 1997: 2). The memory of the drama of the flight, the culture of assistance, the long wait for permits and the different levels of exclusion experienced in other social contexts constitute the network of power that outline the forms of subjection and, simultaneously, 'the conditions of possibility' (Butler 1997: 2) which characterize the existence of these women. So, if becoming an asylum seeker appears to be a process of subjectification, its effects are not necessarily totalizing. As Moore writes, there is space for agency and inventiveness: 'power and ideology may work to produce these subject positions, but they do not determine how individuals will identify with and take up different subject positions at different times, nor do they determine how individuals will be involved in the transformation of discourses of power and difference over time' (2007: 41). By carefully listening to migration stories, I tried to grasp the ways in which women like Rolanda read the power networks in which they were involved, how they lived their assistance relationships with local institutions, and how they carved a path through the intricacy of the bureaucratic apparatus. By identifying the actions that female asylum seekers take to recompose their lives after the flight, it is possible to tackle the trajectory of their subjectivity. One may be vulnerable for economic, social or political reasons, but this does not necessarily imply that one is a victim or a passive subject to be emancipated, as the rhetoric about asylum seeking women seems to suggest. As Das points out, 'to be vulnerable is not the same as to be a victim' (2000: 209).

Rolanda's story sheds light on the social construction of vulnerability (Bourgois 2008) as the by-product of the drama of flight and of experiences in the host country, which asylum seeking women often perceive as a form of abuse.[15] The notion of vulnerability allows us to identify the relationship between migration, the events that occurred after the arrival in the host country, and the desire to reconstruct one's life. In spite of her vulnerability, Rolanda performed practices to cope with marginality. In feminist literature, as bell hooks has emphasized (1991), the notion of margin does not identify merely a place of deprivation: the margin, or the marginal positionality, has a political meaning that enables light to be shed on power networks and on forms of resistance and opposition to them. Marginal positionality encompasses a space in which a new life can be built, imagined, improved.[16] It is in this perspective that I suggest a link between the concept of vulnerability and the theme of fantasy. The latter can be defined as 'ideas about the kind of person one would like to be' (Moore 1994: 66) which allow us to explore individuals' desires for change and the actions that people take to fulfil them. Always, Moore writes, an 'approach to the analysis of agency must include a consideration of the role of fantasy and desire, both with regard to the questions of compliance and resistance and in connection with the construction of a sense of self' (1994: 5). Appadurai (1996) poses a distinction between imagination and fantasy. He defines imagination as a distinctive element of both the modern subjectivity and the modern era, where migrations and mass media, by circulating scenarios of possible lives, make imagination a resource 'for experiments with self-making' (1996: 3) and a 'fuel for actions' (1996: 7). In this sense, imagination becomes 'a social practice' (1996: 31), and a way to explore global cultural processes. According to Appadurai, while imagination is a social and collective process, fantasy has an exclusively private and individualistic dimension, which disconnects it from actions and where projects become 'an escape from reality' (1996: 7). Following anthropology and feminist literature, I consider the concept of fantasy as having a different theoretical genealogy, one which relates to the building of personal subjectivity, and that is far from being an escape from reality. Fantasy is thus linked with agency and embodies an impulse toward change.

Such a perspective arises from a critique of a theory of social action, in which desire, emotions and motivations are not considered in spite of the fundamental role they play in the understanding of individuals' actions. Forms of resistance and action, as well as people's choices, cannot be explained solely in rational and social terms.[17] It is often the ability (or the need) to imagine new lives that, in spite of their impoverished material conditions, enables asylum seeking women to identify resources and carry out projects which help them to face their marginality. As Weiss pointed out, fantasy means planning 'possible lives' (Weiss 2002: 97) because worlds 'must first be imagined, in order to be realized' (2002: 96). In this sense, fantasy becomes a social practice which embodies an impulse towards change.[18] It is the very suffering of exile and of the social marginality experienced in the host societies that pushes asylum seeking women forward. Rolanda's story is hardly understandable unless one takes into account the two dimensions of suffering and desire, because both occupy a central place in her resettlement process. The pain caused by her separation from her daughter, and her hope to see her daughter again as soon as possible, gives voice to Rolanda's emotions and to her fantastic projection into the future. It is precisely this desire that leads her to organize her daily life in order to regain her identity as a mother.

Finally, as feminist anthropology emphasizes, subjectivity is always a multi-positioned process built over time that 'does not have to be conceived of as a fixed and singular identity, but can be seen instead as one based on a series of subject positions, some conflicting or mutually contradictory, that are offered by different discourses' (Moore 1994: 4).[19] Contrasting the stereotype created by the assistance culture of Milan reception centres, Rolanda's story shows the overlapping of different identities with that of asylum seeker. Before migration, she was the wife of a political opponent, a mother, a daughter, and a well-off woman, and after migration she was a woman looking for a job.

Her situation was defined by a set of variables such as gender, culture, education and material conditions. Even after her arrival in Italy, Rolanda always lived her present time by looking forward to the achievement of something different, such as a job and a space to call 'home'. In the way she represented her migration story, both past and future crossed the present time, a point I will further explore by turning, once again, to our conversations during my research.[20]

Centres for Asylum Seekers, from Rolanda's Point of View

> I have wasted so much time in the centre . . . so much time. I've been here for four years. See, I'm still nothing. What I have, I found it by myself. I did it by myself.

Even all these jobs I have now, I got them with the help of a friend of mine. I kept asking and asking, where I should go to find a job. And they would say nothing. What can you do with no money? (Rolanda, January 2007)

Look, I was an independent woman before . . . yes, independent, I did it all by myself . . . and look at me now. (Rolanda, December 2006)

Rolanda's account of her own experiences expresses a view of asylum seekers' life and of the welfare policies meant to support them in which the theme of being abandoned to one's own resources is dominant.

Between December 2002 and June 2005, Rolanda lived in four different reception centres and she often said that the image she had of herself, which was made up of complex belongings, desires, needs and suffering, was poles apart from the one produced by the staff of these institutions. The assistance relationship entailed a double ambiguity. It not only forced Rolanda to feel 'weak' but it also proved incapable of concretely removing her condition of dependence. As Harrell-Bond (1999: 139) puts it, the point is not being helped *per se* – 'all human beings are dependent on others to a greater or lesser extent' – but rather 'the relative powerlessness of the recipient *vis-à-vis* the helper' (Harrell-Bond 1999: 139). One of the major sources of debilitating stress for women like Rolanda, who spent a fairly long period within the structures, is the very way they are helped and the image the helpers project onto their personality (Harrell-Bond 1999: 139). The 'experience of requiring help' often overlaps with the 'pain of being dependent' (Harrell-Bond 1999: 142), as is clearly stated by Rolanda herself:

The way they look at you. They look at you like, you know, you're just a black immigrant. I am . . . look! I was a woman with a lot of things, my family, my shop, Sandra. And now, when you are at the immigration office, or you're at the police station, when you've lived in the centre for a long time . . . the pain won't go away. At the police headquarters you don't even understand what they are asking for, at the centre nobody listens to you, I never talked about my daughter, they would never ask me about it. Go look for a job, but nobody asks. They say 'no'. And you just stay there, like that. (Rolanda, December 2006)

You always have to ask for things, they say no but you've got to ask anyways. You have to ask for food, for a job, for directions where to go. Now it's better, I speak enough Italian, I make a few bucks . . . but before, before I always had to ask but I didn't speak the language. Also ask for clothes. At the centre, you ask, you must ask for everything. You're always belittled! Weak! Poor! But I wasn't weak . . . and now it's a bit better. (Rolanda, December 2006)

Asking for help or showing herself as needy and weak was extremely hard for Rolanda, both with operators in the reception centres and with her social network of acquaintances and fellow countrywomen and countrymen. She often talked about her past: she used to tell job agency operators about the time she spent at her tailor's workshop. She spoke of how happy the girls were under her supervision and described in detail the clothes they created.

She also referred to her future: 'I have to change, I have to get my head straight again before Sandra's arrival'.

In her relationship with the institutions and with employment agencies, Rolanda always perceived herself as a 'poor woman'. This feeling deeply affected her self-image. At the same time, however, this image was in stark contrast with the one that Rolanda offered through her personal narrative of having been an independent woman with a well-compensated and socially respected job and as a mother who could look after her daughter, her house and her family network. This gap, full of pain and laceration, also surfaces in the extracts of Rolanda's accounts I quoted in the beginning of this paragraph. Rolanda evoked the past to protect herself against the weakness which lay at the core of her relationships with assistance structures. The present was a set of temporary strategies and practices necessary to remove marginality and weakness, while her more intimate and real life was projected into the future. Women like Rolanda indeed live waiting for something to happen to fulfil something else. In other words, Rolanda's life expressed itself in fantasies of identity and in terms of what she would have done if only she had a regular and better paid job that would allow her to be a mother again.

Rolanda often talked of herself as a woman who had lost her balance and mental health. She used to cry every time she talked about her daughter. She often used the word 'pain' to describe the torn relationship with both her husband and her daughter. Actually, the pain and the perception of being a woman who had lost her inner balance were a by-product of her migration and of the years she spent in Milan. The long wait for regularization documents, the three years spent living in reception centres, the difficulties experienced in trying to regain a sense of autonomy all nurtured the feeling of 'being nowhere'. 'This head is still not working', she often repeated while touching her forehead with her hand:

> Who knows if I will make it . . . at the beginning I didn't even speak Italian, and I wouldn't even understand what I was supposed to hope for. Then, slowly . . . something, a job with the elder women, but you're always waiting and waiting. Then also . . . after all this time, your strength goes away a little bit. It's a struggle, a struggle to keep the head work well. What am I supposed to do if my daughter comes here and I still feel like this? (Rolanda, September 2006)

Strategies in Spite of Assistance

As I have tried to explain, there was a discrepancy between Rolanda's self-description and the real practices she was embedded in. Above all, the vulnerability caused by her condition as an asylum seeker and by the lack of any structural help from the welfare system, which proved unable to fulfil her expectations (after all, Rolanda only wanted to find a decent job and bring her daughter to Italy) did not block her agency. Although she met with extreme difficulty, Rolanda was trying to build a better future for herself and Sandra. Both the memory of her past and her projection towards the future played a crucial role in resisting the image that the centres stamped on her. Rolanda found alternative resources within informal networks, entering the irregular work market and sharing the house with Perpetua. At this point, her desire for improvement played an important role. Rolanda's flight gave rise to deep suffering, and rather than helping her, the centres actually narrowed her margins of movement. Nevertheless, she strove to regain power over her life. As soon as she arrived in Italy, she began her struggle. While she was in the second and third centre,[21] Rolanda attended some training courses, which actually did nothing to help her find a job. For Rolanda, having a job was important for at least three reasons. The first was that in Lomé she had always worked, and this was a key element of her personal identity and history. The second reason was that only a job could allow her to leave the centres. Last but not least, a regular job could grant her the opportunity to convert her humanitarian residence permit into a job permit, facilitating – as provided for by the Italian immigration law – her family reunion. Therefore she repeatedly asked the educational operators to help her to find a job or to give her essential information on how to find one, explaining the importance of this step in her life project. Her request, however, was never satisfied. Experience taught Rolanda that structures, operators and services were not ready to support what really mattered to her. In her perspective, her dependence on the centres made her feel even more abandoned.

Refugee women like Rolanda achieve concrete outcomes only through the assistance of informal networks rather than that of state institutions. Even if such networks are often temporary and occasional, they nonetheless provide help in finding a house or a job or in giving the information required to move around Milan. Rolanda and Perpetua met in the second centre that Rolanda lived in. Although Rolanda had other friends and acquaintances, she often remarked how complicity or friendship relationships required time and confidence to grow. When daily life is made up of emergencies, of bonds severed by migration and not yet reconstructed, it is difficult to commit oneself to enduring relationships. This was especially true of the period following her arrival, when Rolanda spent most of her time within the centres. She needed a few months to learn the new language and to move through the city. Even in the centres, the sharing of similar migration experiences and of the same spaces did not necessarily give rise to friendly relations.

It was Perpetua who managed to find a house for Rolanda. When we first met, Rolanda and Perpetua had been living together for one year in a flat consisting of a kitchen, two bedrooms and a bathroom. They split the rent for a room in the flat (shared with other two immigrant women), nearly 450 euros per month. Although happy, Rolanda perceived this accommodation as transitory. She still felt as a woman bereft of home and of a private place to live; but living with Perpetua had made her aware of the possibility of carrying on with her life without the assistance of reception structures. She used to repeat: 'after the centre, I have been able to know life, because when you are inside the centre or only have relations with operators, you can't know how life is' (Rolanda, 5 July 2006).

Rolanda got a job in the summer of 2003 when she began working as a housemaid for some Italian families thanks to the help of other immigrant women. Since we first met, Rolanda has been working with increasing frequency, managing to integrate into the occupational world, although only in its most precarious and irregular layers. In the morning, she looked after the house of a well-off woman. In the afternoon, from 5:30 P.M. to 10 P.M., she cleaned the classrooms of a kindergarten. The real aspiration was to get a regular job, which would allow her to obtain a family reunion permit. For this, she was ready to accept even a modest salary. I helped her to translate her curriculum vitae and we spent plenty of time not only visiting job agencies but also gathering information from informal employment circuits like parishes and religious associations, which often act as job intermediaries both for female and male immigrants at the local level. Actually, only in 2010 did Rolanda manage to find a 'regular' job at a cleaning service and to ask for a job permit. At the end of 2010, she was still waiting for a response, and had not yet rejoined her daughter. Due to their vulnerable situation, asylum seeking women cannot but have an association with reception centres. The construction of their subjectivity, however, is not exclusively shaped by the circuits of state welfare.

Memories of their previous life, the projection towards the future (however uncertain the future might be), the resources available through informal relations, and participation in irregular labour markets all play their part. The system of reception and welfare, although indispensable for female asylum seekers during their first few months after arrival, is fraught with ambiguities and contradictions; however, informal social networks and the irregular labour markets, which these women approach in order to reconstruct their lives, also have their own mechanisms of exploitation. Asylum seeking women are subject to multiple forms of social discrimination. For instance, whereas informal networks help women to find a job and a house, often this job is over-exploited and the house is found only after the payment of monetary compensation to the intermediary.

Conclusion

Suffering and vulnerability are the lot of asylum seeking women. Far from being preternatural, both conditions result from specific social and cultural processes, which, in the case of Rolanda, I tried to identify by using the concepts of time, fantasy and subjectivity. Concrete structural conditions and power networks turned Rolanda, and other women like her, into marginal and vulnerable subjects. Made up of disruptions, suffering and desires, her story illustrates the long time taken for the resettlement process and its association with multiple forms of abuse. It also shows not only the difficulties that asylum seeking women face but also the social and emotive resources that propel them to action and change.

The suffering caused by migration is rarely considered as an enduring condition perpetuated and strengthened by reception contexts and bureaucratic relations in the host country. Indeed, pain and displacement stem from both the traumatic memory linked to the experiences lived in the context of origin and from the dynamics occurring in the host country. In this sense, through Rolanda's story, I tried to shed light on the 'political dimension of suffering' (Bourgois 2008: 114), identifying those forms of violence which 'state institutions are, at least partially, responsible of creating' (Beneduce 2008: 24).

Several actions, such as looking for a job or a house, or waiting for a family reunion permit – all crucial elements in the reconstruction of migrants' social life – are complicated by the hiatus between the formal and the substantial aspects of the law and by the paradox of assistance policies which are unable to fill the existential gap produced by forced migration. Reception structures often live off the very weaknesses they produce, nourishing instead of removing vulnerability and other forms of marginality. Rolanda, however, never perceived herself as a victim nor behaved like one. The vulnerability emerging from her story has a political meaning. More than representing a 'narrative of victimization' (Das 2000), her acts and words denounced the social experiences that caused her suffering. These very acts and words show how Rolanda's ability to see herself and act as a multi-positioned subjectivity played an important role in her attempts to positively modify her existence as an asylum seeker. Her projection towards the future was bolstered by Rolanda's relatively young age and by the fact of having Sandra. From the ethnographical point of view, the notion of fantasy – being linked to what one hopes will happen but has not happened yet – helps one to focus on actions and practices that inhabit the time of wait, in which Italian law confines asylum seeking women. By focusing on both time and fantasy, I attempted to introduce an often overlooked dimension – that of the future – into the study of forced migrations. In doing so, I hope to have shown how forced migrations should be understood as processes which do not end when asylum seekers reach their host destination and obtain a permit, but instead continue over time due to the concrete efforts of women like Rolanda, engaged in a daily struggle against their own marginality.

Notes

1 See, for example, Harrell-Bond (1986, 1999); Harrell-Bond, Voutira and Leopold (1992); Malkki (1996); Ong (2003).
2 Milan policies for asylum seekers have changed a lot in the past few years due to legal transformations at the national and local level. Assistance centres are

managed by a variety of non-governmental actors, such as NGOs, non-profit organizations, social cooperatives and the Catholic Church. When I was following Rolanda's story, there were four institutional centres for asylum seeking women and several other organizations which provided assistance to both migrants and refugees. The Decree n. 25 of 28/01/2008 sanctioned the establishment of C.A.R.A. (Centro di Accoglienza per Richiedenti Asilo), whereby asylum seekers who lack documents of identification are hosted while they wait for the acceptance (or rejection) of their request for asylum.

3 In particular, see pp. 49–70.

4 My work on the biographies and daily experiences of asylum seeking women, and on the importance of life stories as a means of exploring social shared experiences takes its cue from Abu-Lughod (1993); Ghorashi (2007); Ong (1995); Zeitlyn (2008).

5 For an in-depth account of the recent political history of Togo, see Ellis (1993); Seely (2009); and Toulabor (1986).

6 This law, which was promulgated in 2002, is better known as the Bossi-Fini Law (Umberto Bossi was the Lega Nord leader and Gianfranco Fini was the leader of Alleanza Nazionale, both right-wing parties).

7 For an in-depth account on immigration and asylum law in Italy, see Einaudi (2007) and Valtimora (2009: 185–220).

8 The seven Territorial Commissions were created by the Bossi-Fini Law. Decree n. 25 of 28 January 2008 and the implementation Decree of 6 March 2008 established another three Territorial Commissions. There are currently Asylum Commissions in Gorizia, Milan, Rome, Foggia, Syracuse, Crotone, Trapani, Bari, Caserta and Turin. The Commission is bound to listen to the testimony of the asylum seekers within thirty days of the reception of their request. A decision must be reached within three days. Waiting times have thus been drastically reduced although the thirty-day rule is not always respected. See the website of the Interior Ministry, http://www.interno.it/mininterno/export/sites/default/it/temi/asilo/sottotema0021/Le_Commissioni_Territorialix_funzioni_e_composizione.html.

9 In Pinelli (2010, 2011) I stress how bureaucratic and care relations have a significant effect on the daily life and subjectivity of immigrant asylum seekers.

10 Holston and Appadurai (1996) underline how the actual possibility of exercising one's own rights (which is a significant aspect of citizenship) is not always consequent to their formal and juridical acquisition (formal aspect of citizenship).

11 Grillo and Pratt (2002) have highlighted the particularity of the Italian context. For an in-depth account on political discourse in the city of Milan, see also Caponio (2006).

12 Recent ethnographic researches have focused on the daily rules, and on the techniques of control and surveillance that characterize reception the camps for asylum seekers. See for instance Szczepanikova (2005, 2012); Turner (2005); Whyte (2011). See also Fassin (2005) for accounts on the governance of the body and the compassionate attitude of assistance culture.

13 Dialogue with the staff, August 2007.

14 The expression 'female immigrant jobs' refers to the occupational niches that the global labour market reserves for immigrant women. See, for instance, Ehrenreich and Hochschild (2002); Anthias and Lazaridis (2000).

15 This refers to the concept of structural violence, i.e., the violence engendered by structures – in other words by ideologies or by the state apparatus, by political violence, or in this case by humanitarian ideology – that fosters forms of suffering and social inequalities. See Farmer (1997, 2004) and Das and Kleinman (2001) for in-depth accounts of this issue.
16 See de Lauretis (1990); hooks (1991).
17 See Moore (1994: 49–70; 2007: 1–42).
18 On fantasy as a social practice, see also Weiss (2002).
19 For a more articulated debate on multi-positioned subjectivity, see de Lauretis (1990); Moore (1994, 2007).
20 On the relation between past and future, see Ricoeur (1985) in which the author is concerned with the notions of 'space of experience' and 'horizon of hope'. In particular, 'space of experience' indicates everything that has happened, and that has become part of the personal experience; 'horizon of hope' refers to hope and fear, desire and curiosity, i.e., all the expressions and feelings that project the person into the future. Like the space of experience, the horizon of hope is linked to the present. Space of experience and horizon of hope are closely connected to each other, but the past is not enough to determine the future, which is made of lived experiences but also of openness and hopes.
21 Women move from one centre to another following the rule established by the Milan municipality on the duration of their stay in each structure. After six months in one place, they are moved to other institutions according to the space available.

References

Abu-Lughod, L. 1993. *Writing Women's Worlds: Bedouin Stories.* London: University of California Press.
Appadurai, A. 1996. *Modernity at Large: Cultural Dimension of Globalization.* Minneapolis: University of Minnesota Press.
Anthias, F. and G. Lazaridis (eds). 2000. *Gender and Migration in the Southern Europe. Women on the Move.* Bridgend: WBC.
Beneduce, R. 2008. 'Introduzione. Etnografie della Violenza', *Annuario di Antropologia* 9–10: 5–48.
Bourgois, P. 2008. 'Sofferenza e Vulnerabilità Socialmente Strutturate. Tossicodipendenti senzatetto negli Stati Uniti', *Annuario di Antropologia* 9–10: 113–35.
Butler, J. 1997. *The Psychic Life of Power. Theories in Subjection.* Stanford, CA: Stanford University Press.
Caponio, T. 2006. *Città italiane e immigrazione. Discorso pubblico e politiche a Milano, Bologna e Napoli.* Bologna: Il Mulino.
Das, V. 2000. 'The Act of Witnessing: Violence, Poisonous Knowledge, and Subjectivity', in V. Das et al. (eds), *Violence and Subjectivity.* Berkeley: University of California Press, pp. 205–55.
Das, V. and A. Kleinman. 2001. 'Introduction', in V. Das et al. (eds), *Remaking the World. Violence, Social Suffering and Recovery.* Berkeley: University of California Press, pp. 1–30.

De Lauretis, T. 1990. 'Eccentric Subjects', *Feminist Studies* 16(1): 115–50.

Ehrenreich, B. and A.R. Hochschild (eds). 2002. *Global Woman. Nannies, Maids, and Sex Workers in the New Economy.* New York: Henry Holt.

Einaudi, L. 2007. *Le politiche dell'immigrazione in Italia dall'Unità a oggi.* Rome and Bari: Laterza.

Ellis, S. 1993. 'Rumour and Silence in Togo', *Africa* 63: 462–76.

Farmer, P. 1997. 'On Suffering and Structural Violence: A View from Below', in V. Das, A. Kleinman and M. Lock (eds), *Social Suffering.* Berkeley, Los Angeles and London: University of California Press, pp. 261–84.

⸺. 2004. 'An Anthropology of Structural Violence', *Current Anthropology* 45(3): 305–25.

Fassin, D. 2001. 'The Biopolitics of Otherness: Undocumented Foreigners and Racial Discrimination in French Public Debate', *Anthropology Today* 17(1): 3–7.

⸺. 2005. 'Compassion and Repression: The Moral Economy of Immigration Policies in France', *Cultural Anthropology* 20(3): 362–87.

Ghorashi, H. 2007. 'Giving Silence a Chance: The Importance of Life Stories for Research on Refugees', *Journal of Refugee Studies* 21(1): 117–32.

Grillo, R. and J. Pratt (eds). 2002. *The Politics of Recognizing Difference. Multiculturalism Italian-Style.* Aldershot: Ashgate.

Harrell-Bond, B.E. 1986. *Imposing Aid. Emergency Assistance to Refugees.* Oxford: Oxford University Press.

⸺. 1999. 'The Experience of Refugees as Recipients of Aid', in A. Ager (ed.), *Refugees. Perspectives on the Experience of Forced Migration.* London: Continuum, pp. 136–68.

Harrell-Bond, B.E., E. Voutira and M. Leopold. 1992. 'Counting the Refugees: Gifts, Givers, Patrons and Clients', *Journal of Refugee Studies* 5(3–4): 205–25.

Holston, J. and A. Appadurai. 1996. 'Cities and Citizenship', *Public Culture* 8: 187–204.

hooks, b. 1991. 'Choosing the Margin as a Space of Radical Openness', in b. hooks, *Yearning. Race, Gender and Cultural Politics.* London: Turnaround, pp. 145–54.

Malkki, L. 1996. 'Speechless Emissaries: Refugees, Humanitarianism, and Dehistoricization', *Cultural Anthropology* 11(3): 377–404.

Mohanty, J. 1993, 'The Status of the Subject in Foucault', in J. Caputo and M. Yount (eds), *Foucault and the Critique of Institutions.* Pennsylvania: State University Press.

Moore, H. 1994. *A Passion for Difference. Essays in Anthropology and Gender.* Cambridge: Polity Press.

⸺. 2007. *The Subject of Anthropology: Gender, Symbolism and Psychoanalysis.* London: Polity Press.

Ong, A. 1995. 'Women out of China: Travelling, Tales and Travelling Theories in Postcolonial Feminism', in R. Behar and D. Gordon (eds), *Women Writing Culture.* Berkeley: University of California Press, pp. 350–71.

⸺. 2003. *Buddha is Hiding: Refugees, Citizenship, and the New America.* Berkeley: University of California Press.

Pinelli, B. 2010. 'Soggettività e sofferenza nelle migrazioni delle donne richiedenti asilo in Italia', in V. Ribeiro-Corossacz and A. Gribaldo (eds), *Sul campo del genere. Ricerche etnografiche sul femminile e sul maschile.* Verona: Ombre Corte, pp. 135–56.

_____. 2011. 'Attraversando il mediterraneo. Il sistema campo in Italia: violenza e soggettività nelle esperienze delle donne', *Lares* LXXVII(1): 159–79.

Ricoeur, P. 1985. *Temps et Récit 3. Le Temps Raconté*. Paris: Editions du Seuil.

Seely, J. 2009. *The Legacies of Transition Governments in Africa: The Cases of Benin and Togo*. Palgrave: Macmillan.

Szczepanikova, A. 2005. 'Gender Relations in a Refugee Camp: A Case of Chechens Seeking Asylum in the Czech Republic', *Journal of Refugee Studies* 18(3): 281–298.

_____. 2012. 'Between Control and Assistance: The Problem of European Accommodation Centers for Asylum Seekers', *IOM (International Organization for Migration)* 2012: 2–14.

Toulabor, C.M. 1986. *Le Togo sous Eyadéma*. Paris: Karthala.

Turner, S. 2005. 'Suspended Spaces', in T. Blom Hansen and F. Stepputat (eds), *Sovereign Bodies. Citizens, Migrants, and States in the Postcolonial World*. Princeton and Oxford: Princeton University Press, pp. 312–32.

Valtimora, A. 2009. *La disciplina dell'immigrazione*. Napoli: Esselibri-Simone.

Weiss, B. 2002. 'Thug Realism: Inhabiting Fantasy in Urban Tanzania', *Cultural Anthropology* 17(1): 93–124.

Whyte, Z. 2011. 'Enter in the Myopticon. Uncertain Surveillance in the Danish Asylum System', *Anthropology Today* 27(3): 18–21.

Zeitlyn, D. 2008. 'Life-history Writing and the Anthropological Silhouette', *Social Anthropology/Anthropologie Sociale* 16(2): 154–71.

Chapter 2

Negotiating the Past, Imagining a Future

*Exploring Tamil Refugees' Sense of
Identity and Agency*

Anne Sigfrid Grønseth

Introduction

This chapter takes as its starting point a follow-up study carried out among Tamil refugees who have moved from the northernmost Arctic coast of Norway to the capital of Oslo in the south. It focuses on how everyday transnational relations and diasporic challenges have an effect upon illness, well-being and identity as these are related to tensions in continuity and change. These tensions are approached analytically using the concepts of embodiment and 'being-in-the-world' (Bourdieu 1989; Merleau-Ponty 1962 [1945]; Csordas 1994; Jackson 1989), which, I suggest, provide avenues for a study of linkages between memories of the past and future visions as these appear to interact with and generate Tamils' experiences of present pain and well-being. Such an analysis is intended to illuminate how individuals may exercise creativity and agency in the formation of life-projects (Rapport 2003) and self-identity within frames of a fractured and conflicting everyday life. This is an agency, I argue, that emerges from the embodied suffering of social relations and experiences of intersubjectivity when one is living in the borderlands between Tamil and Norwegian life-worlds. Furthermore, I argue that future visions not predominantly sustained by a nostalgic longing for the past, but from connecting to others in the here and now, carry potential for relief and well-being.

Following more than ten years of contact with Tamil refugees, including one year of intensive fieldwork (1999–2000) among Tamils who had settled in Arctic Harbor, one of the small fishing villages of Finnmark county, I re-engaged with the Tamils then living in Oslo. From August to December 2007 I conducted frequent and short-term field visits to Tamils in Oslo. I began with contacts with Tamils whom I had met in Arctic Harbor, but also included other Tamils who live in the area and interact with them. My focus for the follow-up research was centred on how the Tamils of Arctic Harbor experienced the move to Oslo, and how they perceived it to affect their senses of illness,[1] health and well-being.

In the following I briefly introduce the Tamils of Norway in the context of refugee and diasporic issues that are seen to highlight those human capacities of agency that affect senses of identity and temporality. Secondly, I present the context of fieldwork as it follows Tamils moving from Arctic Harbor to Oslo in the search for meaningful Tamil wholeness[2] and a sense of community, freedom and opportunity. The third section presents a case study of a Tamil woman, Malar, who experienced her everyday existence as 'living in a tunnel' or in a zone inbetween what are understood as Tamil and Norwegian life-worlds. Such life-worlds are not fixed or totally distinguishable, but rather have floating characteristics that are constantly disputed, negotiated, created and re-created (see also Introduction, this volume). The fourth section offers an analysis which highlights how the experience of living in the borderlands and in between different life-worlds provides an opportunity for individuals to transcend the losses and traumas of the past and alienation in the present and to create new visions and hope for the future. Finally, I draw attention to the way in which studies of migrant well-being and identity can underscore what is seen as a pendular movement between continuity and change that enforces new senses of self and well-being, thus appreciating difference as a part of being human.

Tamils in Norway: Refugees Living in Diaspora

Though the Sri Lankan conflict is beyond the scope of this chapter, I will briefly mention the civil war context for the Tamil refugees in Norway. The Tamil minority situation has been a political issue since Sri Lanka's independence in 1948. Political tensions and discrimination increased when, in 1956, Sinhalese was declared as the official language. In June 1983 there were upheavals in which many were killed and others had to flee their homes. Among different political and guerrilla movements, the LTTE (Liberation Tigers of Tamil Eelam) were the most aggressive and led the opposition fighting for an independent state of Tamil Eelam. The traditional Tamil majority areas of Jaffna in the north and eastern Sri Lanka were declared war zones, and most Tamil people live in exile or as refugees in their own country. Following the end of the war in May 2009, the LTTE dropped its demands for a separate state in favour of a federal solution. Since the civil war ended the Tamil diaspora has continued to protest against the war by urging governments to undertake war-crimes inspections in Sri Lanka.

While acknowledging the tensions and complexities of the civil war and ultimate declaration of peace, the focus of the present chapter is on Tamils from Sri Lanka who are living in Norway as refugees in the diaspora.

According to Statistics Norway, 1 January 2011, 13.1 per cent of Norway's total population consisted of around 460,000 immigrants and their descendants from 219 different countries and self-governed regions (for more on Norway's immigrant populations, see Henriksen et al. 2010). At that time, 157,692 immigrants had refugee backgrounds, of whom 114,760 were refugees themselves and a further 42,932 had arrived as family members to be reunited with them. This total represents about 3.2 per cent of Norway's total population. Of this population, 14,293 have a Sri Lankan background. According to figures from 1 January 2012, a year later, 8,816 individuals were first-generation immigrants and 5,477 had been born in Norway of parents both of whom came from Sri Lanka. Virtually all the Sri Lankans are Tamils.

Being a refugee implies a sense of being forced to escape from life-threatening circumstances, such as political persecution and war; it often implies sudden departures and a need to travel at great risk, together with great uncertainty about one's destination and future prospects (Malkki 1995; Daniel and Knudsen 1995; Jenkins 1996; Sideris 2003; Hammond 2004; Zmegac 2007; Migliorino 2008). The refugee experience can generally be divided into four phases (Desjarlais et al. 1995: 140): the pre-flight period, in which the pressure of the situation increases and a decision is reached to leave; the escape of migrating from one place to another; and the reception period that passes before the person returns to his or her home region, or settles in the asylum country or in some third location in the fourth phase.

This investigation looks into the fourth period of resettlement and long-term residence, with a focus on the daily efforts to adapt and the quest for well-being on the part of Tamil refugees in their new environment (see also Grønseth 2010). The present study confirms how research on refugees generally discusses problems related to cultural differences, acculturation and social ties, and suggests that refugees have a better chance of retaining their psychosocial health if they maintain strong social and community ties and a sense of cultural identity (Desarlais et al. 1995: 143). Difficulties in obtaining appropriate employment can provide an additional long-term stress factor and may threaten one's sense of self-esteem as well as one's standard of living. However, while not disputing such general features, this chapter explores how embodied social suffering (Kleinman et al. 1997) can also be seen as granting access to an existential agency in forming new senses of identity, self and well-being.

As a consequence of migrating under forced circumstances, many refugees tend to maintain a strong hope and desire to return to their homeland when the time is right, such as when the war is over. Even though many Tamils in Norway have permanent residence permits on grounds of family unification, rather than because they themselves sought asylum, similar feelings of risk, uncertainty and the hope of a return are commonly experienced. While Tamils are generally identified as refugees, they also share features with overlapping categories of diasporic or transnational populations. Many Tamils tend to maintain a myth about their homeland; they see their ancestral home as a place of eventual return, they are committed to the restoration of this homeland, and they display a continuous relationship with it (see, for example, Safran 1991; Clifford 1994; Bicharat 1997; Slymovics 1998). Simultaneously, Tamils engage in transnational relations and practices by circulating people, money, goods and information, thus keeping in touch, participating in family events and taking part in decision-making with significant others spread throughout the world (see also Rouse 1991; Schiller et al. 1992). Thus, as Clifford (1994) argues, decentred and horizontal connections may be as important as those formed around a myth of origin and return (see also Brown 1998; Berg 2009; Hintzen 2001; Axel 2002, 2004). Indeed, the linking of transnational diasporics can be fruitfully seen in the ongoing history of displacement, suffering, adaptation and resistance, which may be as important as the idea of a specific homeland of origin.

Understanding Tamil refugees in the light of the diaspora helps us to recognize how they seek to transcend the labels of ethnicity and minority groups which place them within the discourse of the national majority society and structure issues of assimilation and resistance (Clifford 1994; McDowell 1996; Fuglerud 1999; Grønseth 2010). While the notion of diaspora captures the sense of discrimination and exclusion, it also provides a continuum of identification with a worldwide history of cultural and political powers. Migrants in a diaspora can be seen to have a sense of attachment elsewhere, to a different temporality and vision, which can produce a sense of being global, cosmopolitan, or, I suggest, a sense of being equally human. As such, the diasporic perspective fits in with my aim to explore how, under certain circumstances, suffering can provide access to a complex agency that may help one to transgress the (often nostalgic) longing to return, and create new images of the future that can enhance positive senses of self and well-being in the here and now.

The refugee and diasporic experience is always gendered. Recognizing that gender is embedded in institutions that affect major areas of life such as sexuality, the family, education, economy and the state, it appears that gender principles govern conflicting interests and hierarchies of power and privilege (see Glenn 1999). Moreover, there is a need to recognize how gender in a migration and transnational context includes both cognitive and bodily experiences and actions (see Pessar and Mahler 2001). This corresponds with how this chapter examines individuals', such as Malar's, daily negotiations and creations of identity as these interact with values, images and temporality.

Identity and Temporality: An Intergenerational Perspective

In considering identity and temporality, the linkages and ruptures between generations appear crucial in shaping future visions and engagement in the here and now. While holding on to (nostalgic) dreams and hopes of a return to their homeland, there is also a strong bond to Norway experienced through the younger generation who are growing up and who connect themselves in different ways to Norway. Among the 12.2 per cent of the total population in Norway who are immigrants or have parents who have immigrated (as of 1 January 2010), children and young adults with immigrant parents made up 11 per cent of the total population aged 0–24 years (Dzamarija 2010). The proportion of youths of immigrant background starting upper secondary education is lower, and the drop-out rate is higher than among youth of non-immigrant background (ibid.). The parents of children with backgrounds from Eastern Europe, Asia, Africa or Latin America also have much lower income levels than their majority Norwegian contemporaries, primarily due to the fact that many of the families have difficulties in finding employment and have not acquired social security rights (ibid.). According to Statistics Norway, in May 2012, 6.1 per cent of the immigrant population was registered as unemployed, while the majority population registered 1.8 per cent unemployment. The registered unemployment among immigrant men was 5.9 per cent and among immigrant women 6.3 per cent.[3] These statistics include the Tamil population, though among the refugee populations Tamils are generally known to have a low percentage of unemployment, to be hard-working and to be continuing a tradition that takes pride in and values higher education as part of Tamil culture and identity.[4]

However, a report from Statistic Norway (Lie 2004) points out that in 2001, 17.1 per cent of Sri Lankan immigrants (30–44 years old) have a university or college education. This is a lower average than for the total population (30 per cent), the total immigrant population (26.9 per cent), and non-western immigrants (21.3 per cent). These figures, I would like to add, must be seen in relation to the fact that most of the Tamil refugees in Norway were young people who, because of war and flight, had to break off their studies or plans for an education. Yet, the figure for first-generation immigrants from Sri Lanka (19–24 years old) in higher education was 13.6 per cent in 2000 (Lie 2004). This is a little higher than for the immigrant population as a whole. Among persons born in Norway of two parents born in Sri Lanka, the employment rate was very high (48.7 per cent), much higher than for average in the total Norwegian population. It is important to bear in mind that this group (between 19 and 24 years old) is not very large, numbering fewer than fifty individuals (Lie 2004). With respect to employment, Lie (2004) found that in 2001, 61.1 per cent of first-generation immigrants from Sri Lanka were in employment, while for the total population of Norway the figure was 60.8 per cent.[5] Tamil employment is high among both men and women. In 2001, 69.7 per cent of men and 51 per cent of women from Sri Lanka were employed.[6]

Although the Tamil parental generation seeks to pass on a Tamil cultural identity to the younger generation, many Tamil parents realize the complex expectations and demands that their children must deal with. Many of the parents exert strong pressure, demands and social control as a way of ensuring that their children become 'good Tamils', which includes success in education and work. Trying to fulfil often mismatched and high expectations, many young Tamils experience an existential struggle to retain a minimum of self-esteem and a sense of living a worthwhile life (see also Engebrigtsen and Fuglerud 2007). However, the parents also often find themselves facing a similar quandary in seeking to fulfil Tamil local, diasporic and kin relationships and expectations and at the same time making a life for themselves in the here and now. In dealing with such intergenerational issues, many Tamil parents acknowledge the need to engage in the wider society (apart from wage-work) of the here and now so as to support their children in Norwegian education, work and friendships, thereby conceding that their support and engagement (or lack thereof) affect their children's sense of self and well-being in everyday life. As the Tamils struggle with refugee, diasporic and intergenerational issues in everyday life in the borderlands between Norwegian and Tamil life-worlds, what was once taken for granted and is now (nostalgically) longed for can be perceived as something that can be negotiated and transformed into future new visions that may help to enforce a sense of self, relief and well-being.

Tamils in Arctic Harbor: In Search of a Larger Community

As the tensions between the Sinhalese and Tamil populations in Sri Lanka resulted in open conflict and the outbreak of civil war, many Tamils from Sri Lanka escaped and sought asylum as refugees in a wide range of countries such as Canada, the United Kingdom, New Zealand, Denmark, Norway, Switzerland, Germany, Italy and Greece. The countries that were most desirable for resettlement were not easily accessible, and the Tamil refugees' reception in the host countries has varied according to colonial and historical ties and the politics of immigration and integration. For instance, in the United Kingdom, due to colonial ties and interchange, the refugees were received and perceived of as part of an already established Tamil community, which created its own particular challenges (Daniel 1998). In Norway, by comparison, Tamil immigration was almost non-existent until the outbreak of the civil war in Sri Lanka. While this chapter does not allow a thorough history of immigration to be given, I will discuss some major features that relate to the actual study of Tamils in the northernmost Arctic part of Norway.[7]

The first two male Tamil immigrants came to Norway as a consequence of the Norwegian institution Cey-Nor, which established a fishing project in Jaffna in the late 1960s and opened up a passage for employment in the Norwegian fishing industry in the far north. Gradually, these two men managed to arrange for both close and distant relatives to be employed in the local fishing industry. Following the Norwegian immigration ban of 1975, they found a loophole to help their Tamil compatriots by using the important setting up of *Folkehøyskoler,* a Norwegian system of Folk Colleges. After the outbreak of the Sri Lankan civil war in 1983, Tamil immigration increased via this loophole, while some asylum seekers spent months, sometimes years, in the asylum centres that were distributed throughout mostly rural areas of Norway, before finally receiving residence permits on humanitarian grounds (see Grønseth 2010). Many of these mostly young single men and some women took jobs in the fishing industry along the Arctic coast, which they saw as an opportunity to earn money to re-pay debts from escape journeys, to support the family they had left behind, to help pay the dowry for their sisters' weddings and to establish their own young families in Norway through the Norwegian policy of family unification.

Since this chapter starts from the original fieldwork, conducted between 1996 and 2000 among the Tamil population in Arctic Harbor (a pseudonym), all of whom were then working in the low-status job of cutters in the fishing industry, I will very briefly point out a few aspects that characterize the context of this study (see also Grønseth 2010). Arctic Harbor lies inland in a small fjord near the Barent Sea and the open sea towards the North Pole. In response to changes in the fish population, prices and supply, in the mid-1980s many of the local fishing villages experienced a shortage of labour and made a request to the Governmental Refugee Secretary to use refugee labour in the fishing industry. The first Tamils to arrive volunteered and were then selected from the asylum centres. They formed a group of eleven Tamils – including five married couples and one young single man. They were all allocated to a 'host family', who introduced them to local practices such as hiking in the mountains, preparing local dishes and other local ways of life. Since then, Tamils have been invited as workers in the fishing industry and have proved to be a valuable resource in the local communities. As the mayor of a local fishing village expressed it: 'Without the Tamils, our community would cease to exist'.[8]

By the mid-1990s, the Tamil population had reached about 250 people (10 per cent of the total population) in Arctic Harbor. A few other fishing villages had a similarly high percentage of Tamils in the total population. In Arctic Harbor, as elsewhere in the fishing communities in Finnmark, the northernmost county in Norway, the Tamils were offered safety, well-paid jobs and reasonably good housing, as well as an initial invitation to assimilate by taking part in Norwegian ways of life. Tamils responded by establishing a Local Tamil Association[9] to arrange a variety of Tamil activities (sports, computer classes Tamil language and culture) and invited Norwegians to their celebrations and festivals. However, neither approach was successful in terms of social integration. The Tamil population became economically integrated but remained socially segregated (see Grønseth 2001, 2010). In spite of many successful features in re-establishing a local Tamil community, most Tamils expressed a profound longing for Tamil-Hindu temples and kin ties that were not present in the north of Norway (Grønseth 2001, 2010). The greater proportion of Tamils expressed an embodied and deeply felt longing for their homeland and everyday life as it used to be. In often nostalgic ways life was described with a longing for the sounds of people working and chatting, animal and birdcalls, the smell of sweat, heat, humidity and dust, the smell and taste of foods, curries and spices, and the colours and texture of clothing, flowers and earth, together with the laughter, scolding and chatting that went on among the family and in the neighbourhood. Such images and sensations were described as encompassing a deep longing for community (Cohen 1986; Amit and Rapport 2002), kinship and temples. Despite acknowledging many difficulties and facing obstacles and hindrances as part of everyday life, the Tamils were generally nostalgically 'longing for home'.

The Tamils spoke of a deep sense of uncertainty and aloneness, or *tanimai tosam* (Daniel 1989), related to the loss of kin and religious ties. This experience, I have argued elsewhere (Grønseth 2010), must be understood in the light of how Tamils' indigenous social relations are governed by principles of kin and caste as a hierarchy of distinct categories and groups into which one is born (see Pfaffenberger 1982; Dumont 1980 [1966]; Barnett 1975; Bayly 1999; Fuller 1996; Searle-Chatterjee and Sharma 1994; Deepa 2005; and others). Traditionally, kinship, caste and age groups, all embedded in Hindu religion and culture (Dumont 1980 [1966]; Pfaffenberger 1982), regulate village life in South Asia, including Tamil Sri Lanka. When the hierarchy of kinship and caste groups was fragmented and incomplete, as was the case in Arctic Harbor, Tamils' social relations and self-identity became vulnerable and insecure. The Tamils reiterated their deep sense of 'being alone' without kin to confide in and no temples to visit in which to seek comfort and 'peace at heart'.

Illustrative and frequent pains were referred to as headaches, fatigue, dizziness, nightmares, loss of appetite, 'uncertainty', 'aloneness', 'loss of self', and 'no peace of heart'. The aches presented during consultations at the local health centre were commonly focused on physical pains such as painful breathing, hair loss, stomach ache and various bodily pains (muscular) in the shoulders, back, legs and arms. Given that health personnel found it difficult to diagnose and treat the presented symptoms, I have elsewhere suggested an understanding that sees Tamils' aches and pains as related to a wider social and existential world (Grønseth 2010). I have proposed an analysis where Tamils are seen as being forced to re-orient themselves and negotiate in a radically new social and cultural (and climatic) world, which produces a deep insecurity in personal as well as group identity.

The everyday social life of Tamils in Arctic Harbor was characterized by segregation, stigma and exclusion in both Tamil-Tamil and Norwegian-Tamil social relations (Grønseth 2010). Living in this tension, most Tamils expressed a deep desire to return home to their families' villages in Sri Lanka when possible, as this represented ties to gods and kin, which are seen as supplying a fundamental sense of security, comfort, self-confidence and well-being. However, after more than fifteen years of Tamil settlement in Arctic Harbor and Finnmark, most Tamils moved to Oslo, where they sought relief and comfort by connecting with a larger Tamil community which included relations with kin and Tamil Hindu gods. They also saw the move as offering a much sought after opportunity to achieve greater variety in work opportunities and access to higher education for their children. My fieldwork experience among the Tamils in Oslo suggested that they did not perceive the Tamil community and the Tamil Hindu temple as quite so gratifying and fulfilling as they had expected and hoped for. As the case I shall present below will show, some Tamils sought success and pleasure as well as the fulfilment of future visions and life-projects by connecting with the larger Norwegian society. Before turning to this case study, I will briefly describe a few aspects of the Tamil settlement in Oslo and Silver Forest (a pseudonym).

Silver Forest: A Sense of Freedom and Opportunity

Silver Forest is situated in a rather flat landscape previously used for agriculture. It is located about forty kilometres north of Oslo, and among Norwegians is not considered as an attractive place to live, thus offering comparatively low housing costs. Most Norwegians see Silver Forest as being on the 'wrong side of Oslo' and being a 'nowhere place'. The more attractive and high-cost suburbs are traditionally and currently located south and west of Oslo, offering a more varied and hilly landscape, access to the Oslo fjord and an old and stable infrastructure of work, education, health care, cultural entertainment and activities, as well as other much appreciated public and private services, organizations and institutions. However, the Tamils sensed a potential future for themselves in Silver Forest, as it promised opportunities they appreciated in terms of both current and planned new investments in the area.

Although the Tamils in Arctic Harbor were thrown together and experienced tensions in not being with 'the right Tamils to be with', when moving south they generally sought to live together in particular areas of Oslo. I visited the homes of around ten Tamil families who I already knew from Arctic Harbor and discussed how they experienced the move. I visited a few at their work places – kindergartens, grocery shops, schools – and joined the families as the children went to football training, Tamil dance classes and so on. In addition to being with the Tamils from Arctic Harbor, I was introduced and invited home to other Tamil families in the area. Generally the Tamils praised Silver Forest because it gave them a sense of 'overview and safety'. They appreciated Silver Forest as a small community compared to the city of Oslo, and praised the short walking distance to most shops, schools, kindergartens and so on. The Tamils valued the housing structure which consisted of smaller villas, undetached houses and comparatively modest blocks of flats. The area has many nice roads and spaces with trees, lawns and flowers, but also rather messy constructions of roundabouts, fuel stations, multi-storey car parks and warehouses. As the Tamil population in Silver Forest grew, the Tamil community established a local Tamil association that offered Tamil Saturday school at the local school, Tamil aerobics for women, yoga classes and a few other services for the Tamil community. Moreover, Silver Forest is close to the Tamil Hindu temple and to other places where the larger Tamil Association organizes events and gatherings. 'Living in Silver Forest and commuting is easy', many Tamils repeated.

For these Tamils, living in Silver Forest, which was perceived as both apart from and part of the capital city of Oslo, was experienced as being less prone to stigma from Norwegians and felt to give a sense of belonging to the Tamil community, as well as to the larger community of immigrants. This was explained with reference to the many other immigrant groups of colour living in areas in and surrounding Oslo, who made the Tamils a less visible and identifiable group. The Tamils said they felt 'mixed into a multicultural population', which gave them a sense of 'freedom and opportunity'. Many Tamil adolescents stated that they preferred the larger Tamil community, as it gave them a sizeable social milieu in which to make friends and acquaintances. They also felt they had 'come closer to Norwegians ways', since there was a greater degree of interaction, as well as exchanges and flows of knowledge, between distinct groups of youths. However, none of the Tamil youth I spoke with engaged in any close friendships with Norwegians. Both boys and girls stressed that they lacked time for friendship, with either Tamil or Norwegians, as they felt the heavy demands on them to fulfil their parents' expectations to maintain the Tamil language and cultural identity. Some felt 'overloaded', as they needed to learn both Norwegian and Tamil language and culture, and had little free time at their disposal after doing Norwegian schoolwork and taking part in Tamil activities. A few teenage girls said they felt their parents sought to impose 'control and isolation' on them, as they were generally (though with some exceptions) not allowed out to meet friends on their own after school hours (see also Engebrigtsen and Fuglerud 2007). Several girls and boys complained about bodily pains and headaches, which the boys were inclined to attribute to uncertainty and frustration, while the girls tended to speak more in terms of fatigue and sadness. However, most young people had a positive outlook on their future. In different ways they tended to trust their parents to 'in the end both support and restrict' their individual aspirations and desires in order to make 'what will become a good life'. As one boy aged seventeen said:

> In the end, I need to figure out my own way, be it Tamil or Norwegian. I need to be me, wherever I am, in Oslo, London, Chennai, Singapore or Toronto. I have relatives everywhere. But, this [Norway] is where I have grown up. I will do education, marry and live here. My parents will respect me. When they are old, I will support them. We need to stay together.

Looking to the future, the Tamils thought of Silver Forest as offering a place where their children could complete senior high school within the municipality and eventually go on to higher education at college or university in Oslo, still within a relatively short distance. The parental generation was usually resigned to having to find work in Silver Forest or in neighbouring municipalities as cleaning assistants, till staff, taxi-drivers, pizza delivery staff, hospital porters and assistants at homes for the elderly, kindergartens and primary schools. Although they remained in low-status work as they had in Arctic Harbor and Finnmark, they appreciated the greater variety of such work and the sense of at least having potential opportunities for education and other work. The Tamils pointed out that the municipality was enjoying a period of economic growth, expanding its welfare services, and they referred to ongoing constructions of roads, terminal buildings, an already established large hospital and homes for the elderly, which together offered many, varied, and new jobs and prospects. And, importantly, the Tamils perceived Silver Forest as being placed on the 'right side' of Oslo, as it is only about twenty kilometres from the international airport, which makes international flights easily available. This facilitates significant visits to kin and 'good Tamil Hindu temples' (mostly in Tamil Nadu, India), as well as Ayurvedic and other healing experts for various illnesses and misfortunes.

In sum, by living in Silver Forest, the Tamils were situated close to vital Tamil networks – both national and international – and within easy access to activities, events and festivals. From these descriptions, it is shown how they sought to enhance their social positions in Norway both individually and as a group through education, work and economic and material wealth, while also securing a Tamil identity and loyalty to Tamil values as these are negotiated and practised within the local and worldwide Tamil diaspora. Closeness to the Tamil association, Tamil Hindu temple and international airport were seen as crucial for the experience of Tamil wholeness and community. Simultaneously, the stress on jobs and education, together with the quest for 'freedom and opportunity', introduced an avenue for engagement with others which simultaneously maintained and challenged their Tamil identity and traditional ways of 'being Tamil'.

In order to investigate challenges to self- and group identity and the crafting of life-projects further, I suggest that a focus on temporality, with its links to senses of self and well-being, is vital. By employing concepts of embodiment, creativity, agency and intersubjectivity, I hope to explore how memories of the past and experiences in the present have the potential to motivate and give direction to the ongoing creation of a new here and now, as well as hopes and visions for the future. As the Tamils who had moved from Arctic Harbor to Silver Forest engaged and connected with an ongoing social life and practices in the wider Norwegian multicultural society, many felt a greater sense of freedom and agency. From this, I suggest that Tamils' engagement in diverse and multicultural relations provided them with the potential to generate future visions that changed from nostalgia to include altered practices and meanings. In the following, I will introduce the case study of a migrant woman in her mid-forties called Malar which illustrates how, under certain circumstances, Tamils experience a greater sense of well-being when they engage in practices that aspire to a future including multicultural relations in which differences are conceived as part of a shared and human everyday life. Some of the factual information concerning places, work, education and family relations has been changed to create anonymity. However, the extracts of Malar's narration demonstrate her – and what I believe to be many other Tamils' – motivation, capacity and drive for personal change and inclusion in the wider Norwegian society.

Malar: 'I walk through a tunnel to balance the life I lead in Norway'

One of my Tamil informants who had moved from Arctic Harbor to Silver Forest recommended that I meet with a Tamil woman in Silver Forest who, he said, 'served the Tamils'. I met Malar in her home, a nice house at the end of the road. Malar appeared to be a well-adjusted, engaged and busy woman. She spoke fluent Norwegian, was dressed in Norwegian clothing, and greeted me in the Norwegian manner. As well as the usual furniture of sofa, coffee table, dining table and so on, her living room contained office facilities like a fax machine, computer, printer, telephones and papers. She was eager to get going with our conversation, served up tea and biscuits, and pointed out that she had a tight schedule for the day. I asked her to tell me about her life in Oslo. She began her story from the time when she arrived in Norway.

When Malar came to Norway, she and her two young sons joined her husband in a small valley village. While obtaining guidance and support from professionals and neighbours on how to run a household in Norway, and being included in local traditional activities such as knitting and weaving, Malar and her family felt 'not only generous helpfulness', but also 'intrusive demands' giving little space for 'being our Tamil way'. Feeling the weight of the expectation of assimilation, Malar said they felt even more nostalgic about traditional Tamil ways. Recognizing that they could not expect to move back home to their village in Sri Lanka, Malar and her husband decided that the prospects for a good life were not to be found in the small valley village. The family moved to Silver Forest in a quest for improved well-being, as Malar referred it as being 'part of the Tamil community', in which she could 'visit the Tamil-Hindu temple', 'feel able to live my own life', and 'secure a Tamil identity and a future for my sons'. However, she also said that she did not experience the relief, comfort, freedom and opportunities there that she had expected and came to realize that she not only wanted to immerse herself in the local Tamil community, but also saw a need to acknowledge the Norwegian and Tamil community as a whole. She and her husband recognized the need to engage in Norwegian contexts and acquire a Norwegian education. Malar completed senior high school, and entered higher education. Reflecting on her life she said:

> I am not going to collect bad karma. I will do good, and serve my people. I do not want to be reborn. The world is so terrible. I have lost a lot. The war has taken my

family, my house, my life. I have lost everything. I [have to] walk through a tunnel to balance the life I lead in Norway. Both sides are pressing me. I need to be Tamil with the Tamils – and Norwegian with the Norwegians.

Malar said that she had 'suffered a lot'. In the valley village she had been to the local health centre for consultations. When she told the doctor about her sleeplessness, dizziness, headaches, fatigue and pain, they examined her body. She had been given all kinds of X-rays, blood tests and other examinations, but the doctors had found nothing. She had been encouraged to seek psychiatric help, but Malar had refused. She said, 'We have no tradition of psychiatry. We seek Ayurvedic practitioners and guidance for meditation'. Malar said she felt terribly 'lost and alone'. Most of all she missed the local temple in her home village, where she had found peace and consolation. When she came to Oslo, she found that the Tamil Hindu temple there did not provide what she needed. She, like many other Tamils, preferred to turn to her household shrine for *puja* and worship. Malar said:

The possibility for meditation, to cry and seek relief, is not there. The temple in Oslo only resembles a temple. The Oslo temple is only a social meeting place. It is full of decorations and people dressing up. It is not a place to seek peace for your soul. I'd rather stay alone and use my own puja room in my house. So do many Tamils.

Today, Malar said, she sought comfort in dedicating herself to her life project of carving out a future life for Tamils in both Norway and Sri Lanka. She served the Tamils in her local community and sought out avenues for what she called 'multicultural relations'. She saw a need for the Tamils to involve themselves more deeply with Norwegians as well as with other migrant groups. Malar involved herself in the Tamil Association and offered to assist in classes and discuss how to deal with Norwegian issues. Together with others, she acted as a bridge-builder and cultural by offering assistance to the forming of municipal integration programmes at different levels in the municipality. By involving herself in 'multicultural relations', particularly with Norwegians, Malar hoped to achieve her goal of helping her own people. She wanted to build an orphanage in Sri Lanka and contribute to developing Norway into a society which Tamil children like her sons could 'feel part of'. Malar said she had a 'future vision':

I have a goal. It lights up in front of me in the dark tunnel of my everyday life. It helps me bear the pain of adjusting to the small Tamil community and the Norwegian majority society. I need my own way through the tunnel. In the lightening at the end of the tunnel I see my goal. I want to build an orphanage in my home country. And, I want to do something for Norwegian society to help it to become a multicultural society. My boys need to be supported, not restricted. The Tamils need to search for ways into Norway. Or else our children will not survive. We need to help our children.

Visiting my friend from Arctic Harbor somewhat later, I asked him why he had wanted me to meet this woman. He said, 'She knows the Tamils. She knows how we suffer. Most importantly, she can tell you what we need'.

'Living in a tunnel': Migrants' Everyday Life between Memories of the Past and Hopes for the Future

In presenting the case of Malar, an active and purposeful woman, I seek to illustrate what I see as an agentive and conscious engagement in many Tamils' lives and narratives on the part of both women and men. I suggest that some features of Malar's engagement and agency appear in numerous other Tamils' everyday lives, though not necessarily always as outstanding and vigorous. Nonetheless, there are several Tamils (some among my informants) who share a similarly high awareness and engage in various kinds of organized activities to assist and improve Tamil affairs in both Sri Lanka and Norway (see, for instance, the Tamil Resource and Counselling Centre, Tamil Youth Organisation Norway, Norwegian Tamils Health Organisation, and Norwegian Council of Eelam Tamils).

By starting from a study of Tamils' illness and well-being, I see an opportunity to explore how, under certain circumstances, future visions can transcend the hopeless and nostalgic and become a vision that includes new practices, new others and new identities. The case of Malar illustrates how embodied social experiences and practices contribute to the here and now perceptions of being-in-the-world and the forming of hopes, dreams and future visions. Recognizing the perceptive and sense-making body is an approach that understands suffering as containing a kind of knowledge about human life that the intellect cannot sufficiently grasp (Nussbaum 1986: 46). Pain and suffering are expressions of a body that intentionally communicates about its being-in-the-world and addresses what Lacan (1992) and Nussbaum (1986) refer to as a certain unspeakable or suffering knowledge about society, values and social relations. I suggest that this is a kind of experience that comes from the perspective of 'living in between' or 'on the borders' (Jackson 2009; Grønseth 2010) between two life-worlds, in this case Norwegian and Tamil, and how these life-worlds are in a sense overlapping and mixed in the present.

The embodied and emotional experience of living in the borderlands is in Malar's case described as 'living in a tunnel' that gave her a sense of 'being under pressure' and in 'need of balancing between' what she perceived as distinct life-worlds. Malar's life on the borders, as was true for many Tamils, generated a sense of insecurity and uncertainty in the here and now. This, I suggest, is related to the way in which profound tensions and frictions between the past and the present are linked to experiencing confusing individual life-worlds and the difficulties in creating new future visions. While dealing with Tamil relations as they are ruptured and distributed in a worldwide diaspora, and mistrust and envy among Tamils in Norway (Grønseth 2010), Malar suffered from being disconnected and from a lack of someone to confide in. Through her suffering, Malar recognized a need for Tamils not only to connect to the Tamil life-world as it resembled 'being at home', but also to the people of the here and now and thus to engage in Norwegian and 'multicultural relations'. Malar experienced the pain and the pressure of balancing life in the tunnel, or living on the limits in between, and acknowledged that what appear as essential distinctions may change and become connected. As I suggested in the Introduction (this volume), the zone in between shows how distinct phenomena and their identities are not things in themselves, but result from a process in time and space, thus ready and open to connect with others. Given the openness and readiness to connect with others, meaning and practice do not appear to spring from one single individual, but from interaction between several others. Taking this view, I propose that, through involvement in practices with others, we create and re-create future visions.

Malar's experiences of pain and suffering, related to living her everyday life 'in a tunnel', give her access to a kind of agency that creates new meanings and practices in search of opportunity, well-being and identity. This kind of everyday agency does not necessarily enhance new meanings and well-being, but can also lead to disruption and self-destruction. However, this approach is inspired by a view that recognizes the body as perceptive, active and sense-making (Merleau-Ponty 1962 [1945]; Csordas 1994; Jackson 1989; Introduction, this volume). Changing position and engaging in new practices, as Malar and other migrants have done, effect perceptions of self and other and, I suggest, open up a space for new identities, imaginations and visions of a possible new future. The links and interactions between past, present and future in Malar's experience and imagination are understood as offering her a zone of ambivalence and vagueness between memories of the past, nostalgia and hopes for the future. In this dynamic, I see an opportunity for agency, as it comes from pain and suffering together with imaginations and hopes, which allow Malar to create a new identity and future life for herself. Simultaneously, it appears that she suffers with her sons and recognizes a need to make it possible for the younger generation to re-create their senses of identity and well-being as Tamils and Norwegians, but above all as human beings.

Carrying with her embodied and conscious Hindu ideas of *karma*, Malar was determined not to be reborn into what she experienced as a 'terrible world' in which 'the war had taken her family, her house, her life' and she had 'lost everything'. Malar searched for ways to 'do good, and serve her people'. At the end of the tunnel, Malar saw a light that threw shades of brightness into the dark tunnel of her everyday life. Envisioning the light, Malar transcended some of her pain of the here and now and reached towards a future in which she imagined the fulfilment of what had become her life-project. She associated the light with accomplishing her vision. Experiencing the present as containing losses, traumas and memories of the past, as well as uncertainties, ambivalences and the pressures of living in between, Malar can be seen as looking for a future that provided a new beginning for her sense of self and well-being within experiences of her present everyday life. While Malar stretched herself towards the light and her goal, she experienced living in between as less pressing. The demands from the sides of the tunnel were experienced as less contradictory. When her future vision threw light onto her everyday life, the tunnel, or border zone, widened and the oppressive walls were lowered. She felt free to negotiate and adjust to being Tamil for the sake of herself, her sons and her fellow human beings.

Moreover, engaging in Norwegian and individualized relations is understood as generating a linkage between the tenses in which the future becomes ever more crucial in motivating and making sense of the present (Adam 2004, 2006; Øian 1998, 2004; Berge 1992). This relates to how, in a study of young unemployed adults in Oslo, Norway (Øian 1998, 2004), self-identity is observed as being closely linked to images of oneself in the future. Similarly, the future aim of 'helping our children' gave Malar the motivation and direction for creating a life-project and a self-identity that bridges the two life-worlds as well as the past and the present. Although in contradiction to how unemployed Norwegians create an individualistic future image of themselves (Øian 2004), the case of Malar, and many other Tamils, illustrates a more collectivistic future image by including the children and future generations. In addition, Malar's collectivistic and intergenerational future image can be seen to match Tamils' sense of self and personhood as they are commonly associated with dependent social and religious relations more than with the autonomous and independent individual, although these differences are always balancing between the two poles (see also Grønseth 2010; Kakar 1997; Morris 1994; Marriot 1990; Mines 1988). However, by creating a collective intergenerational future vision that motivates and directs an individual life-project, Malar is seen as having reduced the sense of insecurity and confusion in her present everyday life and having created a space and time for agentive practice. Rather than just holding onto practices linked to future images based on nostalgia, Malar became involved in new Norwegian and multicultural relations and practices which gave her sensations of pleasure, accomplishment and future success.

On an interpretive level, Malar's embodied and painful experience of the past, and of the here and now, made her acknowledge difficulties in social relations that created a 'need to help our children'. In response, she sought to build an orphanage in Sri Lanka and to find 'ways into Norway'. For Malar, I suggest, these visions and aims helped her to link the past to the future and as such to supply meaning and a sense of well-being in the present. Theoretically, the case of Malar illustrates how imagined and memorized places interplay in the experience and narration of past and the future equal to, and sometimes more than, the actual place of the here and now, that is, Oslo. This, I suggest, addresses how experiences and senses of time are linked to space by human agency, creation and narration (see Merleau-Ponty 1962 [1945]; Ricoeur 1980). Thus, exploring agency and creation as it links time and space recognizes how narration reveals our care, concern and pre-occupation with things in everyday life of existential significance (see also Introduction, this volume). Acknowledging the existential dimension further shows how time is not a linear measure, but is related to human experiences and sensations which always take place in the body and in space. To reach her goal and future vision, Malar recognized a need to engage in relations and practices in the borderlands. By interacting with both Norwegians and Tamils, Malar was exposed to and engaged with the mixed and indistinguishable quality of living in between (Jackson 2009), which can generate potential new wholes and identities. Human experiences such as Malar's from the zone in between self and other, together with her narration of human existential concerns in everyday life, interconnect time, place and body, thus illustrating how images and senses of identity, self, pain and well-being are flexibly created and re-created.

In the migrant context, connecting and engaging with the larger society thus holds the potential to create future visions that transcend past memories and nostalgia. Holding such a future vision, I further suggest, generates new practices and meanings, linking the tenses in ways that together reduce pain, and increase well-being and self-identity in the present. By becoming involved in the borderlands between the Tamil-Hindu and Norwegian life-worlds, Malar recognized on an interpretive level how practices of mutuality do not erase differences but construct human identities.

Concluding Remarks

In conclusion, I would like to draw attention to the point of departure for this study and the chapter's focus on well-being and identity as this links to a movement between past, present and future, or continuity and change. As the Tamils were torn away from the traditional principles that regulate social and religious relations, they experienced insecurity in the here and now of social relations and self-identity. Some of the pain and suffering that many Tamils reported is understood as being linked not only to ruptures in social and religious bonds, but also to breaches between the past, present and future. As the body carries memories and traumas from the past and is thrown into a present characterized by unfamiliar Norwegian practices, the Tamils painfully experienced the violation and confusion of a vast and sudden change. As part of this experience, many Tamils suffered nostalgia and did not see any future other than a return to what they had left. They rebuilt what resembled their lost past, but found little relief or joy in doing so. However, when entering the border zone between the Tamil and Norwegian life-worlds, it becomes possible to see that things are not distinct by independent individual identities in themselves, but by their relation to others. By engaging in the border zone, the human disposition to connect is activated and potentially creates future visions that generate new practices with new identities, well-being and prosperity.

Thus, I suggest that the Tamil informant from Arctic Harbor wanted me to learn what he himself could not yet articulate, but sensed as a future vision with promises of greater well-being as being both Tamil and human. While living in Arctic Harbor, he had dreamt of a return to a peaceful Sri Lanka. Living in Silver Forest, he was now moving towards a hope of greater inclusion and well-being in Norway. As he said:

> I suffer, and I suffer for my children. We cannot lock them up in the Tamil community. Our children are forced to oppose our values. They are struggling to make their own space and dreams. We need to help them. We must all – Tamils, Norwegians and everyone – look for a future together.

Notes

1 Illness is understood to encapsulate the individual's experience of having and dealing with a disease (as it represents a biological pathology), or more vaguely feeling sick and unwell in spite of not being able to come to any clear diagnosis (see Kleinman 1980).

2 Tamil wholeness refers to a coherent meaningful wholeness that is commonly shared by Tamils, which includes cultural values and meanings connected to Tamil social practices, structures and life-worlds. When seeking refuge in Norway, the Tamils tend to experience social structures, relations and life-worlds as splintered and fractured, as they cannot sufficiently maintain and re-establish elements that are felt to be crucial in order for them to experience a meaningful wholeness (see Grønseth 2010).

3 Among the majority population the percentage of unemployment is 2.0 among men, and 1.5 among women (May 2012, Statistics Norway).

4 Tamils' emphasis on hard work and higher education must be seen in relation to how Tamils in the north and east of Sri Lanka had the opportunity to acquire education in high-standard Christian schools, which in turn gave them access to positions in the government and state administration during the period of British colonization.

5 The high percentage of Tamil employment must be seen in relation to the age composition of the Tamil population in Norway. There are few elderly Tamils, and most of the population is aged between 30 and 45 years old.

6 This also demonstrates that the difference between the percentages of women's and men's employment was much higher (18.7 percentage points) than among other immigrant groups (8.1 percentage points). However, in the third quarter (July-September) of 2003, there was a 17.3 per cent unemployment rate among first-generation Sri Lankans, 12.5 per cent for men, and 23.9 per cent for women (Lie 2004).

7 For further details on Tamil immigration to Norway, see Fuglerud 1999; Grønseth 2010.

8 *Verdens Gang*, 16 October 1996.

9 The Tamil diaspora is well known for its well-organized networking. In Norway there are local Tamil Associations wherever a reasonable number of Tamils have gathered. The structure of these associations is quite informal and they are run by Tamils who take it upon themselves to lead and organize Tamil activities (Tamil language, dance, Hindu religion, ceremonies and events). Sometimes the local association arranges events together with other local associations and can, under certain circumstances, network on a national (Norwegian) level. The associations do not admit to any political or similar agenda other than to offer a minimum of activities to maintain cultural continuity and identity while in exile. However, there have been local and national disturbances among many Tamils concerning a supposed link between the Tamil associations and the LTTE (Liberation Tigers of Tamil Eelam). Although any possible links are only informal, there is no doubt that many supporters and activists in the LTTE are also active in running the Tamil Associations. See also Grønseth 2010.

References

Adam, B. 2004. *Time*. Cambridge: Polity Press.
_____. 2006. 'Time', *Theory, Culture and Society* 23(2–3), 119–26.
Amit, V. and N. Rapport. 2002. *The Trouble with Community: Anthropological Reflections on Movement, Identity and Collectivity*. London: Pluto Press.
Axel, B.K. 2002. 'The Diasporic Imaginary', *Public Culture* 14(2): 411–28.
_____. 2004. 'The Context of Diaspora', *Cultural Anthropology* 19(1): 26–60.
Barnett, S.A. 1975. 'Approaches to Changes in Caste Ideology in South India', in Burton Stein (ed.), *Essays on South India*. Hawaii: University Press of Hawaii, pp. 149–80.
Bayly, S. 1999. *The New Cambridge History of India IV. 3: Caste Society and Politics in India from the Eighteenth Century to the Modern Age*. Cambridge: Cambridge University Press.
Berg, M.L. 2009. 'Between Cosmopolitanism and the National Slot: Cuba's Diasporic Children of the Revolution', *Identities: Global Studies in Culture and Power* 16(2): 129–56.
Berge, T. 1992. 'Life is Another Place: on Relations between Past, Present and Future' [Livet er et annet sted: Om samspillet mellom fortid, nåtid og framtid], *Journal of Norwegian Anthropology [Norsk antropologisk tidsskrift]* 3(2): 118–34.
Bicharat, G. 1997. 'Exile to Campatriate: Transformations in the Social Identity of Palestinian Refugees on the West Bank', in Akhil Gupta and James Fergerson (eds), *Culture, Power and Place: Explorations in Critical Anthropology*. Durham, NC: Duke University Press, pp. 203–33.
Bourdieu, P. 1989. *Outline of a Theory of Practice*. Cambridge: Cambridge University Press.
Brown, J.N. 1998. 'Black Liverpool, Black America and the Gendering of Diasporic Space', *Cultural Anthropology* 13(3): 291–325.
Clifford, J. 1994. 'Diasporas', *Cultural Anthropology* 9: 302–38.
Cohen, A.P. 1986. *The Symbolic Construction of Community*. London: Routledge.
Csordas, Th. (ed.). 1994. *Embodiment and Experience: The Existential Ground of Culture and Self*. Cambridge: Cambridge University Press.

Daniel, V.E. 1989. 'The Semiotics of Suicide in Sri Lanka', in B. Lee and G. Urban (eds), *Semiotics, Self and Society*. Berlin: Mouton de Gruyter, pp. 67–100.

———. 1998. 'Suffering Nation and Alienation', in Arthur Kleinman, Veena Das and Margaret Lock (eds), *Social Suffering*. Delhi: Oxford University Press, pp. 309–58.

Daniel, V.E. and J. Chr. Knudsen (eds). 1995. *Mistrusting Refugees*. California: University of California Press.

Deepa, S.R. 2005. 'The Ethnicity of Caste', *Anthropological Quarterly* 78(3): 543–84.

Desjarlais, R., L. Eisenberg, B. Good and A. Kleinman. 1995. *World Mental Health: Problems and Priorities in Low-Income Countries*. Oxford: Oxford University Press.

Dumont, L. 1980 [1966]. *Homo Hierarchicus: The Caste System and its Implications*. Complete Revised English Edition. Chicago and London: John Hopkins and The University of Chicago Press.

Dzamarija, M.T. (ed.). 2010. *Children and Youth with Immigrant Parents: Demography, Education, Income and Work-Market. [Barn og unge med innvandrerforeldre: demografi, utdanning, inntekt og arbeidsmarked.]* Oslo: Rapport 12/2010 Statistics Norway.

Engebrigtsen, A. and Ø. Fuglerud. 2007. *Youth in Refugee-Families. Family and Friendship – Security or Freedom? [Ungdom i flyktningefamilier. Familie og vennskap – trygghet eller frihet?].* NOVA-rapport 3/07. Oslo: NOVA.

Fuglerud, Ø. 1999. *Life on the Outside: The Tamil Diaspora and Long Distance Nationalism*. London: Pluto Press.

Fuller, Chr. J. (ed.). 1996. *Caste Today*. SOAS. Studies on South Asia: Understandings and Perspectives. Delhi/New York: Oxford University Press.

Glenn, E.N. 1999. 'The Social Construction and Institutionalization of Gender and Race: An Integrative Framework', in M.M. Ferre, J. Lorber and B.B. Hess (eds), *Revisioning Gender*, pp. 3–43. Thousand Oaks, CA: Sage Publications.

Grønseth, A.S. 2001. 'In Search of Community: A Quest for Well-Being among Tamil Refugees in Northern Norway', *Medical Anthropology Quarterly* 15(4): 493–514.

———. 2010. *Lost Selves and Lonely Persons: Experiences of Illness and Well-Being among Tamil Refugees in Norway*. Carolina: Carolina Academic Press.

Hammond, L. 2004. *This Place Will Become Home: Refugee Repatriation To Ethiopia*. Cornell, NY: Cornell University Press.

Henriksen, K., L. Østby and D. Ellingsen. 2010. *Immigration and Immigrants 2010*. Oslo: Statistics Norway.

Hintzen, P.C. 2001. *West Indian in the West: Self-representations in an Immigrant Community*. New York: New York University Press.

Jackson, M. 1989. *Paths toward a Clearing: Radical Empiricism and Ethnographic Inquiry*. Bloomington: Indiana University Press.

———. 2009. *The Palm at the End of the Mind: Relatedness, Religiosity, and the Real*. Durham and London: Duke University Press.

Jenkins, J. 1996. 'The Impress of Extremity: Women's Experience of Trauma and Political Violence', in Carol Sargent and C. Brettell (eds), *Gender and Health: An International Perspective*. New Jersey: Prentice-Hall.

Kakar, S. 1997. *The Inner World: A Psychoanalytic Study of Childhood and Society in India*. Oxford: Oxford University Press.

Kleinman, A. 1980. *Patients and Healers in the Context of Culture: An Exploration of the Borderland between Anthropology, Medicine, and Psychiatry.* California: California University Press.

Kleinman, A. and M. Lock (eds). 1997. *Social Suffering.* California: University of California Press.

Lacan, J. 1992. *The Seminar of Jacques Lacan.* Book VII, edited by J.A. Miller. New York: Morton.

Lie, B. 2004. *Facts about 10 Immigrant Groups in Norway. [Fakta om 10 innvandrergrupper i Norge.]* Oslo: Statistics Norway.

Malkki, L. 1995b. *Purity and Exile: Violence, Memory and National Cosmology among Hutu Refugees in Tanzania.* Chicago: University of Chicago Press.

Marriot, M. 1990. 'Constructing an Indian Ethnosociology', in McKim Marriot (ed.), *India through Hindu Categories.* London: Sage Publications, pp. 1–39.

McDowell, Chr. 1996. *A Tamil Asylum Diaspora: Sri Lankan Migration, Settlement and Politics in Switzerland.* Oxford: Berghahn.

Merleau-Ponty, M. 1962 [1945]. *Phenomenology of Perception.* London: Routledge & Kegan Paul.

Migliorino, N. 2008. *(Re)constructing Armenia in Lebanon and Syria: Ethno-cultural Diversity and the State in the Aftermath of a Refugee Crisis.* New York/Oxford: Berghahn.

Mines, M. 1988. 'Conceptualizing the Person: Hierarchical Society and Individual Autonomy in India', *American Anthropologist* 90: 568–79.

Morris, B. 1994. *Anthropology of the Self: The Individual in Cultural Perspective.* London: Pluto Press.

Nussbaum, M. 1986. *The Fragility of Goodness: Luck and Ethics in Greek Tragedy and Philosophy.* London: Cambridge University Press.

Øian, H. 1998. *Free from Work and Loss of Leisure: Young Unemployed in Oslo Meeting the Post-industrial Wage-work-regime's Demands of a Linear Career. [Arbeidsfri og fritidsløs. Om unge arbeidsledige i Oslo og deres møte med det etterindustrielle lønnsarbeidsregimets krav om lineære karrierer].* Oslo: University of Oslo.

_____. 2004. 'Time Out and Drop Out: On the Relation between Linear Time and Individualism', *Time & Society* 13(2–3): 173–95.

Pessar, R.P. and S.J. Mahler. 2001. *Gender and Transnational Migration.* Conference Paper on Transnational Migration: Comparative Perspectives. Princeton University, 30 June–1 July 2001.

Pfaffenberger, B. 1982. *Caste in Tamil Culture: The Religious Foundations of Sudra Domination in Tamil Sri Lanka.* Syracuse, NY: Maxwell School and Foreign and Comparative Studies.

Rapport, N. 2003. *I'm Dynamite: An Alternative Anthropology of Power.* London/New York: Routledge.

Ricoeur, P. 1980. 'Narrative Time', *Critical Inquiry* 7(1): 169–90.

Rouse, R. 1991. 'Mexican Migration and the Social Space of Postmodernism', *Diaspora* 1(1): 8–23.

Safran, W. 1991. 'Diasporas in Modern Societies: Myths of Homeland and Return', *Diaspora* 1(1): 83–99.

Schiller, N.G., L. Basch and C. Blanc-Szanton (eds). 1992. *Towards a Transnational Perspective on Migration.* The New York Academy of Sciences. 645. New York: The New York Academy of Sciences.

Searle-Chatterjee, M. and U. Sharma (eds). 1994. *Contextualising Caste: Post-Dumontian Approaches*. Oxford: Blackwell.

Sideris, T. 2003. 'War, Gender and Culture: Mozambican Women Refugees', *Social Science & Medicine* 56(4): 713–24.

Slymovics, S. 1998. *The Object of Memory: Arab and Jew Narrate the Palestinian Village*. Philadelphia: University of Pennsylvania Press.

Zmegac, J.C. 2007. *Strangers Either Way: The Lives of Croatian Refugees in Their New Home*. London: Berghahn Books.

Chapter 3

Narrating Mobile Belonging

A Dutch Story of Subjectivity in Transformation[1]

Maruška Svašek

((The recording equipment is set up – 23 seconds))
M: OK. So let's start the interview. So I just told you the idea is to – erm – // you were just going to tell me about the story of your life and how you became the person whom you are today/. And /ehm/ I'm not going to interrupt you and you can just start, probably – eh – , with your very first memory.
A: – Mmh mmh –
M: And then just continue as you like.
A: Yes.
M: Yeah?
A: OK.
M: And if there's any, you know, if you're, sometimes if there's silences that's no problem. If you like need some time to think.
A: Ah. – Right, OK, so will I say who I am and?
M: Yeah.
A: Or not, yeah?
M: Yeah you can, yeah.
A: OK, well I am – ehm – Anna de Groot[2] and I was born in – ehm – Holland – ehm – thirty-eight years ago and – ehm – I – ehm – lived in B. with my mother and my brother – in – ehm – a very nice (green) area in a terraced house and – ehm – my mother divorced my father, when I was five and – ehm – my brother was nine then and – erm – she raised us and – ehm – I went to – erm – a, a nice primary school, a Montessori school where we would, – ehm – my mother would bring me there every day on the bicycle, together with my brother.

This is the beginning of an interview I conducted in 2008 with 'Anna', a Dutch migrant whom I got to know in Northern Ireland, and whose life story will be central to this chapter. Her self-narrative is interesting as she discusses her 'migrant experiences' in the wider context of her trajectory as a mobile person. Her story, in other words, does not only demonstrate that certain experiences of migration are enveloped by desires, hopes and fears that are directly related to emigration, but also brings out some of the more general issues around human mobility. An important theme that links the two dimensions is that, as human beings move through time and space and cross boundaries of family dwelling, neighbourhood, town and country as part of their everyday lives, their perceptions of their personal pasts and futures may change. As we shall see, in the case of Anna, a variety of pre- and post-migration dispositions affected her sense of well-being as her life enfolded.

In the interview, Anna talked about experiences within and beyond the boundaries of family life and friendship circles, and she discussed her travels abroad. The trips included several shorter European holidays, a six-month period as a language student in Spain, and a longer tour to India and Nepal with her Northern Irish boyfriend. In 1993, she decided to follow the latter to Northern Ireland, get married and study geography at Queen's University Belfast. Over the next fifteen years, the couple had three children, bought a house in a coastal town not far from Belfast, and played with the idea of obtaining a small holiday cottage just over the border in the Republic of Ireland. They were clearly 'settled'. Anna's husband, 'Danny', had a tenured job at the University of Ulster, and the family had no intentions of leaving. In 2008, however, Danny was offered a professorship at a Dutch university, and the opportunity motivated him to further develop his career beyond Northern Ireland. Initially, Anna was quite hesitant about returning to her homeland, going back to a place she thought she had 'left forever', having to uproot herself and the children. She did, however, slowly warm to the idea when visiting the Netherlands to look into housing and schools. Imagining a possible return made her reflect critically on her life in Northern Ireland and, gradually, 'Holland' became a promising alternative. The interview took place a few days before their move to the Netherlands and reflects her changed state of mind.

The aim of this chapter is two-fold. First, I am interested in the ways in which Anna projected and reflected on past, present and future subjectivity during the interview. To throw light on her narrative performance of self, I shall analyse a selection of descriptive, argumentative and reflective narrative fragments, focusing especially on the emotional dynamics of her story. Following Leavitt (1996: 531), I shall adopt a perspective on emotions 'that takes their complexity as every day concepts seriously' and understands them as 'experiences that we recognize as involving both cultural meaning and bodily feeling'. I shall argue that producers of biographical narratives tend to actively evaluate their life-as-lived-so-far, making judgements about the positive and negative impact of past predicaments and choices on their unfolding everyday lives.[3] As will become clear, both remembered and newly felt emotions frame and produce such judgements.

The chapter's second aim is to assess Anna's changing perception of belonging to and well-being in Northern Ireland as her departure became more imminent. The analysis explores how her understanding of her migrant status altered when she considered her changed future, a future that rather unexpectedly would take her back to her old homeland. Having known her for eight years, I was in a good position to compare her most recent view to chats and discussions we had had over the years. Scheduled not long before her departure, the interview opened up an affective space in which she could more openly feel and reveal ambiguities about her past life as a 'non-native' in Northern Ireland. In the interview, she discussed her sense of alienation, a topic she had occasionally mentioned but underemphasized during earlier meetings.

In the last four years before her departure, Anna had lived the life of a full-time housewife, carrying the main responsibility for the running of the household and the care for her three children. Most of her friends were mothers of her children's classmates and she enjoyed chatting with them over a coffee, and helping out with special school activities. She spent (to her annoyance) much of her time in the car, taking her children to and from school, piano lessons and football practice, and other children would often come over to play and have a sleep-over. For many years, she travelled once a week to another town to teach an evening course in Dutch, a welcome break from the hubbub of everyday life. I met with Anna about once every two months, often in her house for a coffee or a meal and mostly while her husband was away at a conference. Being a working mother myself, and the wife of a husband who lived abroad, I enjoyed family time with Anna and her children, and appreciated the familiarity of our shared Dutch background and the mutual acquaintances we had. We also met each other's mothers when they were over for visits, which gave us a better insight into the other's family background and each other's attempts at emotion management during the reunions.[4] Our shared predicament as migrant mothers in Northern Ireland deepened our friendship and mutual empathy (see also Grønseth and Davis 2010; Svašek 2010c: 75).

Before turning to Anna's account, it is important to note that life trajectories are partly determined by structural possibilities and constraints, governed by legal regulations, national and international politics and global economics. Restrictions and opportunities that limit or allow people's geographic mobility influence the content of their autobiographical accounts (Schütze and Schröder-Wildhagen 2012; see also Brown 2005; Burrell 2006; Jordan and Brown 2007). A middle-class Dutch citizen who voluntarily travelled and resettled within the Europe Union, Anna found few obstacles on her way. Her verbal reflections, in other words, differ considerably from stories told by some of the other migrants and refugees that feature in this edited collection, who have experienced 'Europe' as an almost unreachable hostile space of surveillance and bureaucratic regulations, and/or as a safe alternative to their homelands in which they were persecuted (see also Schubotz et al. 2012).

Subjectivity, Mobility and Emotions

The interview with Anna was conducted for a large collaborative research project in which EU-based individuals, including migrants from numerous countries, were asked to tell their life stories (Miller et al. 2012). In earlier publications on migration and expulsion (Svašek 2002, 2005, 2008, 2010a, 2012), I have taken a processual approach to subjectivity, regarding individuals as dynamic thinking, feeling and interacting bodies that project and experience changing, sometimes contradictory notions of being (see also Conradson and McKay 2007). This approach defines emotions as processes by which individuals, who move through time and space, relate to their surroundings through embodied modes of engagement, impressed by and impacting upon their changing human and non-human environments. In the process, subjectivity is experienced in different ways, and notions of self are defined, reconsidered, and redefined.

To explore the complex relationship between emotions and subjectivity, it is useful to take a multi-dimensional view, defining emotions as 'discourses', 'practices' and 'embodied experiences' (Svašek 2005; Svašek and Skrbiš 2007).[5] This approach has several methodological implications when analysing life stories. The Foucauldian perspective of 'discourse' outlines how cultural categories of emotions and the notion of emotivity itself produce knowledge about the world and the self in that world. These discourses are often historically and group specific, but certain general or highly individualized features can often also be distinguished. Exploring emotions at the level of discourse means analysing how specific emotional statements and emotion words in speech events shape and produce judgements about self and society, and how they are used pragmatically to define a communicative context.

The dimension of 'practice', derived from Bourdieu's theory of practice, draws attention to the performative nature of emotions, both in terms of learned, internalized behaviour (habitus) and the more deliberate, 'acted out' politics of emotions. From this perspective, biographical interviews are understood as performative practices, as narrators act out, manage and reflect on a complexity of emotions through their stories, taking multiple roles of storyteller and actor(s) that feature in the accounts. These practices are also strongly informed by less conscious affective economies and discursive regimes that are embedded in power relations and cultural ideologies (Ahmed 2004a, 2004b). The outlook of 'embodied experience' explores physical aspects of emotional experience, and regards the multi-sensorial process of unconscious and conscious bodily perception and interaction as central to the emotional process (Csordas 1994; Lyon 1995).

When life stories are told in an interview situation, the use of emotion terms, the changing tone of voice, and the fluctuating emotional density and bodily enactment of the story can all shed light on the ways in which a biographical storyteller evaluates past instances of mobility from a present-day perspective.

Mobile Selves: Transit and Transformation

The focus on discourses, practices and embodied experiences of emotions reinforces a processual view on subjectivity that regards individuals as persons in transit and transformation. Moving through space and time (i.e. being in transit), people are engaged in social, political and emotional processes, experiencing new situations and reacting to new challenges and demands. This is of course a more general human phenomenon, not necessarily a migrant condition. Through adaptation, negotiation and improvisation, individuals take on – or may be forced into[6] – contextually specific roles and identities. While these transformations may be temporary and situationally specific, people may also undergo more fundamental personal changes. To give an example, asylum seekers may fall into depression during years in limbo as they wait for a refugee status. Another example, applicable to both migrant and non-migrant groups, is when new parents, influenced by the changed family demands and ways of being, come to define themselves as parents.

Individuals may make more or less conscious attempts to 'experiment' with subjectivity, creating particular affective possibilities that enable specific experiences of self.[7] The transit to new environments can, of course, also cause unwanted feelings of confusion, threat, and alienation.[8] Affective routes are intricate and multifaceted and cannot easily be classified as 'positive' or 'negative'. Consequently, when exploring the emotional dimensions of transit and transformation, it is essential to acknowledge the complexity, inconsistency and ambiguity of mobile belonging and non-belonging. It is also important to realize that people who decided to leave their homeland and resettle elsewhere started their affective lives before they even considered emigration. Pre-departure emotional discourses, practices and embodied feelings that shaped earlier senses of self often affect people's experience and self-narration as 'migrants'.

Being Human through Narrative Performance

So how can self-narratives be analysed to gain a better insight into the emotional dimensions of human mobility and subjectivity? Mary Chamberlain and Selma Leydesdorff (2004: 230) have argued that 'the plots and themes we select and through which we choose to recount our lives have effectively prefigured the way we see ourselves'. Story telling is part and parcel of the human condition, and helps migrants and non-migrants alike to make sense of their (sometimes ruptured) lives. The biographical method developed by Fritz Schütze, used in this chapter, is based on the assumption that there is 'a deep relationship between identity development of an individual and his/her narrative rendering of life historical events'. This means that clues about changing subjectivity can be found through detailed analysis of autobiographical story fragments and narrative performative acts.

Schütze's method is quite specific and provides clearly defined instructions regarding the autobiographical story telling process.[9] The main idea is that unsolicited material provides a purer insight into the interviewee's own self-historical *gestalt*, or all-encompassing view of her/his life (Schütze 2008a, 2008b). To distil a meta-narrative of self from interview material, the life story is transcribed in detail, typing up all utterances (including incomplete sentences and words), silences (through the inclusion of hesitation marks), verbal emphases (underlining emphasised words), and giving some indication of emotional expression (referring to them in brackets). In addition, various text features are distinguished, including different communicative schemes of presentation and process structures (Domecka 2008; Domecka et al. 2012). These are regarded as important ordering principles that can throw light on the dynamics of personal experience, self-perception, self-performance and transformation. This chapter shows how Anna used various narrative features to evaluate her migration experiences against the background of her longer-term life trajectory.

Having experimented with the method as interviewer and interviewee, I can state that the recalling of personal experiences with the aim of giving an overall account of one's life in a limited time period (autobiographical interviews generally take between one and two and a half hours) is quite a challenge that requires creative improvisation and active emotion management. Biographical narration forces the narrator into a performance of self through reflective engagement with personal memories, including evocative memories of self-perceived success and failure. The mnemonic process of recalling one's life involves remembering and re-experiencing both happy and painful emotions, and forces the interviewee to make quick decisions about what to disclose and what to keep for oneself. The intensity of remembering and verbalization makes it impossible to be in full control of what is being said, which means that interviewees may surprise themselves with the development of their own storylines.

The performance has a strong creative element, as complex and mixed feelings need to be translated into words, sentences and plots, a process which has different levels of complexity. On the one hand, the format of the life story gives space to relatively 'fixed' stories that have been told many times before, and that may follow particular generic rules, such as the relatively detached genre of the curriculum vitae. At the other end of the spectrum, the narrator will be challenged to verbalize previously unspoken or rarely discussed past events that may be painful, which is often signalled by the use of linguistic contradictions, hesitations, and self-corrections.[10]

The relationship between the interviewer and the interviewee also influences what is being said in autobiographical interviews (Svašek and Domecka 2012: 111). Anna was quite open to me as we were both females with a somewhat similar background (partly due to migration) who considered each other as friends. Evidently, our acquaintance also had its limitations. I was very familiar with some parts of her life story (for example, Anna having been a student at Queens and having three children), and as she told me after the interview, this meant she had not felt the need to discuss them in detail. No doubt such forces, deriving from the social and emotional dynamics of the interview event, influence narrative self-presentation (Davies and Spenser 2010; Spencer and Davies 2010).

Stories of Self and Fluctuating Emotional Density

As we will discover in the analysis of Anna's story, interviewees tend to move between descriptive, argumentative and reflective narration, and may 'work through' confusing life events, as they try to unravel and understand earlier experiences. Particular parts of biographical narratives are characterized by different levels of emotional density. While some fragments may be relatively neutral and straightforward ('I began secondary school in 1956'), others may consist of highly emotional outbursts ('I hated that!'). Not surprisingly, biographical storytellers are regularly directly affected (being moved to tears, feeling embarrassment, bursting into laughter) by the plots of their own unfolding stories. As noted earlier, it is important to observe indications of this process during biographical interviews through sensitivity to emotionally loaded body language (laughter, tears, facial expressions, tension in body parts), by noticing the frequency of particular emotion words in the narrative, and by picking up on deliberate evocative acts, aimed at the interviewer.[11] The fluctuating emotional density of Anna's story revealed certain ambiguities that were directly related to her longer-term history of transit, which included experiences of emigration and imminent remigration.

Pre-migration Contrasts: Childhood and Family Dynamics

The interview with Anna was conducted one evening in my house in Northern Ireland and lasted about an hour and a half. She agreed to speak English as she was fluent and felt comfortable with the language. On one or two occasions we switched to our mother tongue, trying to find a proper translation of Dutch expressions. The interview demonstrated how particular narrative features and degrees of emotional density helped Anna to describe and reflect on her transit and transformation within local, translocal and transnational contexts. She started off by talking about her childhood using several contrast sets, a common feature in autobiographical narratives. As a structuring device, it allows speakers to compare and evaluate everyday experiences, including contrasting emotional experiences in different locations. The issue of human mobility is central here, as she was able to make a comparative judgement because she had moved into and out of different social settings. The fact that Anna's parents were divorced and that her mother worked framed her comparison. Although she stressed that she had a happy and secure childhood, she vividly described the families of friends she stayed with after school, comparing them to her own family. She referred, for example, to the 'cosiness' of one of the families, frequently marking them as 'nice' and 'very nice'. It is important to note here that the Dutch word for cosy, '*gezellig*', is an emotionally loaded, culturally specific term, commonly used by Dutch people to indicate a deep sense of harmony derived from enjoying the company of others (*een gezellige familie*) or a pleasant, warm environment (*een gezellig huis*) (McCrum 2007: 237). Anna smiled when she recalled:

> I remember my – best friend had a very *nice* house, I remember that – erm – and a very big garden with swings in it and that was very interesting. Compared to my sort of more normal house, I remember she had this this big swing and she had a really nice big family with – erm – *nice cosy* big family with lots of children and we would have *nice* food to eat and it always had *a very nice cosy feeling*. – Erm – and she had a father, I remember that really well, that she had a father which I didn't have and it was *a very nice together family*. So I would have stayed with her a lot of the time, she was my best friend and she was called 'Karin'.

The words 'a very nice together family' produced a contrast to her own home situation, characterized by the lack of a father, tensions between her brother and mother, and a relatively strict upbringing. Later on in the interview, Anna used another contrast set, comparing the free lifestyle of some of the families she visited to her own.

> A: the girl in the family became my best friend for a *long, long* time, until, really I think until I left Holland. And we used to do everything together, we would well play in the street and later we would go out in the street and I would be in her house all the time, and again she was a family that I felt was *a lot, very different from mine, because they would, there would be a lot more things allowed*, there would be /ehm/ you know they could always watch TV whenever they wanted to have it. I remember they had a day that they would eat chips, they would, I don't know all these things, we could play upstairs and do whatever we liked to, we could go downstairs and we could go into the fridge and slice sausages up and pretend it was food and
> M: ((Laughter))
> A: And it was *a very nice, free house, compared to sort of my own, when I was called back it was always a lot more strict.*

Moving beyond the spatial and social boundaries of her family gave her the opportunity to experience alternative social ambiances that were, however, not always liberating. She used to stay with 'a lot more conservative friend', in whose home 'you weren't allowed to do as many things and *it wasn't as – cosy, the house wasn't as messy. . . .* I didn't like that so much because – *I'd always felt I was shifted around* to different people that I had to stay with'.

Her evaluation of the different households she stayed in and the fact that she had no full control over her mobility was not only communicated through choice of words and tone of voice, but also by the use of contrasting facial expressions, smiling and talking with an upbeat voice, or frowning and slowing down. The underlying argument was that she had longed for an affective space that was more stable and less restrictive. Having known Anna for eight years, I could easily recognize this portrayal of her childhood self as a justification for the choices she had made as an adult. I was familiar with the informal atmosphere she normally created in her own home in Northern Ireland, and knew that she had given up on her PhD to look after her children, not wanting to be a working mum. While gender specific affective regimes played a role in her self-definition as main care provider, her choice against paid employment can thus not simply be understood as a result of traditional gender expectations.

Although on the whole, Anna described what seemed to have been a reasonably happy childhood, her references to school life indicated a recurring feeling of 'living between two worlds', of not fully belonging to a specific social circle. She described, for example, that friends with whom she played after school attended a different school, which meant that her social worlds of 'school' and 'neighbourhood' were not connected. She also pointed out that she had felt 'out of place' at primary school, partly because the other children came from more affluent families and 'had nice, you know, families with a father who was always there and cars, and we never had a car, we always had to do everything on the bicycle'. As we shall see, in her story, the theme of 'non-belonging' was further developed in later sections.[12]

Wider Social Circles, Less Dependent Mobility: Trying out New Directions

Secondary school offered Anna opportunities for more self-experimentation, escaping temporarily from what she saw as a sober and restricted family life. Interestingly, having grown older and become a mum herself, her story expressed ambiguous feelings about the choices she had made in her teenage years, showing a clear discrepancy between 'Anna as narrator' and 'Anna as story carrier' (see Schütze 2008a: 45). Taking an ironic, observing approach to her past experimenting, changing self, she reflected on her temporary transformation into a more 'tacky' person, and laughed a lot when describing what at the time had seemed exciting.

And – erm – but then we met other girls, I got other friends and they were very, . . . different, they were a lot more conservative and they were a lot more sort of – erm – going to night club girls and I got very friendly with two of them. We were a group, with two of them and we were very close, but *they really sort of changed me as well and I became a lot more – well a lot more like, you know I find this really interesting, you know a lot more with putting make up on and I remember I put – erm – ((tuts)) those curling things, – a perm in my hair ((laughing))*. And my mum, again my mum of course told me (???) that because I was much more like – erm – well I don't really know the word for it, but somebody who would like to go to nightclubs and *a lot more tacky than I used to be*. But I found this, *I felt I had found my new identity, not my kind of identity, but I found this was all very new to me.* To put nail polish on and all that sort of things and we would go and look for boys. I must have been 14 I think, something like that. And I had my hair all dyed very blonde and *I must have looked awful ((laughing))*

Moving between descriptive and evaluative statements, she spoke about feelings of empowerment as she successfully took on an 'alien' role. Partly driven by the urge to fully belong, she acted out a self that would bring her closer to her new friends. It was equally important to demonstrate her ability to become her own 'independent' person, departing from dominant family norms – a common process during puberty. As noted earlier, in the interview she distanced herself from her earlier teenage perceptions of self, labelling the social circles she had found herself in as '*burgerlijk*', a derogatory word for a common, lower middle-class, conservative lifestyle.

Tourism, a particular brand of cross-border mobility, had been an important means of her transformation.

I remember we went on our first holiday together to – erm – ((tuts)) I think to Spain or somewhere, the three of us. And we had a very nice time about going to nightclubs and all these kind of things, *and I, it all those things did feel very I think they felt very alien to me but they also, I really felt, oh wow somehow I could actually, I actually can belong to these people.* I suppose in my family *I always felt that I was quite different but with those girls I thought, if I, you know they really are, they are, what you should be like and I can be part of that. I was quite, somehow quite proud of that I think.* – Erm – And that lasted for quite some years I think.

She again used a contrast set to evaluate different experiences of subjectivity. Opposing nature oriented family outings to her Spanish package holiday experience, she created opposing images of her 'alternative', sober self (a self promoted by her family) to the more tacky self that had been an exciting, but ultimately less influential, teenage experiment. Anna pointed out that during her teenage years she had not been interested in school, an attitude that fitted her 'tacky' personae. She justified her 'past self' saying that secondary school had 'not been very satisfying', and that she had had no clue what to do when she received her Diploma. She tried some temping work in a bistro and travelled with a boyfriend to Malta, rather naively planning to stay there 'forever'. She presented the trip as a failed and totally unrealistic attempt to do something with her life, calling it a 'fiasco', and recalled that she had soon returned to the Netherlands to her job in the bistro.

A New Action Scheme: 'Serious' Travel Abroad and Attaining Freedom

One of the features distinguished in biographical analysis is the 'biographical action scheme', a description of a deliberate attempt to take a new trajectory.

Action schemes are characterized by formulations of clear intentions and a positive mood of thinking and planning, and the narrator's tone of voice is generally upbeat (Schütze 2008a: 26). It is not surprising that past movements across state borders that lead to a longer, more or less successful stay abroad are often phrased as premeditated plans to change one's life. As we saw earlier, the 'fiasco' of Malta was presented in the interview as a dead end. In what follows we will see that it was also framed as a preamble, leading to more cross-border mobility and genuine transformation.

Following the negative evaluation of her post-school 'uncertainty and failure to escape', Anna continued in a more cheerful voice. She pointed out that she had still wanted to go abroad, but had been better planned, starting to save money to pay for a six-month language course in Spain. The life story opposed this new movement to her earlier trip to Malta evaluating as an immature, badly planned and failed attempt to start an independent life. The subsequent account was a story of personal success and growth towards adulthood and a cosmopolitan mind-set. She first explained how hard it had been, arriving on her own in a place she did not know.

> I remember even for myself it felt like *a very big thing* because I remember very well arriving – with an enormous suitcase and the hostel that I had booked, – either didn't exist or was full and I had to find something else. And at nineteen I remember I *felt really quite lost* in this big, well it wasn't a very big city but it was a big university town and I didn't know anybody or couldn't speak Spanish of course.

She soon found her way, making friendships and experiencing a new lifestyle, which she described as 'liberating'.

> – Erm – but very soon I met people and I got into the course and I remember it felt *extremely – ehm – . . . liberating to be away and to being able to do all these things myself* and to, I don't, it gave me a *very good feeling that I could actually do all these things on my own* and I was managing really well and I was learning the language really quite well and I was learning all about history in Spanish and all these things. And I made very nice friends of course from all over the world. It was *a really nice eye opener* to meet all these – new people and – erm – *more interesting people* than maybe the people I had been sort of met in secondary school, they weren't really, they never really felt like long lasting people, I was still in touch with them, but they, I have to say when I lost contact with them, which was I suppose, they kept up the contact very well, but I could have let go really the moment I arrived in Spain, I think I met so many nice people there and *it was such a good experience to be there and to, well just live in another country was just wonderful, away from, there is more to Holland than just, you know, my streets in B. and my small family in a way.*

She met her future husband who had come over from Northern Ireland on an exchange programme, and described him, again using a discourse of 'liberation'. Her laughing reinforced the message that she had been positively amazed.

And so I met him there and he was another *liberating* person in my life, because ((laughing till +)) he was so *free* and so (+) open and – erm – so *adventurous*, I was really, I was really *overwhelmed* by that.

The theme of 'breaking constraints' was further developed in the account as she outlined a new affective route, pointing out that the relationship had given her the possibility of exploring a new sense of freedom. During their stay in Spain, the couple decided they wanted to travel more, and they moved to London to earn money for a trip to India and Nepal. Anna described her life in London as 'even better' than the experience in Spain, as it was a choice for 'real life' abroad. It was

> *more serious*, because we both looked for jobs and that actually gave me even a better feeling because *now I really lived abroad but in the real life abroad*. You know and we shared a house with six other English people and you know, so it was really nice to be part of that – erm – English life I suppose and I had a job there and it was really, *it was sort of very real in a way it felt like, like it to me.*

Anna presented the move to London as a transformation from a relatively safe and guided educational foreign experience to a more serious, independent confrontation with real life that tested and strengthened her new sense of transnational freedom.

It is not uncommon that positive work experiences and intimate relations outside the homeland eventually result in emigration. In the interview Anna stressed that she 'liked being abroad away from Holland', had 'no desire to go back', and that having to go back at that point would have 'sort of made me, a bit sad'. Her choice of words ('liked', 'no desire', 'sad') clarified the significance of emotions to her increasing detachment from the Netherlands. In the context of her whole life story, the references prepared her audience (myself) for the story of eventual migration.

The trip to India and Nepal introduced Anna and Danny to a world outside Europe and forged the growing bond between them. During the interview, the story of their travels allowed Anna to further comment on her metamorphosis from a rather insecure local girl into a more independent cosmopolitan person. Looking at her body language, I could see that the memories evoked extremely positive feelings. She glowed as she evaluated the trip as 'a wonderful experience' and, more importantly, as a test of character and strength.

> it was *very nice* – erm – well for all the reasons of, of *the challenge* of it and the, the poverty and the different religions and the different culture and the, *trying to cope* with all the illnesses on your own and the – *being able to do all that.*

The next part of the story functioned as a short interim, as a proverbial silence before the emotionally storm of the account of 'settling in Northern Ireland'. She stated that the decision to leave her homeland made her focus on a new life away from her family and old friends. After their Asian trip,

Danny started his PhD in Belfast and Anna returned to the Netherlands to do an English teacher training course, qualifying her to start a university degree in Belfast. By now '[they] knew [they] would like to stay together', and her new action scheme and affective focus accommodated that aim. Significantly, she mentioned that she no longer enjoyed the company of her old friends as 'they also sort of *felt quite shallow, or sort of, not really what I wanted any-more out of friends I think*'. She explained that when she was abroad, she had not really missed her family 'that much'. In the context of her life story, this evaluation justified her decision to migrate to Northern Ireland.

Settling in a New Country: Conflicting Memories and Increased Emotional Density

The narrative of 'settling in Northern Ireland' was long and detailed, and compared to many other parts of her story, emotionally dense. The upbeat theme of liberation made way for a discourse of alienation and 'betweenness' (Fortier 2000: 16) and an imagined future of problematic belonging. Rather tellingly, the account started off with a statement about cultural difference, about having to get married because of Danny's family background.

> And then of course I arrived here and because Northern Ireland being so reli-gious and well my husband's family being so religious, my husband, my husband thought it would be a better idea for us to go and get married because we couldn't live together otherwise.

Getting married at this point in her life was not really what she had expected to do, but she constructed the decision as a strategy to accommodate the situation. Yet although she might have justified it quite easily to herself, she still had to face her mother in the Netherlands. The latter, Anna commented, was 'totally against that idea, because of course she had a, she had broken up her own marriage and we didn't know each other that long'. Interestingly, Anna had felt she could best convince her mother by saying that she really wanted to get married, hiding the fact that her decision had been a pragmatic one. Her body language showed that she felt uncomfortable, remembering the event. Breaking up sentences and contradicting herself, she explained:

> I couldn't really say to her that it was because – otherwise we couldn't live together, so I had to say to her that I really wanted to get married, which wasn't really the case, I would have been very happy just to live together, but I knew for him that wasn't possible, but I also, I did want to live together.

Tensions in transnational families are common, and several studies have shown that both migrating kin and their relatives abroad employ emotional tactics and affective strategies to keep uncomfortable truths hidden (see, for example, Ryan 2008; Svašek 2010b; Velayutham and Wise 2005). Anna's con-scious choice to put on an act for her mother created what can be regarded as a split self, a double act that failed to fully suppress her own feelings of ambiguity about marrying into a conservative religious family. In the life story, Anna tried to deal with this duality by presenting it as a fact of life she simply had to deal with. She justified her solution, explaining to me that it showed she had become an independent adult, ready to make decisions against her mother's advice. Her feelings of ambiguity did, however, bubble up when she continued her story. After stating that she got married straightaway when arriving in Northern Ireland, she made a jump back in time to the first and only other time she had visited Northern Ireland while living with Danny in London. The narrative shift in time was telling, as it introduced a new affective theme to her story: feelings of non-belonging to her new social environment. Again, such feelings are not only felt by many migrants, but are part and parcel of the (mobile) human condition.

Background Constructions as Indicators of Biographical Work

The account of this first visit to Northern Ireland functioned as a 'background construction', evaluating an occasion when Anna met Danny's family for the first time during a family wedding. In Schütze's perspective, the insertion of background constructions in main biographical narratives commonly indicates that a narrator is dealing with changing subjectivity and inconsistencies in self-presentation (Schütze 2008a: 27, 34). In his view, such passages are important means for creative 'biographical work', defined as an inner activity of mind and emotional psyche, essentially constituted by conversation with significant others and oneself (ibid.: 28). As we shall see, Anna's background construction explained to herself (and to me as audience) why she had felt unsure about permanently moving to Northern Ireland in 1993, feelings that had not been mentioned when she first brought up the theme of migration in the interview. In the context of the whole interview, the background construction also predicted and justified her eventual return to the Netherlands. The account allowed her to express doubts about her marriage, and contradicted the following statement she had made earlier:

> the alternative would have been us living separate and me living in a house full of Northern Irish girls and him living in a house full of boys. And I didn't like that idea, you know coming from Holland I, you live together and, but I thought well OK *I kind of knew that I didn't mind getting married. I liked the idea of getting married.*

The account of the visit created a more complex picture of her decision to get married and began in London, when Anna had asked a friend for advice on what she should wear when invited to the wedding of one of Danny's Northern Irish relatives. The friend had lent her a short sleeveless black dress and it was in this outfit that she first met her boyfriend's parents.

> I remember I arrived here and the next day we had to go to the wedding and *I remember I just felt so out of place suddenly* when I wore that dress, because they

had all sort of come together, that it was totally, it was black, it was too short, I had no tights. *And I remember Danny's mother looking at me in disgust ((laughing))*

Anna laughed as she remembered her *faux pas*, and I laughed, feeling empathy (remembering my own blunders in connection with my English in-laws), but she had clearly been terribly embarrassed. Confusing the time sequence, she evaluated the event as a wake-up call that had made her realize that her later move to 'Northern Ireland' would not be another liberating trip.

> there was, I *remember that was the start of, it dawned on me that I, this was a different place, I was going to, well that was the first time I had, of course I wasn't really intending to live there then, but I did remember feeling totally awkward in the whole family. Which I had never, I have never felt awkward living abroad with other people, because always somehow I was totally accepted.*

She remembered her feelings of alienation and awkwardness, and stressed how hard it had been to act in a role she had not been comfortable with.

> But with this thing, with his family, it was a different thing, we had to sleep in different rooms, everything *was alien suddenly to me.* I remember eating cereal in the morning, *I felt alien* and the way they spoke was, the colloquial language I had to, *I half understood them* and they talked to me as if I should understand everything. The dress, they've never really said anything about, but *I knew it was totally, absolutely wrong.* I can't remember much of the wedding, apart from that it was hours of standing about with, *sort of behaving really fake* and – and endless photographs that had to be taken it was and it was *boring.*

The occasion of the biographical interview clearly made Anna reflect on the feelings of non-belonging she had felt during that first visit, feelings she had most likely tried to forget when moving to Northern Ireland in 1993.

> And that I felt, *I did feel awkward*, now I did, I think I did when I came down, when we got married, when I really moved here, to go and start in Queen's. *I was a bit hesitant about, sort of coming over here remembering that sort of strange family.*

Anna visibly relived the event as she remembered and narrated it, which signalled its emotional intensity. The detail of the account and the fact that she returned to it again later on in the interview demonstrated its symbolic relevance to her life story, told at a time when she was leaving Northern Ireland.

The Wedding: More Biographical Work and Deep Reflection

Tellingly, she described her own wedding as an occasion that needed a 'solution', unconsciously framing it as a potential problem. She needed to manoeuvre carefully, accommodating her new family-in-law but at the same time not compromising too much to lose her sense of personal identity. An example is her choice of wedding dress. Writing this chapter in July 2009, I wondered whether her experience with the black dress during her first visit to Northern Ireland had influenced this choice, so I emailed her about this. She replied:

> Yes [my choice] was a bit traditional in that it was a white dress. Bought in Miss Selfridge, so not a real wedding dress but it *was* long and white. I definitely took his family's opinion into account, but *did* want to choose one according to my own taste. I can show you the photo album his sister made for me, then we can laugh a lot because that's what I do every time I look at those pictures. It was such a silly event.

It should again be noted that Anna was interviewed just a few days before leaving Northern Ireland. Her departure gave her the space to more emphatically express her uneasiness with her husband's family than she had possibly done on other occasions, allowing her to reflect on the pressures caused by specific cultural expectations. In the account that followed, several elements symbolized Anna's non-belonging: the unwanted wedding presents, her conscious act of gratefulness, and her parents-in-laws' disappointment about their son's choice of wife.

> A: We had to go and look at the presents and they were *all absolutely hideous* crystal vases and mahogany tables, and a rocking chair.
> M: ((Laughing))
> A: And it was all standing in the good room, I remember they had this good room here that is only used for visitors and only used for occasions like weddings, and all the presents were standing out there. I have realized that they were for us and then we had one evening that everybody came who had given presents and *we all had to sit there and be very thankful and look at the presents.*

The memories of the frictions brought up feelings of discomfort. In a subsequent reflective passage, however, she came to the conclusion that it was mainly cultural differences (her family-in-law being conservative Protestants), and not personal dislike, that had caused the difficulties. She distanced herself from her feeling of alienation, expressing understanding and empathy for her parents-in-law.

> I think they were, on the whole they were *disappointed* he didn't get married from somebody from the same church and from the same village and you know *who had the same understanding of, of everything really* and so the wedding really felt, *it was a very bad start I think from coming to live here because they just felt I wasn't, I wasn't a girl for, I wasn't a local girl who would think about things the same way and I wouldn't bring up my children the same way* and – erm – .

Anna ended this section with the words: 'So why am I saying all this? Oh I talked about how I came to Ireland wasn't it?' These sentences signified a sense of 'waking up' from deep thought, a common feature in biographical interviews that also signals a realization that specific reflections need to be placed in the context of the whole life story. She answered her own question as follows:

It wasn't how I feel about living here. – Erm – well I think, I think I talk about the wedding because that's sort of, – erm – what is the right word for it? . . . Says it all about, how I feel I suppose how I feel I don't fit into that Northern Irish society, life, society I think.

Importantly, she softened the statement, pointing out that the relationship between herself and her parents-in-law had improved as both sides had come to accept each other's differences. The account made clear that quite a bit of kin work and emotional management had been necessary to achieve this transformation.

I think it's better now after, how many years is it? 15 years of living here, I feel a lot more part of his family, but it's with a lot of effort and with a lot sort of – erm – put on feelings that I try to be part of them and I try and understand them or, and they it goes both ways, I think they try and understand me more. I think there have been times that they really couldn't understand me and didn't want to understand me and the same went for me, but I think we've gone through some sort of we've, we have neutral understanding now of like OK we're both different, but you're part of our family and we'll accept you because you, well you're married now into the family.

Return Migration: Picking up the Theme of 'Transformation and Liberation through Mobility'

The 'return to the Netherlands' was a logical end narrative in the interview. Anna used the section to make some statements about feelings related to her foreigner status in Northern Ireland. She felt that her return to the Netherlands had changed her sense of self as it had made her accept that she would always remain an outsider in Northern Ireland.

I don't think I'll ever feel that I'll, I am really part of it or that I feel really at home here.

Interestingly, we had both complained about 'not fitting in' when meeting up as friends over the past eight years, but I had never heard her express her feelings with so much conviction.

I think now that we're going to go back to Holland in the summer I think all those things, also are a lot more obvious now I think, that I know that if I would stay here I will always stay a foreigner. I still, when I still, when I meet new people, even although maybe they don't often can figure out my accent anymore, they don't really know where I'm from. They kind of know I'm foreign, and even through looking at me I can see that they think, 'she's not one of us'.

She admitted not knowing whether returning to the Netherlands would increase her personal sense of belonging, but emphasized that being in the Netherlands on a more permanent basis might satisfy a (perhaps unconscious) longing for familiarity.

I think – now that we go back to Holland, I somehow and I don't know what it's going to be like here, to go and live there. But I do think that now I will feel more like I'm going to go home and I don't mean because my family is there, but I think – partly because – I don't know I think because of the language, the familiarity I think with how people – erm – interact with each other somehow, *it seems so familiar suddenly when I'm back in Holland and I do notice that here I really try and be like the Northern Irish people, which is still not, after all those years, it's still, it's not, it hasn't become part of me, myself.*

Her expectations were not based on the naïve assumption that she would easily reintegrate into an unchanged society, but on the realization that trying to fit into Northern Irish society had, at least to some extent, constrained her.

the idea then of going back to Holland, which *might be a complete illusion because things might have changed totally* but it gives me like, suddenly it gives me sometimes when I think of it, *it gives me a feeling where I suddenly, I can sort of breathe out and let go. ((Takes deep breath)) But I can be myself again, whereas maybe all those years I've really put on trying to be someone else that I'm not really.*

An Underlying Story of Personal Transformation through Mobility

In the remainder of the interview, Anna countered this contrast between real and fake selves ('myself' and 'someone else that I'm not really') through an account of dynamic subjectivity that emphasized personal growth and change. She argued that she had changed as a result of her experiences outside the Netherlands, and hoped she had become a more independent person.

I wonder if now// well I'm, I suppose I'm hoping for that too, that I've grown so much to be my own person with my own thoughts, that I can now go back to Holland in a way that I can be my, you know the sort of the, the, well the Anna that I would like to be, without them [i.e. her family] telling me or anybody telling me what to do or maybe society having expectations on me.

Interestingly, this is the first time she mentioned her children in the interview, defining the move to the Netherlands as an escape from Northern Irish protestant culture and as an opportunity to familiarize them with particular Dutch traditions that had shaped her. Even though she had tried to introduce her children to elements of 'Dutch culture', such as *Sinterklaas*, she knew she could not fully reproduce the Dutch homeland experience while living in Northern Ireland (Svašek 2010c: 82–83). As Anne Marie Fortier (2000) and Ahmed et al. (2003) noted, migrant attempts to engage with homeland traditions are always marked by distance from the homeland, and should not be understood as direct replications of identity.

In Anna's narrative, produced when she was about to remigrate to the Netherlands, distance (in time and space) was regarded as a chance to have grown into a more independent person.

> So it would be nice to go back to Holland now and you know a large part of that society is sort of a bit like the way I think about things. Not all of it of course, but hopefully and maybe *because I'm now older or because I've lived here, I can choose those things a lot better rather than being you know, having them formed just by, by the society or something like that.*

Consciously moving toward the end of her autobiographical account, she repeated being happy about the return to her country of origin. She speculated about the role reversal, with her husband now becoming a 'foreigner'. As the last sentences of biographical interviews ('pre-coda argumentation' in Schütze's terminology) often condense the underlying message of life stories, it is worthwhile presenting the full text.

> on the whole I'm sort of . . . *relieved to get out of the tightness of being here* I think, after all those years. And I'm really *sad* that I've, it's been, I've had a *wonderful time* here too, but it's been – erm – a bit of a *struggle* sometimes I find, and it's, it could have been, – I could have chosen an easier society, I think somehow I am very. It feels like that. I feel it's been// but maybe that is perhaps that is just being, that is *maybe just being, you know living in another, really living in another culture.* Like I think when I went to Spain it was more like a sort of a half student holiday life and then when we went to London, that was sort of real living in another culture and India of course, that was such a sort of a complete culture shock, but that gave me an interest in that whole side of . . . life in the world, in a way. But being here I suppose, *I wonder if it would, would have been equally difficult had I got married to somebody from France or from Spain or, you know, like a different country, maybe it's just very difficult to live in another culture, any other culture and when you have to live with the family and all the expectations that they put on me, I've found that very hard. I still always put it down that it's such a religious, tight, insular society, I still put it down to that and maybe that isn't it. Maybe it's just difficult to just live in another culture,* this is why I think it will be interesting to see how my husband will feel like in Holland, because that is supposed to be a lot more tolerant, but *he might not feel it like that. Because, after all, he's going to be a foreigner there.* So I think, I think that's, I can't think of anything else really that.

Conclusion

Anna's story demonstrated that emotions, conceptualized as discourses, practices and embodied experiences, not only shape subjectivity in everyday mobile life, but also play an important role in the production of autobiographical narrations. Remembered, re-experienced and newly felt emotions, expressed in narrative accounts, describe and evaluate histories of situated selves in the performative context of the interview. Autobiographical storytelling provides a rather particular space for active re-engagement with the past, as the genre stimulates the narrator to produce a chronological account of transit and transformation through time and space, constructed through the narrative sequencing of significant life events. As the example of Anna's story showed, the storyline often roughly follows biological/social phases of childhood-adolescence-adulthood, reconstructing a more or less orderly succession of stories of location and relocation within and (in the case of migrants) across state boundaries.

Autobiographical narration, however, also tends to break the illusion of chronological mobility, as the task of uninterrupted life storytelling challenges the narrator to select, connect, compare, oppose and interweave accounts of personal experiences. As Anna's narrative demonstrated, this means that story lines are often interrupted through emotional associations, background stories and meta-reflections that judge not only past subjectivity but also comment on the story in the making and, in Anna's case, analyse the psycho-social development of self. With regard to the latter, it is important to note that the method of autobiographical narration tends to be welcomed as an opportunity of deep self-reflection by people who are familiar with performative genres of one-to-one self-disclosure (Svašek and Domecka 2012). For migrants like Anna, who have had to deal with unfamiliar cultural expectations, the occasion of the interview offers a chance to reflect on the challenges of belonging and non-belonging in a foreign environment.

Anna's story referred to temporarily transformative experiments (specifically during her teenage years) that had enriched her experience of mobile existence, but that had had no long-lasting effect on her personal development. In addition, she also spoke of more fundamental processes of change. She evaluated these through embodied emotional practices with different degrees of reflective intensity, ranging from involuntary stutters and nervous laughter to thoughtful, and at times quite passionate, arguments about the conditions and consequences of some of her past actions.

In the meta-narrative of her story, she created an image of someone who had felt a strong desire to adopt a secure but free and outward looking lifestyle, longing to belong through transnational mobility. The argument was that she had chosen a life outside the Netherlands to realize this. She claimed that, actively negotiating her position as a migrant wife in a mixed marriage, more or less successfully coping with culturally specific expectations, she had come out of the process as a stronger and more confident person. Developing the notion of psychological growth, she concluded that, returning to her homeland, she would be in a better position to control her own and her children's future transformations.[13]

As Anna developed her story of migrant belonging and non-belonging, her frequent use of emotion words, the changing tone of her voice and the temporary display of particular feelings demonstrated what was stated at the beginning of this chapter, namely that human beings are fundamentally emotional beings, also when recalling life experiences and translating them into narrative performance.

As noted earlier, Anna's understanding of emotivity, loosely defined as the interplay of meaning and feeling, was tied in with her processual understanding of personhood as self-realization. In her view, that was influenced by popular psychological notions of self making, situationally felt emotions boosted or threatened her sense of personal freedom. Verbal references to feelings of 'cosiness', 'happiness', 'sadness' and 'confusion' all related to her understanding of herself as a person who had moved through various phases of relative restriction and liberation. In the narrative, references to and verbal interpretations of specific remembered and re-experienced emotions signalled what she saw as positive or negative developments in personal development. Told at a particular moment in her life, just before the return to her homeland, the self-narrative meant to convince herself that she had had enough; that it was time to leave.

While Anna's story is most of all a story of migration and remigration, it is also a story that many non-migrant readers of this chapter will be able to relate to. After all, as mobile beings in transit and transformation, people cannot but face issues of belonging and non-belonging. As members of a language-centred species, human beings are also more generally inclined to tell stories about themselves, verbalizing and working through pasts of stability and rupture. Their accounts are not only produced as autobiographical narrations in interview settings, but also intersperse and inform everyday activities.

Notes

1 The research for this chapter was funded by the European Commission and forms part of a large collaborative Framework 7 Project, entitled 'Euroidentities – The Evolution of European Identity: Using Biographical Methods to Study the Development of European Identity' (see http://www.euroidentities.org/). I would like to thank Robert Miller, Markieta Domecka and Dirk Schubotz for their useful feedback on an earlier version of this chapter, and thank other members of the international research team who made comments during discussions about this particular interview. I am also extremely grateful for insightful remarks to several versions of the chapter by Anne-Sigfrid Grønseth.

2 Not her real name. All names in this study have been anonymized, and some information has been changed.

3 Named emotions such as anger, fear, shame, love and disgust often function as evaluative judgements, reflecting normative values (Nussbaum 2001: 4; Heatherington 2005: 147; Parkinson 1995). Emotions therefore play a central part in autobiographical narrative performance, when narrators reflect on their own past and present behaviour, and ponder about decisions that may affect future self-manifestation.

4 See Baldassar 2001; Ramirez et al. 2007; and Svašek 2010b for analyses of transnational reunions and return visits that highlight the need for emotion management.

5 The discourse of 'romantic love', for example, is encoded in cultural scripts that
people are confronted with when growing up in particular socio-historical settings. The norms underlying this particular discourse (which is, of course, changing as people contribute to it in different ways) are expressed though specific
practices. 'Romantic love' between two lovers can, for example, be expressed and
activated through a special dinner for two and a gift of red roses, rather specific
traditions that have been promoted globally (though not reaching everywhere)
by the popular media. Discourses of emotions commonly inform practices of
emotions, and vice versa. Romantic feelings expressed and evoked by perfor-
mances such as intimate dining, for example, are also inherently physical. The
bodily sensations of erotic attraction and 'warm' feelings can be perceived as
manifestations and indicators of romantic attachment, and influential discourses
of 'romantic love' may portray these embodied experiences as natural symptoms.
For studies that include a focus on physicality and embodiment in their theoretical perspective on emotions, see for example Lyon 1995 and Csordas 1994.

6 It should not be forgotten that these processes take place in contexts of power.
In transit and transformation, situated bodies gain various degrees of ownership
over arising situations.

7 In a study of Australians in London, Conradson and Latham (2007: 232) pointed
out that moving out of known social and geographical settings enabled their
informants to experiment with new lifestyles, allowing them to 'work upon' the
self 'in modest but nonetheless significant ways'.

8 This implies that new experiential contexts generate affective possibilities that
may (or may not) contribute to a person's situated feelings of well-being. Recent
anthropological work on well-being amongst migrants and refugees has stressed
that experiences of alienation and being misunderstood in the new country of
settlement may contribute to ill-health and feelings of non-belonging (Grønseth
2001; Grønseth and Oakley 2007). In a study of Tamil refugees in Norway, Anne
Sigfrid Grønseth (2006: 149) argued that 'when Tamils are forced to reorient
themselves and negotiate a radically new social and cultural world, this might be
seen to enforce a deep insecurity in personal as well as group identity'.

9 Before the interview starts, the interviewer explains the general theme of the
research but points out that, in telling his or her life story, the interviewee may
mention anything that has made him or her into the person he or she is today.
Crucially, interviewees are told that they may take as long as they feel is necessary to tell their story. During the first phase of narration, the interviewer
does not intervene in the narration and provides only limited, mostly non-verbal,
responses. Once the interviewee indicates that the story is finished (this narrative
fragment is called 'coda'), the interview moves to a second stage, when some additional questions concerning the interviewee's biography are asked in reaction to
themes the narrator has brought up in the first phase of the narration. During the
third and last phase of the interview, the researcher asks more explicit questions
relating to the theme of the research project, which in our case was the theme of
'Europe' and 'European identity'.

10 In my own experience as autobiographical narrator, at moments when 'difficult'
topics appeared on my story's horizon, I tried to keep control by quickly moving
on to other, emotionally less complex topics. In more extreme cases of past suffering, a process of 'fading out' may indicate a strong sense of self-alienation
(Schütze 2008a: 6).

11 Emotional interactions between the speaker and the listener are in my view part and parcel of the performance, with the interviewer showing expressions of empathy, concern and amusement, especially when the narrator seems to expect a reaction.

12 It is rather striking that in quite a few interviews conducted for the Euroidentities project (of which Anna's interview was part), interviewees in similar positions to Anna (having migrated to other European countries and/or having married foreigners) mentioned experiences of non- or partial belonging during childhood and adolescence. It is not unlikely that, at least in some cases, the experience of not-fully-belonging to local contexts boosted a desire to escape the limitations of single national geographic/social settings. Alternatively, these earlier experiences may have been rationalized during the interview as moral justifications for the sometimes unwelcome decision to migrate or marry a foreigner.

13 When I asked Anna, after she had ended her account, to describe herself in a few words, she produced a discourse of 'personal development', emphasizing how she had gone through various phases: '/Err/ well, I think I have, – err – from a very, I think a very – protected kind of quite insecure child that I was, maybe due to my upbringing and the way, maybe because my dad left and things like that and maybe because we were a family that was slightly more, in a sort of – err – a family that was more maybe – erm – not in the mainstream/. I think I was always quite a, yeah quite a protected child, protected upbringing and a quite an insecure child. And I think that stayed with me up until I'd moved away I think from Holland, I think it was only then that I started to be, maybe become an adult. Now I don't want to say I'm an adult now, but I think – I've grown up to be a lot more like my own person I think and I do think that is thanks to going abroad. But I'm sure there was a reason for me going abroad, I think I had to get away from maybe, I don't know if it was family, but circumstances too, sort of maybe escape I think. And I think I've, I've grown up a lot and I'm still quite insecure I suppose but I think I'm much more aware of that now and more – /erm/ I think I've become much more of a person who can actually – erm – decide much better what I want to do and – erm – have a better idea of what I want now. And I do think that's thanks to being, living abroad and having to, maybe having to adapt to other people. I, I don't know, but yeah I don't know I find it hard to say how I see myself, but I see myself as a lot more ((7 seconds silence)) knowing a lot more what I want in life, I think, yeah.'

References

Ahmed, S. 2004a. *The Cultural Politics of Emotion*. Edinburgh: Edinburgh University Press.

_____. 2004b. 'Affective Economies', *Social Text* 79, 22(2): 117–39.

Ahmed, S. et al. 2003. *Uprootings/Regroundings: Questions of Home and Migration*. Oxford: Berg.

Baldassar, L. 2001. *Visits Home: Migration Experiences between Italy and Australia*. Melbourne: Melbourne University Press.

Brown, P. 2005. *Life in Dispersal. Narratives of Asylum, Identity and Community*. Unpublished Doctoral Thesis, University of Huddersfield.

Burrell, K. 2006. *Moving Lives. Narratives of Nation and Migration among Europeans in Post-War Britain*. Aldershot: Ashgate.

Chamberlain, M. and S. Leydesdorff. 2004. 'Transnational Families: Memories and Narratives', *Global Networks* 4(3): 227–41.

Conradson, D. and A. Latham. 2007. 'The Affective Possibilities of London. Antipodean Transnationals and the Overseas Experience', *Mobilities* 2(2): 231–54.

Conradson, D. and D. McKay. 2007. 'Translocal Subjectivities: Mobility, Connection, Emotion', *Mobilities* 2(2): 167–74.

Csordas, T.J. (ed.). 1994. *Embodiment and Experience. The Existential Ground of Culture and Self*. Cambridge: Cambridge University Press.

Davies, J. and Spencer, D. (eds.) 2010. *Emotions in the Field. The Anthropology and Psychology of Fieldwork Experience*. Palo Alto: Stanford University Press.

Domecka, M. 2008. 'Autobiographical Narrative Analysis'. Unpublished document, Queens University Belfast.

Domecka, M., M. Eichsteller, S. Karakusheva, P. Musella, L. Ojamäe, E. Perone, D. Pickard, A. Schröder-Wildhagen, K. Siilak and K. Waniek. 2012. 'Method in Practice. Autobiographical Interviews in Search of European Phenomena', in R. Miller (ed.), *The Evolution of European Identities: Biographical Approaches*. Basingstoke: Palgrave Macmillan, pp. 21–44.

Fortier, A.M. 2000. *Migrant Belongings. Memory, Space, Identity*. Oxford: Berg.

Grønseth, A.S. 2001. 'In Search of Community: A Quest for Well Being among Tamil Refugees in Northern Norway', *Medical Anthropology Quarterly* 15(4): 493–541.

_____. 2006. 'Experiences of Illness: Tamil Refugees in Norway Seeking Medical Advise', in J. Helle and I. Làzàr (eds), *Multiple Medical Realities. Patients and Healers in Biomedical, Alternative and Traditional Medicine*. London: Berghahn Press, pp. 148–62.

Grønseth, A.S. and D.L. Davis (eds). 2010. *Mutuality and Empathy. Self and Other in the Ethnographic Encounter*. Wantage: Sean Kingston.

Grønseth, A.S. and R. Oakley. 2007. 'Introduction. Ethnographic Humanism: Migrant Experiences in the Quest for Well-Being', *Anthropology in Action* 14(1–2): 1–11.

Heatherington, T. 2005. '"As if Someone Dear to Me Had Died": Intimate Landscapes, Political Subjectivity and the Problem of a Park in Sardinia', in K. Milton and M. Svašek (eds), *Mixed Emotions: Anthropological Studies of Feeling*. Oxford: Berg, pp. 145–62.

Jordan, B. and P. Brown. 2007. 'Migration and Work in the United Kingdom: Mobility and the Social Order', *Mobilities* 2(2): 255–76.

Leavitt, J. 1996. 'Meaning and Feeling in the Anthropology of Emotions', *American Ethnologist* 23(3): 514–39.

Lyon, M.L. 1995. 'Missing Emotion: The Limitations of Cultural Constructionism in the Study of Emotion', *Cultural Anthropology* 10(2): 244–63.

McCrum, M. 2007. *Going Dutch in Beijing. The International Guide to Do the Right Thing*. London: Profile Books.

Miller, R. et al. (eds). 2012. *The Evolution of European Identities: Biographical Approaches*. Basingstoke: Palgrave Macmillan.

Nussbaum, M. 2001. *Upheavals of Thought: The Intelligence of Emotions*. Cambridge: Cambridge University Press.

Parkinson, B. 1995. *Ideas and Realities of Emotion*. London and New York: Routledge.

Ramirez, M., Z. Skrbiš and M. Emmison. 2007. 'Transnational Family Reunions as Lived Experience: Narrating a Salvadoran Autoethnography', *Identities. Global Studies in Culture and Power* 14(4): 411–32.

Ryan, L. 2008. 'Navigating the Emotional Terrain of Families "Here" and "There": Women, Migration and the Management of Emotions', *Journal of Intercultural Studies* 29(3): 299–314.

Schubotz, D, M. Svašek, R. Miller and M. Domecka. 2012. 'Into and Out of Europe: Dynamic Insider/Outsider Perspectives', in R. Miller (ed.), *The Evolution of European Identities: Biographical Approaches*. Basingstoke: Palgrave Macmillan, pp. 201–10.

Schütze, F. 2008a. 'Biography Analysis on the Empirical Base of the Autobiographical Narratives: How to Analyse Autobiographical Narrative Interviews', in *European Studies on Inequalities and Social Cohesion* 1–2: 153–242.

Schütze, F. 2008b. 'Biography Analysis on the Empirical Base of the Autobiographical Narratives: How to Analyse Autobiographical Narrative Interviews', in *European Studies on Inequalities and Social Cohesion* 3–4: 5–77.

Schütze, F. and A. Schröder-Wildhagen. 2012. 'European Mental Space and its Biographical Relevance', in R. Miller (ed.), *The Evolution of European Identities: Biographical Approaches*. Basingstoke: Palgrave Macmillan, pp. 255–78.

Spencer, D. and J. Davies (eds) 2010. *Anthropological Fieldwork. A Relational Process*. Cambridge: Cambridge Scholars Publishing.

Svašek, M. 2002. 'Narratives of "Home" and "Homeland". The Symbolic Construction and Appropriation of the Sudeten German Heimat', *Identities. Global Studies in Culture and Power* 9(4): 495–518.

_____. 2005. 'Emotions in Anthropology', in K. Milton and M. Svašek (eds), *Mixed Emotions. Anthropological Studies of Feeling*. Oxford: Berg, pp. 1–24.

_____. 2008. 'Who Cares? Families and Feelings in Movement', *Journal of Intercultural Studies* 29(3): 213–30; 331–45.

_____. 2010a. 'On the Move: Emotions and Human Mobility', *Journal of Ethnic and Migration Studies* 36(6): 865–80.

_____. 2010b. *Who Cares? Emotional Interaction, Support and Ageing in Transnational Families*. Report for Changing Ageing Partnership, Belfast: Queens University.

_____.2010c. 'In "The Field". Intersubjectivity, Empathy and the Workings of Internalised Presence', in D. Spencer and J. Davies (eds), *Anthropological Fieldwork. A Relational Process*. Cambridge: Cambridge Scholars Publishing, pp. 75–99.

_____. (ed.). 2012. *Emotions and Human Mobility. Ethnographies of Movement*. London: Routledge.

Svašek, M. and M. Domecka. 2012. 'The Autobiographical Narrative Interview. A Potential Arena of Emotional Membering, Performance and Reflection', in J. Skinner (ed.), *The Interview. Anthropological Approaches*. Oxford: Berghahn, pp. 107–26.

Svašek, M. and Z. Skrbiš. 2007. 'Passions and Powers: Emotions and Globalisation', *Identities. Global Studies in Culture and Power* 14(4): 367–84.

Velayutham, S. and A. Wise. 2005. 'Moral Economies of a Translocal Village: Obligation and Shame among South Indian Transnational Migrants', *Global Networks* 5(1): 27–47.

Chapter 4

Well-Being and the Implication of Embodied Memory

From the Diary of a Migrant Woman

Naoko Maehara

This chapter focuses on the memories, perceptions and emotional processes of a Japanese migrant woman called Naomi[1] who migrated to Ireland in October 2006 when she was in her late forties. She grew up in the south of Japan, went to university in Tokyo for five years, and lived in two or three other cities before migrating to Ireland with her Irish husband and three children. I met her for the first time at a dinner party in the spring of 2007. Since then, we have spent some time together at different social occasions; at friendship gatherings, where we met other Japanese-Irish couples and their children; at a multi-cultural course in a women's centre, where we sat together; and also on a Japanese online community, where we shared diaries and comments. Through personal communication, her diaries, and interviews, I will explore her early experiences of migration, particularly her emotional responses to the new environment.

In focusing on an individual migrant's psychological process, I will begin by outlining the phenomenological perspectives of Henry Bergson (2004 [1912]). Bergson's work reminds us to take into account the dialectical relationship between memory and perception. Following Bergson, I explore how memory operates in the context of migration and transnational processes. In the latter part of this chapter, I will integrate some literature from emotion studies to examine how the past is shaped by, and shapes, the basis of the individual's current feelings. Through this case study I shall suggest that examining the rich detail of the psychological processes of individual migrants is necessary for an understanding of the dynamic complexities of their experiences and subjectivities.

The Embodied Mind and Memory: The Phenomenological Approach of Bergson

In his book *Memory and Matters* Bergson (2004) poses a fundamental challenge to the Cartesian dualism and cognitivism in seeking to show that the nature of the human mind is largely determined by the form of the human body. His approach to memory has been tremendously influential on several generations of French philosophers, while it has also seen a renewed presence in recent works of psychology and the philosophy of mind (Middleton and Brown 2005). In what follows, I sketch some of the most significant features of his work, and how these theoretical assumptions can be applied to the empirical concern of this study.

For Bergson, perception is not a means of getting the world 'inside' the brain, as if it were some form of storehouse or container; nor is it a means by which the nervous system serves as an apparatus to shape representations of the world. Think for instance of the burning sensation in your fingers as you touch the stove. If you burn your fingers your brain gets the message to withdraw your hand very quickly. Through the nervous system we receive stimulation, transfer and interpret impulses, and send appropriate instructions to the muscles and glands. The brain is thus to be regarded as an instrument which receives movement, interprets the eventual action from a number of possibilities, and executes movement. In this sense, he sees the emergence of conscious perception as the means by which 'the fluid and mobile continuity of the real' is divided and selected in relation to the lived body. What we see is neither things as they really are, nor a simple reflection of our prior understandings; instead, it is 'the aggregate of images', 'an existence placed halfway between the "thing" and the "representation"' (ibid.: vii–viii).

The body is also a part of the aggregate of the material world, 'an image which acts like other images, receiving and giving back movement' (ibid.: 4–5). We as organisms are nourished by mixing images of external objects or bodies, while simultaneously shaping our perceptions of these images. Our neural pathways develop through experience, and remain bound up with the rest of the material world. As he argues: 'There is no perception which is not full of memories' (ibid.: 33). In processing sensory information we mingle a thousand details from our past experience. In this way, memories are not conserved in the brain; but they are 'in' time and are linked to creative duration and to perception.

The presence of the past can manifest itself in two ways, as Bergson distinguishes two main types of memory: 'habit memory' and 'recollection memory'. The first type of memory denotes 'motor mechanisms' or what psychologists call procedural memory, for instance, remembering verse by rote learning (ibid.: 91). It is automatic, inscribed in the body, and ensures an appropriate reaction; it is '*habit interpreted by memory* rather than memory itself' (ibid.: 95). The second type of memory is a more explicit form of 'independent recollections' (ibid.: 87), characterized as 'memory images' or 'representations', such as the memory of the lesson in which we learn the verse (ibid.: 91). Both memories serve the requirements of the present. In the case of habit memory, the past is stored in a cerebral mechanism, and is used for present action by releasing automatic movements adapted to circumstances. The operation of independent recollection is completely different. The representative memories of the events of our daily life are recorded as they take place in a unique time and place, regardless of utility and practical application. The brain actualizes only those images that are likely to be relevant to the needs of the present.

For Bergson, psychological recollection is not just a biological function like the process of simple re-excitation or pure reproduction; it is imaginatively constructed through moment-by-moment mappings of the body, self and the world. A lived body is embedded in the flux of time, and in the requirements of the present that inform its constant movement within the dimension of the past and horizon of the future: 'Thus is ensured the appropriate reaction, the correspondence to environment – adaptation, in a word – which is the general aim of life' (ibid.: 96). Without this coordination of memory-images and a present perception by the adaptive consciousness, our life would be inexplicable and less meaningful. Bergson also notes that there are always dominant memories which exist as 'shining points round which others form a vague nebulosity'; 'These shining points are multiplied to the degree in which our memory expands' (ibid.: 223). Personal recollections are contemplative and dynamic; they can evoke the chains of well-established habitual practice, and serve in 'pure memory' which begins to shape the present perception: '[w]e start from a "virtual state" which we lead onwards, step by step, through a series of different *planes of consciousness*, up to the goal where it is materialized in an actual perception' (ibid.: 319).

Bergson's model of memory and perception provides a useful perspective for exploring how memory operates in the mind of an individual who is embedded in multiple cultures and places; how migrants' perceptions enact and relate to their experiences of pre-migration. A number of researchers now acknowledge how migrants' subjectivities are inextricably bound up with more sensuous forms of bodily experience (Gardner 2002; Lee 2000; see also the Introduction in Wise and Chapman 2005). For example, Gardner (2002) implies that in the case of Bengali elders in London, the physical sensations of feeling too cold, of snow or freezing rain, of smells and taste are often incorporated into their experiences of discontinuity and rupture. Wise (2010) also demonstrates that globalization and increased mobility can bring discomfort not only to migrants but to local residents as well. For longer-term elderly residents of one Sydney suburb, their discomfort is clearly embodied and experienced through unfamiliar sights, smells, spaces, and language. As Wise argues, the mismatch of the senses of migrants and local residents are deeply intertwined with their memories as re-experienced in the present. But how are migrants' perceptions and senses affected by their 'consciously felt' goals, feelings and ideals in their lived experiences? As is described in what follows, Bergson's treatment of memory as duration draws our attention to the agency of the conscious human subject.

In this chapter, I shall focus on the case of Naomi, a recently arrived Japanese migrant woman in Ireland. Following Bergson, I will begin by describing how at times Naomi failed to coordinate the past with the present, not being able to navigate and 'actualize' the past in memory-images. Since the new environment in the new country did not evoke the rest of her history in her homeland, she faced a strong sense of loss and disorientation in the early days of her migration. Her case also demonstrates how her habitual responses, socially and culturally patterned, are infused with her goals and desire in a given time, being immediately available to conscious reflection in real-time.

Japanese Wives and Mothers in Ireland

Before addressing Naomi's case, let me briefly describe the context of my research. Naomi is one of my research participants, one of forty women who migrated from Japan to Ireland and Northern Ireland and married Irish/ Northern Irish men during the period between the 1990s and 2000s. My fieldwork, mainly based on participant observation and life story interviews, was conducted between early 2007 and late 2009. I initially met some of the women at the Japan Society in Belfast, and encountered others through a social networking website. Living in Co. Derry, I have made a number of trips to spend time with these women who live all over Ireland, from Donegal in the north to Kerry in the south. They largely come from middle-class backgrounds and from different parts of Japan. Their ages vary from those in their late twenties to those in their late forties. More than half of them are full-time mothers, and others teach the Japanese language, work in Japanese companies, or continue to work in their own professions (as accountants, nurses, etc.). A few of them also do part-time work in shops or cafés.

Naomi's and my other respondents' migrations to Ireland reflect specific socio-cultural and historical contexts of Japan, as well as the contemporary globalized, deterritorialized world where 'distances, and boundaries, are not what they used to be' (Hannerz 1996: 3). With its growing prosperity from the mid-1990s to the mid-2000s, Ireland attracted an increasing number of Japanese tourists, students and workers, at a time when Japanese interest in Ireland and Irish culture, as well as the consumption of Irish goods and cultural artefacts, was also increasing. In Japanese metropolitan areas, Irish-related organizations hold cultural events such as St. Patrick's Day's parades. There are workshops for Irish music, dance and cooking; there are shops that sell 'Irish' brands (from crafts, jewellery, sweaters, to food and drink); and there are books or articles written in, or translated into, Japanese, on the topic of Ireland/Northern Ireland. Many 'Irish pubs' have also sprung up and it is estimated that more than forty such bars exist in the Tokyo area alone. The promotion of Ireland as a tourist destination, as well as the growth of its heritage sector, invoked images of a distinct sense of Irish landscape, and of a continuous and stable Celtic and Gaelic past (Cusack 2001). The designs and commodities of difference reproduced deep-rooted stereotypes about Ireland/the Irish: 'Irish warmth and friendliness, a relaxed attitude toward life, and the innate ability to tell a great story'; 'the Irish as a welcoming people'; and 'the simple, unsophisticated Irishman' (Zuelow 2005: 194–95; O'Connor 1993). Wulff's (2007) analysis of Irish travel advertisements also identifies the motifs of 'peaceful country life, childhood summers, and a happy, old fashioned past' (2007: 532).

The past two decades in Japan have seen significant transformations in its sociocultural and economic conditions, transformations prompted by two major events: the end of Japan's post-war boom and the end of the Cold War. Regarding the former, the Japanese economic bubble came to an abrupt end in the early 1990s, and growth slowed markedly in the following ten years which has been termed Japan's 'Lost Decade (*Ushinawareta Jūnen*)'. With the rise of unemployment, a recession, and the decline of industry, a sense of loss was felt by many people in Japan (Abe 2001). The acceleration of economic globalization further deepened the sense of loss and uncertainty about the future. It prompted the Japanese to reconsider their taken-for-granted relationships with the United States (including Japan's military alignment with the U.S.), while it brought a growing sense of anxiety about American hegemony (ibid.; also Glosserman 2005). It was during this 'Lost Decade' and the prolonged recession of the 2000s, and against the backdrop of globalization, that something like an 'Irish boom' developed in Japan, and nostalgic images of Irishness started to attract Japanese consumers.

Naomi and my other respondents shared certain expectations towards, and fantasies about, Ireland and Irishness. These included thinking that it offered a better family environment, a more relaxed way of life, or better gender equality. Naomi, like others, spoke about how she 'could not expect much regarding children's education in Japan'; 'Japanese education is full of problems and puts a heavy burden on children'. She also reflected on the periphery status of Ireland, as well as its scars of colonialism: 'I prefer to live in a place with the experience of being dominated, like Ireland was when it was controlled by England, rather than in a place which has been dominating other nations, sometimes even without realizing it. I think you could learn to feel other people's pain more'. Some of my other respondents talked in a similar way about how they were tempted to live in a remote, unexploited place like Ireland, where they could hope to live peacefully in a pre-modern space.

Ortner argues (2005: 31) that cultural and social formations always shape, organize, and provoke 'modes of perception, affect, thought, desire, fear, and so forth that animate acting subjects'. While the global imaginary and cultural logics of desire significantly shape the Japanese women's subjectivities, the case study in this chapter seeks a psychological perspective on what individual actors make of these processes. How can the collective imaginations associated with Ireland evoke memory and/or emotion for a given person? How do public meanings gain directive and motivational force (D'Andrade and Strauss 1992) for any given person?

Migration and the Disruption of Embodied Memory

In Japan, Naomi had been involved in NGO activity for over ten years. She wrote and translated articles about issues of development in Asia and Africa, particularly about the issue of debt in developing countries. She was also actively engaged in the grass-roots Green movement, and in anti-war activities in Japan. Since migration did not cut her off from all these connections, she spent most of the first two years in Ireland continuing to be involved with a Japanese NGO, flying back to Japan to attend conferences and meetings, and translating and writing articles. However, it seems that the maintenance of social as well as career connections with the homeland sometimes caused her a dilemma about her present and future direction: whether she should keep in touch with her old life or focus on building up new connections in Ireland. The following diary fragment was written during her first summer in Ireland. It reveals how she reacted to the new physical environment and the weather, in particular, the coolness of an Irish summer.

9 August 2007 Memory of 'war'
Today is the day when the atomic bomb was dropped in Nagasaki.
  I don't know how the weather is in Nagasaki today, but certain images are imprinted on me, the images of a commemoration ceremony under a flaming sun, silent prayer, an oath of peace, and the offering of flowers to the deceased.
  Every August, I automatically think of 'the atomic bomb', 'the second world war', 'a visit to the *Yasukuni* shrine[3] by the prime minister and government officials, and the discussions and protests against them, and I feel that this season has come again. But I can't feel such a feeling this year.
  Only when my friend (in Japan) wrote to me that she was going to visit Nagasaki on 9 August and her plan for the *obon* holiday,[4] I realized in my head 'oh my God it's already this season', but without any sense of reality.
  Maybe my memory of war . . . although I don't have first-hand experience of it off course . . . my relived memory through films, books, and the experience of visiting Okinawa, has been associated with the strong heat of the summer. This may be why in this weather – sometimes a bit warm, but sometimes a bit cold – I can't turn my thoughts towards it as I did before.
  Although I used to think that I would be the same wherever I lived in the world, I realize, and this is quite upsetting, how strongly my over-forty-years experiences of Japan has soaked into me, to a deep level, deeper than the fact that I miss Japanese food.
  P.s. I'm a bit jealous of my friend who wrote how tasty the beer was in the Japanese hot summer.

In this diary she reflected on how the memories of the Second World War and attending the annual commemorations were deeply associated with the strong heat and sunlight of August in Japan, and how it was difficult for her, in the cool, rainy Irish summer, to recall such personal memories. She can of course know these past events as 'facts' without being able to navigate and 'actualize' them in her ongoing life.

The notion of 'place memory' offered by Casey (2000) is also revealing here. Inspired by Bergson and other thinkers (including Heidegger and Merleau-Ponty), Casey focuses on the role of body in memory of place: 'To be embodied is . . . to have not just a point of view but a place in which we are situated' (ibid: 182). He argues that the lived body, as psycho-physical in status, uses the physical features of place in the act of remembering, and what we remember through our bodies is often indissolubly place-bound (ibid.: 188–89). This remembering is achieved through establishing and maintaining a deep familiarity, or what he describes as 'in-habitation': 'an effectuation and a culmination of bodily being-in-place' (ibid.: 191–93). For Naomi, in the early days of her migration, the physical, material, and interpersonal dimensions in Ireland remained unfamiliar, 'un-attuned' places, with which she could not feel 'at ease' (ibid.: 190). At the same time, her lived past was increasingly disconnected from her ongoing life in Ireland. An unfamiliar place did not evoke any meaningful memories or associated feelings, as she repeatedly wrote: 'I can't feel such a feeling this year' and 'I can't turn my thoughts towards it as I did before'. And this upset her, since these past experiences were meaningful for her, closely tied to her social networks, personal interests, values, and desires. A sense of loss arises through the erasure of a familiar place, the disruption of body memory which is deeply orienting and informs us where to go, which route is possible or desirable.

Migration has brought Naomi new ecologies of place which have constrained her over forty-year-old embodied memories, and it seems that a split sense of self has arisen from her different modes of awareness. In discursive, reflective thought, she was ready to settle down in Ireland, uprooting herself from Japan. Her parents had already died, and she had no close relatives left in Japan. She said that it was she, rather than her Irish husband, that had always wanted to move to Ireland. She thought that migration would bring her family a better life than in Japan, particularly in terms of the children's education and lifestyle. However, her body functioned at a deeply pre-reflective level, expressing a sense of loss and disturbance. She began to be aware of this, as she wrote 'how strongly my over-forty-years experiences of Japan have soaked into me, to a deep level'. Finding herself having such a strong sense of loss, she wrote, 'this is quite upsetting'. For her, this was a confusing, uncanny experience.

Her sense of loss and disturbance also seemed to have manifested itself in some physical symptoms. During her first summer in Ireland, she wrote about being depressed, 'lying in bed all day long', which she had never done before and which she found surprising. She wrote that she felt miserable and had anxiety and a sense of loneliness, which she never expected to have before migrating to Ireland. Although she knew that she had had a lot of positive experiences since coming to Ireland, she said that she could not remember such things when she was not well. In the second winter, just after coming back from Japan, her symptoms included a constant headache and feeling depressed again. Since she always liked to practice Japanese folk medicine, rather than modern western medicine, she consulted her friend, a fortune-teller in Japan, on the phone. She was told that she should keep her body warm by taking a daily *koshiyu* (hip bath), which is a Japanese traditional way of bathing, said to be good for one's health. After taking this advice, and when the spring eventually came, her symptoms became better. She said, 'in theory, I didn't care about the rain in Ireland and I thought I would get used to the cold. . .'.

For recently arrived migrants, like Naomi, the disruption of place memory is a major obstacle in their search for well-being. According to Sarvimäki (2006) who was inspired by Heidegger, well-being is considered as 'comprising a sense of familiarity and authenticity in the everyday unfolding life, as well as orienting towards the future and realizing one's potential' (Biong and Ravndal 2009: 5; Sarvimäki 2006). Her early experience of migration may thus be characterized as a loss of her authentic 'self' within an unfamiliar environment in Ireland. Being unable to 'actualize' well-established memories leads to a sense of disorientation and emotional dissonance. Such embodied memories, even though they belong to the latent or tacit dimension of our being, play significant roles in constructing a sense of authenticity: 'we could not be who we are, nor do we know what we do, without them' (Casey 2000: 163).

The Interplay between Emotion and Memory: The Cognitive Perspective

Before describing some of the ways in which Naomi has tried to readjust her memories, or gradually 'tune' her body into a new place, let me mention some of the recent studies on emotion. I will apply here Milton's ecological perspective on emotion (2002, 2005) which I find particularly useful when mixing the perspectives of emotion and memory. It also resonates well with the phenomenological works of Bergson and Casey whom I described earlier.

Following from William James, Milton views emotions as being integral to perception, the subjective experience of particular physiological conditions, which themselves emerge from various stimuli without conscious or reflective process. She argues that the initial bodily reaction (affect) to a stimulus will take place 'through which an individual human being is connected to and learns from their environment' (2005: 31). For example, she describes how she 'learned to fear snakes' during fieldwork in Africa, as a result of which her leg muscles always automatically tightened when she walked through long grass. This effect continued for a while after her return to Ireland, where there are no snakes (ibid.: 36). She states: 'Through their engagement with different environments, people learn to love, hate, fear, or be disgusted by different things, so their bodies react differently when these things are encountered' (ibid.). In her view, 'emotions are ecological phenomena that link us to our environments and enable us to learn from them' (ibid.: 37). Such bodily reactions (affect) can be interpreted or perceived in consciousness as different feelings depending on the context in which they occur. For example, in some cultures people cry both at weddings and at funerals, but they have learned to perceive the same bodily reactions (i.e. tears) as conveying different meanings – joy or sorrow – depending on the context. They also learn how to express their emotions; for instance, in some contexts, tears are shed openly, but in others, they may be suppressed (ibid.: 37).

Milton's view of emotion has been much inspired by the work of the neuroscientist Damasio (1999). Briefly, Damasio demonstrates that we, as organisms, have learned how to respond to certain stimuli – particularly those that are potentially useful or potentially dangerous from the point of view of our survival – with certain responses which we call emotions (ibid.: 56–57). Since birth, we have learned to associate different objects and situations with particular emotions, either positive or negative. This association occurs in either of two ways. First, a stimulus might be linked to particular emotions through one of our senses. For example, through the sight of a familiar place or face, particular objects or situations might be conditioned by certain feelings. This happens automatically, not consciously. Second, particular objects or situations might be represented as particular mental images conjured up from memory. For instance, particular objects, such as a hill, might be perceived with certain positive emotions through remembering the fact that one used to love hiking. This happens in the thought process. In either circumstance, Damasio argues, emotions are shaped by 'learning': 'A form of learning known as conditioning is one way of achieving this association' (ibid.: 58).

If emotions are shaped by 'learning', or as Milton summarizes, 'human beings learn by receiving information from their environment and remembering it' (2005: 35), what would happen to what migrants have 'learned' in their home environment when they move to unfamiliar ecologies of place? Migration from one country to another inevitably involves the disruption of embodied memory – memory of how to respond to particular stimulus. For recently arrived migrants, unfamiliar objects or situations often may not be prescribed to cause any significant emotions, but may evoke only some neutral emotions. Migrants may also continue to react to some familiar objects or situations with particular affective states without being consciously aware of it. Such embodied knowledge of home places, however, might not be welcomed in the new environment where they are often expected to 'learn' new ways of conditioning and associations. A recent study describes this:

> migrants are prone to experience a sense of emotional destabilization as their emotional dispositions, learned 'back home', may not be accepted in their new

locations. They may feel the pressure to hide what they regard as 'natural' feelings, or they may feel forced to express them in newly coded ways. (Svašek and Skrbiš 2007: 374–75)

Language is certainly one of the important dimensions in which people emplace themselves in the sensuous materiality of the world. In their studies on the 'bilingual's two sets of memories', Schrauf and Rubin (2003) offer interesting reflections on the effects of language and culture on autobiographical memory. They argue that for 'people who grow up in one place and move in early adulthood or later to another country', second language acquisition and acculturation result in complex psychological processes, including cognitive and affective elements, which inevitably affect remembering (2003: 121):

> Immigrants of long standing . . . may have a sense of loss as the linguaculture of their homeland recedes from them and becomes less accessible even in memory. In cognitive terms, the reasons for this may be a lack of rehearsal of old memories and a consequent loss of content. From their reflections, it would seem that it is not the loss of this or that memory that they principally mourn but the fading of the network itself. And the fading of the network may amount to the fading of that network of memories that undergird the identity tied to the culture of origin – that particular curriculum vitae of memories. This results in a sense of loss of identity, or a replacement of it by another. (ibid.: 140)

A sense of loss shaped by the disruption of embodied knowledge seems particularly evident if a migrant has limited capacity for the local language, and no access to her mother tongue. Using a second language all the time, some of the Japanese women I interviewed had lost fluency in their native tongue. One, Yuki, in her forties, for instance, described this experience: 'Losing my mother tongue . . . I feel *nasakenai* (miserable, woeful). I'm losing my own language, even though my English is still poor'. She had not visited Japan for seven years, and had rarely had an opportunity to use Japanese in her daily life. The Japanese adjective *nasakenai* is commonly used to describe a miserable person or circumstance in a sorry, or poor, state. Her feelings of inadequacy emerged from her inability to communicate well with others (in either language), and also her inability to give form and structure to her experience without access to the networks of association which she previously learned (see also Westen 2001). Her narration, as well as Naomi's diary described earlier, suggests how migrants, whether they are aware or not, may lose the sensory apprehension of the world which they used to associate with certain feelings and memories.

What can migrants do in order to re-emplace themselves in the sensuous materiality of the world? For some of the Japanese migrants, the use of the Japanese language seems one way to do so. One of the interviewees, Yoko, who was engaged to an Irish man, spoke about how she read Japanese novels every night so that she could not only recall Japanese words she was forgetting but also 'think in a Japanese mode': 'Using English all the time . . . when I'm at work or at home, watching TV, I feel I am in an English mode. I want to have some time on my own, even it is short, to think in Japanese'. Yoko's need to 'think in a Japanese mode' at the end of the day is her way of re-emplacing: 're-experiencing past places' (Casey 2000: 210). As Casey (2000) notes, 'in remembering we can be thrust back, transported, into the place we recall' (ibid.: 201). For other migrants, established ethnic communities may help them to create a sense of continuity, and in this case there is little need for nostalgia. Law (2001) describes, for instance, how Filipino domestic workers in Hong Kong try to re-emplace themselves in the new place through creating familiar sights, sounds, tastes, aromas and so on.

In either case, however, the issue of emplacement inevitably involves new bodily ways of being in a new environment. In order to establish new relationships in the new county, migrants are required to build up new memories—i.e., learn new ways of conditioning and associations. For the women in my study married to Irish men, it was crucial to learn to cook Sunday dinner or Christmas meals, and to communicate properly with their in-laws and the locals. They came to feel it was quite normal to live in houses with fireplaces and carpets, having cups of tea after each meal, and wearing sweaters and socks during the summer, even though they had never done any of this when they lived in Japan. In developing a bodily attachment to the new sensuous materiality of the world in Ireland, some of my respondents even felt disoriented or alienated when they first went back to Japan. In order to create a sense of homeliness, as Wise (2010) notes, 'we need to grow new bodies, new sensory responses, emotional, affective grammars' (2010: 935). How to respond and manage these tasks will vary from one to another. However, as Howes (2004: 7) puts it, 'What, indeed, can a disembodied existence or a desensualized world mean to us who only live through our bodies? Are we not better off sticking our fingers in the soil to determine our location by smell?'

The Attunement of the Body in a New Place

Now, I want to go back to Naomi's case, paying special attention to how her past is shaped by, and shapes, the basis of her current feelings. Two and a half years after migration, when I asked Naomi to cooperate on the photo-diary project in February 2009, her diary expressed more positive emotional orientations than was previously the case.[5] I asked her to take photos every day, and write comments on them for about ten days. The photos could show any aspect of her life, as long as they were personally meaningful for her, for example, people, scenery, or objects which may trigger any kind of positive or negative feelings. She was very cooperative. After collecting the photos and diary from her, I also conducted an interview. In what follows, I analyse some of these photos,[6] diary fragments, and her narratives by focusing on two dimensions: her emotional responses to, and perceptions of, the new physical and social environment; and her attempts at redefining the past and the future.

Fig 4.1 *The morning glow*

Building up New Memory: The Perceptions of, and Bodily Responses to, the New Environment

On the first day of her photo-diary project, Naomi took a photo of the cloudy sky outside her house, showing the morning glow, cloudy with different colours (Figure 4.1). She wrote:

> Got up at half seven, which wasn't so early but I could taste the atmosphere of the dawn. Like *Keruto no Hakumei* (*The Celtic Twilight*), many Irish seem to love the colours blue, green – especially bluely green and purple – I know this from working in the shop, maybe it's because they often taste the dawn of autumn, winter, and spring and the dusk of summer.

The hours of sunlight are much shorter during the winter in Ireland than in the south of Japan. Her body still 'expects' light and blue skies at half seven in the morning, but in Ireland in February, it is cloudy and still a little dark. This photo-diary however expresses her relatively positive feelings, as she wrote that she could 'taste' the somehow mysterious atmosphere. Her sense of ease appears enough to be able to stretch to thinking about *The Celtic Twilight*, a W.B. Yeats' collection of folktales and myths, and the colours she thinks Irish people favour. Through this imagination appears her growing sympathy with the culturally shaped physical world in Ireland. 'Attuned space', Casey explains, is 'a space with which one feels sympathetic at some very basic level – in contrast with the indifferent site-space of cartography or rational geometry' (2000: 192). Her new surroundings in Ireland have been appropriated, and have become her own with her ongoing life where she can feel at ease (ibid.).

Some of the other fragments, however, do not express such a growing sympathy but instead a sense of unease created by mismatched habituated expectations. For example, on the same day, Naomi took a photo of a sandwich she was making (Figure 4.2), and wrote:

> Today is the day I have to work at the shop. I'm preparing lunch: The same kind of sandwich every day. There is little variety of food here, and I feel a bit unsatisfied anyway.

In the south of Japan, where she is from, food is cheaper than in Ireland, and there is more variety of vegetables and fish in the shops. The average Japanese person does not eat sandwiches for lunch, but rather, if they are at work, rice and other dishes in a *bento* box. The sandwich she is making does not satisfy her body memories – memories of taste, smell, texture, or feelings of eating a greater variety of vegetables and fish for lunch, and remains the object of her negative feelings.

In another fragment (Figure 4.3), she also wrote about her frustration about how moving house in Ireland is a slow, badly-organized process.

Fig 4.2 *Sandwich*

Fig 4.3 *Telephone not working*

When moving to a new house, she wrote, there was a problem with both the telephone and the Internet company, and it took over a month to get it sorted out before she was able to use the telephone again. Her frustration emerges from her habituated expectations of Japanese ways which are 'more organized' and 'more responsible'. 'An Irish way' appears 'unreasonable', and 'disorganized'. Such a negative affective response to 'an Irish way' is perceived as something problematic, as she continued:

> In Japan, everything is done smoothly under the hidden system and we don't have to know what is happening. Like the application in the PC, you just have to know how to use it, but don't have to know about the process. Here, I often encounter inconsistencies and need to be aware of them. That's a good thing in a way, but I still don't understand the pace of this society. I'm always impatient maybe because I'm Japanese?

In this reflection, she gets some distance from her own affective states, and questions them. She questions her habituated expectations, and is aware that there is something problematic about the negative meanings attached to 'Irish ways'. It is interesting to wonder why 'the sandwich' remained as a negative object, while 'an Irish way' was more open to reflection and questions.

One explanation for this seems to lie in Naomi's ongoing interpersonal relationships in Ireland. Significantly, other diary fragments have positive emotional associations. For example, underneath the photo of foreign women whom she met every week in the women's centre, she wrote: 'These women from various countries, who were supposed to be supported "migrant women", are very positive and strong! So much positive stimulation I've got from them'. Through the help of the people whom she met in the women's centre, she also opened a fair-trade shop, which she had dreamed of doing for a long time, selling crafts from the slums of Kenya. This seems to have opened new opportunities for her to meet other people living in the local area, as she wrote: 'Since I went to the women's centre and started to run the fair-trade shop, I've had real opportunities to mix with the locals'.

Outside work, she has also enjoyed playing the Irish fiddle. She learned the violin in her childhood and started to practice Irish tunes just before migrating to Ireland. While attending fiddle classes, she also started to join informal sessions in a pub (Figure 4.4). She wrote: 'This is my favourite time these days . . . These people in this session were very welcoming, even though I'm no good and a foreigner, that's why I could continue playing'.

Such positive perceptions of new friends and acquaintances reflected how she tried to 'learn' new ways of conditioning and associations in Ireland. Chamberlain and Leydesdorff (2004) argue that migrants, in seeking to establish new relationships in the new place, may be 'required to forget, or at least relegate, the past so that the memory of what is here and now – and thus identification with the present – becomes dominant' (2004: 229). In her case, her growing sympathies with the people whom she met in Ireland helped her to create a sense of belonging and future, navigating positive perceptions of living there. In the next section, I describe how her perceptions and emotions are also navigated through selective identifications with particular memories.

Fig 4.4 *Music session*

Creating a Sense of Continuity: Restructuring the Past and the Future

There were certain motifs in Naomi's diary which contrasted images of prototypical 'Japaneseness' and 'Irishness'. For instance, among other photographs, there was the one of her family, her children playing some music and her husband listening to them comfortably (Figure 4.5). With this photo she expressed her positive feelings and some recollections:

> all my children have started to learn music, Irish music. They still have some trouble with English, but because of that, we spend more time together than we used to . . . Whether the handicap is good or bad all depends on your way of thinking. I already had such an attitude as *saio ga uma* (which is a Japanese saying which roughly means that 'Joy and sorrow are today and tomorrow'). But since I came here, I've really developed such an attitude.

The saying, *saio ga uma*, connotes a kind of relaxed, easygoing, or determined attitude – that one should not be very pleased or very worried, nor should be too up or too down, because nobody can predict what will happen next. She seems to use it as an antithesis to the mainstream Japanese value of rationalism. In the interview, I asked her how she had gained such a *saio-ga-uma* attitude, and she replied that it was since she met her husband. She said that she was previously the kind of person 'who thought too much and

Fig 4.5 *Music and family*

couldn't help seeking a solution as soon as possible', and that she 'knew this wasn't good for her'. Her previous attitude and personality were, she explained, 'the typical Japanese ones of her generation after rapid economic growth – your failure is your responsibility, or is down to your lack of effort'. She contrasted this attitude with her husband's and that of Irish people in general:

> I don't know whether my husband's attitude comes from his Irishness or just his own personality ... but ... I wonder if there is such an attitude among Irish ... because of their history of hardship ... because there were many things which they had to put up with ... So, in a sense, I've become a very lazy person now. . .

The 'laziness' of her husband, Irish people, and herself appeared as a positive attribute in contrast to the negative one of 'Japaneseness'. These contrasted images of Japan and Ireland may reflect the media images of Irishness, as well as ones of Japaneseness, circulated and disseminated across the globe. In the past decades Ireland has been marketed with images of unexploited nature and pre-modern space. Irish men often also appeared on the films as 'quick-tempered' and 'humorous'. These stereotypical images of Ireland and the dominant representations of Japan and Japanese men are completely different. During the bubble economy in Japan in the 1980s, in particular, the term *karoshi* was commonly used to refer to death caused by the stress of overworking. Japanese men have often been represented in the media, from news coverage, TV to film, as 'corporate warriors', or as technologically advanced yet emotionless people (Morley and Robins 1995). The prevalence of these images of Japanese 'workaholic' men in the media, and of the critiques of their lives and values, might have helped Naomi to distance herself from any kind of identification with Japaneseness and instead, to create a desire for Irishness.

Another diary fragment also shows how such an evaluative division between Irishness and Japaneseness was reshaped and sustained through evoking more personal meanings. With the photo of the drum that her son plays (Figure 4.6), she expressed how she and her children could enjoy music and art in Ireland, something which they could not do in Japan:

> One of the good things in Ireland I think is that music, art, and poems are encouraged, and there are lots of opportunities to enjoy these things ... The good thing is also that you can make noise at home. When I visited Japan last year, I had to be worried about the noise of my fiddle when I was practicing. It would be difficult to play music in such an environment. Even more so if the instrument was a drum.

Her positive feelings associated with art and music experienced in Ireland were triggered through recollecting her negative experiences in Japan during the previous visit. The subsequent interview also revealed that her positive affective responses to life in Ireland were more deeply rooted in her earlier life experiences. She talked about how her childhood and her life in her

Fig 4.6 *Drum*

twenties were 'dark' periods. From her stories, it seemed that her mother had high expectations of her and her brother, and always wanted them to get good academic grades. Both she and her brother learned classical music from an early age, but her mother became very opposed to her brother's playing music because he neglected his studies in school. She explained how music and art were looked down on at that time:

> In my parents' home town, people were obsessed with children's education. For them, the most desirable profession was a teacher, who might become a headmaster in the future. Someone like a musician or an artist, they would think, 'what kind of job is that'?

She said that her brother rebelled against her mother, almost to the point of 'domestic violence', although those words were not used. Because of the tension between her mother and brother, she initially avoided any conflict: she 'went to university as expected, to study law to become a lawyer'. However, since university, she had started to question her previous life, and became estranged from her mother. They did not reconcile before her mother died. Her father, who had 'always been quiet', also died before she migrated. She had no other close relatives in Japan. Her only brother lives in Europe where he is a musician. Her memories of emotional estrangement from her parents, childhood, and cultural expectations in Japanese society have all shaped and sustained the foundation for her positive affective reactions to life in Ireland and her desire to create a sense of belonging there.

At the end of her diary, she commented: 'Now I'm trying to broaden the circle of connection of people – particularly people who are concerned with environmental issues and sustainable lifestyles – and I think I've found the direction I'd like to go to in this place'. Here, she interweaved other past experiences from her later life—for instance, working in a Japanese NGO, and networking with people in various social activities. These memories of Japan seem to have been mixed with her current perceptions, helping to create a sense of familiarity and continuity with the future. As Birth (2006: 181) notes, 'The existence of the past in contemporary consciousness is the result of cultural and psychological processes at work in the present'. In her case the remnants of the past confronted her and produced a coherent narrative of the past, the present and the future.

The Researcher and the Researched: Empathy and Intersubjectivity

In closing, it is important to reflect briefly on questions of method: what sorts of issues were involved in researching another person's affects and emotions. In other words, as Hollan asks (2001: 57), how can I be sure that the senses, perceptions, and bodily experiences I have discovered in Naomi's diaries and narratives are really hers, and not my own physiological, sensual, and perceptual projections or preoccupations? Since I cannot directly experience what she experiences, what I have described in this chapter can be considered as a tentative translation of her remembrance and feeling-tones. Such an anthropological translation inevitably involves what Wikan (1992) termed 'resonance' between the researcher and the researched:

> an effort at feeling-thought; a willingness to engage with another world, life, or idea; an ability to use one's experience . . . to try to grasp, convey, meanings that reside neither in words, 'facts', not text but are evoked in the meeting of one experiencing subject with another or with a text. (ibid.: 463)

As I mentioned above, Naomi and I had known each other for about two years. Both of us come from the south of Japan; both our husbands are Irish; and we both came to Ireland recently – she migrated in October 2006 by which time I had been there for three years. We had shared some similar experiences as Japanese migrant women living in Ireland: for instance, the Irish weather, diet, and 'Irish ways'. The 'photo-diary' method applied in this study seems to work well in such an empathetic translation. 'Taking photographs', as Oliffe and Bottorff (2007: 852) note, involves 'a physical, as well as a cognitively active process', and 'constructing and reconstructing rather than telling a static or exclusively verbal story'. Through this method I hoped to capture her everyday experiences which could not be fully captured through the standard interview method or participant observation. I also hope that I captured some of her unarticulated embodied views of self and others, as well as ordinarily private details and everyday flows of feelings.

I must also acknowledge that such 'shared feelings' or 'emphatic understanding' are far from unproblematic and are not an end to understanding (Leavitt 1996: 530). My description of Naomi has developed during the course of research and through the interacting processes between the researcher and the researched (Davies 1999; Peacock and Holland 1993; Grønseth and Davis 2010). For example, my PhD in anthropology may have shaped Naomi's career-oriented future narratives significantly. Naomi and I also shared an interest in Irish music, and this may have helped her to take photos related to music. Our age difference may also be one of the factors which explains her relatively positive feelings when producing photo-diaries. My description of Naomi is not her life-world as has been transparently understood by an anonymous researcher, nor simply my own personal fantasy projected onto it; it is, however, as Throop (2003: 127) also indicates, 'the confluence of partially created, partially received precepts, concepts, ideas, memories, feelings, motivations, and actions' (ibid.: 128) between us, whose personalities, life experiences, and ages are different, but who nevertheless have shared some similar experiences as Japanese migrant women married to Irish men.

Conclusion

Here I would like to sum up my discussion of migrants' memory, perceptions and emotional processes. In the former part of this chapter, inspired by Bergson, I described how migration inevitably involved the disruption of embodied memory – the memory of how to respond to particular stimulus. For recently arrived migrants like Naomi, a sense of loss and disorientation emerged as they were unable to 'actualize' significant memory images of home places within an unfamiliar environment. Although she was aware of some positive aspects of migration regarding her new life in Ireland, her difficulty in navigating such memories and associated feelings led her constantly to negative affective states. She could not orient herself towards the future or realize her potential, and this was a major obstacle to her search for well-being.

In the latter part of this chapter, which was based on the photo-diary project, I focused on how Naomi gradually overcame such confusion and disturbance by building up new memories, or 'attuning' the body in the new place. In building up new memories – i.e., learning new ways of conditioning and associations – she has gradually created a sense of familiarity and authenticity in Ireland. While her sense of unease sometimes appeared to be caused by mismatched embodied knowledge (such as 'sandwiches' and 'Irish ways'), her narratives expressed many more positive emotional orientations and positive perceptions of life in Ireland. This partly reflected her ongoing interpersonal relationships with family, friends, and acquaintances in Ireland. On the other hand, her positive perceptions of her new life were also shaped by her past experiences – i.e., memories of emotional estrangement from her parents, childhood, and cultural expectations in Japan. In renewing her identification with particular personal histories and memories, she also managed to produce coherent self-representations, drawing a sense of continuity into the future narrative.

Through her case, I can suggest how the subjectivities of individual migrants are shaped and reshaped dynamically through their relationships with the physical and social environment, and through the intrapersonal processes of memory and symbolic formation. Each migrant creates a sense of belonging or non-belonging in the new place in a different way, according to her/his ongoing experiences and embodied past. Her/his perceptions of the new environment will be shaped through embodied memories 'learned' back home, shaping different feelings. Naomi's case also suggests that migrants, in order to establish new relationships in the new environment, learn new sensory responses and emotional associations. In building up new memories, i.e. learning new ways of conditioning and associations, they also restructure their past in order to integrate continuities and discontinuities. It is with this achievement of new bodily being-in-place, or 'in-habitation', that migrants may be able to start to improve or achieve their well-being.

Notes

I am grateful to Naomi (not her real name) for generously sharing her experiences. I also thank Anne Sigfrid Grønseth for many useful suggestions on earlier drafts of this article, and many thanks to Maruška Svašek, my supervisor, for her feedback and encouragement during the research and writing process.

1 Not her real name.
2 For a good analysis of Bergson's work, see for example Middleton and Brown (2005).
3 *Yasukuni* shrine is a Shinto shrine in Tokyo, dedicated to the soldiers and others who died fighting on behalf of the Emperor of Japan. Controversial visits there during the 2000s by Prime Minister Junichiro Koizumi were widely reported in the Chinese media and led to widespread anger among Chinese youth. Many in the international and Asian community saw the visit as representing support for Japanese militarism, and a denial of the war crimes carried out by Japan in the Second World War.
4 *Obon*, or *bon*, is a Japanese Buddhist custom to honour the spirits of one's ancestors. This custom has evolved into a family reunion holiday during which people return to their ancestral homes and visit and clean their ancestors' graves. It is also the time when the spirits of ancestors are supposed to revisit the household altars.
5 My photo-diary project was inspired by the photo-elicitation method used by some researchers (e.g., Harper 2002; Oliffe and Bottorff 2007).
6 Unfortunately, the original images taken by Naomi could not be used in this chapter because of their low resolution. In the publication process, the author asked

Naomi to retake the photos with the same themes. The images used in this chapter are those taken by her in March 2013, and are slightly different from the original ones.

References

Abe, K. 2001. *Samayoeru Nationalism: Orientalism, Japan, Globalization*. Kyoto: Sekai Shiso Sya.

Bergson, H. 2004. *Matter and Memory,* trans. N.M. Paul and W.S. Palmer, originally published in 1912. New York: Dover.

Biong, S. and E. Ravndal. 2009. 'Living in a Maze: Health, Well-being and Coping in Young Non-western Men in Scandinavia Experiencing Substance Abuse and Suicidal Behaviour', *International Journal of Qualitative Studies on Health and Well-being* 4(1): 4–16.

Birth, K. 2006. 'The Immanent Past: Culture and Psyche at the Juncture of Memory and History', *Ethos* 34(2): 169–91.

Casey, E.S. 2000. *Remembering: A Phenomenological Study.* 2nd ed. Bloomington: Indiana University Press.

Chamberlain, M. and S. Leydesdorff. 2004. 'Transnational Families: Memories and Narratives', *Global Networks* 4(3): 227–41.

Cusack, T. 2001. '"A Countryside Bright with Cosy Homesteads": Irish Nationalism and the Cottage Landscape', *National Identities* 3(3): 221–38.

Damasio, A.R. 1999. *The Feeling of What Happens: Body and Emotion in the Making of Consciousness.* London: Heinemann.

D'Andrade, R.G. and C. Strauss (eds). 1992. *Human Motives and Cultural Models.* Cambridge: Cambridge University Press.

Davies, C.A. 1999. *Reflexive Ethnography: A Guide to Researching Selves and Others.* London: Routledge.

Gardner, K. 2002. *Age, Narrative and Migration: The Life Course and Life Histories of Bengali Elders in London.* Oxford: Berg.

Glosserman, B. 2005. 'Anti-Americanism in Japan', in David I. Steinberg (ed.), *Korean Attitudes toward the United States: Changing Dynamics.* Armonk, NY: M.E. Sharpe, pp. 34–45.

Grønseth, A.S. and D.L. Davis (eds). 2010. *Mutuality and Empathy: Self and Other in the Ethnographic Encounter.* Wantage: Sean Kingston.

Hannerz, U. 1996. *Transnational Connections: Culture, People, Places.* London: Routledge.

Harper, D. 2002. 'Talking about Pictures: A Case for Photo Elicitation', *Visual Studies* 17(1): 13–26.

Hollan, D. 2001. 'Developments in Person-Centered Ethnography', in C.C. Moor and H.F. Mathews (eds), *The Psychology of Cultural Experience.* Cambridge: Cambridge University Press, pp. 48–67.

Howes, D. 2004. 'Introduction: Empire of the Senses', in D. Howes (ed.), *Empire of the Senses.* Oxford: Berg, pp. 1–20.

Law, L. 2001. 'Home Cooking: Filipino Women and Geographies of the Senses in Hong Kong', *Cultural Geographies* 8(3): 264–83.

Leavitt, J. 1996. 'Meaning and Feeling in the Anthropology of Emotions', *American Ethnologist* 23(3): 514–39.

Lee, S.S. 2000. 'Dys-appearing Tongues and Bodily Memories: The Aging of First-Generation Resident Koreans in Japan', *Ethos* 28(2): 198–223.

Middleton, D.J. and S.D. Brown. 2005. *The Social Psychology of Experience: Studies in Remembering and Forgetting*. London: Sage.

Milton, K. 2002. *Loving Nature: Towards an Ecology of Emotion*. London: Routledge.

_____. 2005. 'Meanings, Feelings and Human Ecology', in K. Milton and M. Svašek (eds), *Mixed Emotions: Anthropological Studies of Feeling*. pp. 25–41. Oxford: Berg.

Morley, D. and K. Robins. 1995. 'Techno-Orientalism: Japan Panic', in D. Morley and K. Robins (eds), *Spaces of Identity: Global Media, Electronic Landscapes and Cultural Boundaries*. London: Routledge, pp. 147–73.

O'Connor, B. 1993. 'Myths and Mirrors: Tourist Images and National Identity', in B. O'Connor and M. Cronin (eds), *Tourism in Ireland: A Critical Analysis*. Cork, Ireland: Cork University Press, pp. 65–85.

Oliffe, J.L. and J.L. Bottorff. 2007. 'Further Than the Eye Can See? Photo Elicitation and Research with Men', *Qualitative Health Research* 17(6): 850–58.

Ortner, S. 2005. 'Subjectivity and Cultural Critique', *Anthropological Theory* 5: 31–52.

Peacock, J. and D. Holland. 1993. 'The Narrated Self: Life Stories in Process', *Ethos* 21(4): 367–83.

Sarvimäki, A. 2006. 'Well-being as Being Well – A Heideggerian Look at Well-being', *International Journal of Qualitative Studies on Health and Well-being* 1(1): 4–10.

Schrauf, R.W. and D.C. Rubin. 2003. 'On the Bilingual's Two Sets of Memories', in Robyn Fivush and Catherine A. Haden (eds), *Autobiographical Memory and the Construction of a Narrative Self: Developmental and Cultural Perspectives*. London: Lawrence Erlbaum Associates, pp. 121–45.

Svašek, M. and Z. Skrbiš. 2007. 'Passions and Powers: Emotions and Globalisation', *Identities* 14(3): 367–83.

Throop, C.J. 2003. 'On Crafting a Cultural Mind: A Comparative Assessment of Some Recent Theories of "Internalization" in Psychological Anthropology', *Transcultural Psychiatry* 40(1): 109–39.

Westen, D. 2001. 'Beyond the Binary Opposition in Psychological Anthropology: Integrating Contemporary Psychoanalysis and Cognitive Science', in C.C. Moore and H.F. Mathews (eds), *The Psychology of Cultural Experience*. Cambridge: Cambridge University Press, pp. 21–47.

Wikan, U. 1992. 'Beyond the Words: The Power of Resonance', *American Ethnologist* 19(3): 460–82.

Wise, A. 2010. 'Sensuous Multiculturalism: Emotional Landscapes of Inter-Ethnic Living in Australian Suburbia', *Journal of Ethnic & Migration Studies* 36(6): 917–37.

Wise, A. and A. Chapman. 2005. 'Introduction: Migration, Affect and the Senses', *Journal of Intercultural Studies* 26(1–2): 1–3.

Wulff, H. 2007. 'Longing for the Land: Emotion, Memory, and Nature in Irish Travel Advertisements', *Identities: Global Studies in Culture and Power* 14: 527–44.

Zuelow, E. 2005. *Ireland's Heritages: Critical Perspectives on Memory and Identity*. Aldershot: Ashgate.

Chapter 5

Towards a 'Re-envisioning of the Everyday' in Refugee Studies

Christina Georgiadou

Introduction

> By forging a new relationship to emergent objects of knowledge and means of knowing, we once again come across the older imperative 'dare to know', which we must understand in a new way today, savoring its complex bittersweetness. And we must find a way to live with what we find – that is, to integrate the quest for knowledge (of nature, of injustice and folly, and of the self) with a ceaseless search for ways to apply this knowledge to the care of the self and of others.
>
> (Biehl et al. 2007: 32)

What is the value of bringing to light and studying individual cases of refugees who are creatively trying to cope with the conditions of their lives? What kind of new insights can anthropological occupation with individual lives generate in a discursive space already overcrowded by journalistic, literary, political, and academic representations of refugees? According to Marcus (1998: 197), 'modernist (or postmodernist) ethnography is supremely aware that it operates in a complex matrix of already existing alternative representations'. It is a challenge, thus, for ethnography to address existing representations of forced migration in a critical manner.

There are at least two good reasons for trying to create anthropological analytical space around personal stories of forced migrants who inventively try to actualize their life plans. The first relates to dominant narratives that circulate across media, aid agencies and academic communities, producing and reproducing the category of 'refugee' as a special part of humanity whose qualities are epitomized in the category itself. For Abu-Lughod (1993: 7), processes of generalization and typification result in making '"others" seem simultaneously more coherent, self-contained, and different from ourselves than they might be'. Feldman (1994 in Malkki 1997: 235) criticizes mass, depersonalized images generating 'anonymous corporeality' and he stresses that this kind of representation 'functions as an allegory of the elephantine, "archaic" and violent histories of external and internal subalterns'. Counteraction to representations of 'anonymous corporeality' can arise from 'ethnographies of the particular' (Abu-Lughod 2006: 473), that focus on particular individuals trying to deal with particular conditions of life. For Abu-Lughod, this kind of ethnographic writing is a choice connected with 'tactical humanism' for it 'encourages familiarity, [...] helps to break down "otherness", [...] actively facilitates identification with and sympathy towards others' (Abu-Lughod 1993: 29–30).

The second reason implying a need for alternative ways of representation is the dominance of 'problematic' mass images in the discourses about forced migration. Refugees are usually represented either as people with nothing but problems or as themselves constituting a social problem for the receiving societies. Victimization is employed by media as 'infotainment' for commercial purposes (Kleinman and Kleinman 1997: 1) or by 'clinical and philanthropic modes of humanitarianism' (Malkki 1997: 248) as a way of justifying their existence. On the other side of the coin, 'hydrophobic' and 'military' metaphors presenting refugee movements as 'tides' or 'invasions' (Daniel 2002: 273) depict an image of a social menace that has to be confronted and administered by 'robust' political decisions. What is missing from the picture, either way, is the moral core of the experience of suffering (Biehl et al. 2007: 11), the value of efforts for resilience and the kind of creativity implied in reconstructing a new life in exile. If we accept that ethnography is 'more than the record of human experience', being a 'moral, allegorical and therapeutic project' (Denzin 1997: xiv) that asserts 'moral optimism' as a 'primal act of faith in humankind' (Trouillot 2003: 135), then we need an alternative politics of ethnographic representation that would analytically elaborate on those aspects of the experience of individual refugees.

An alternative politics of knowledge and representation may require an alternative politics of research, a special way of engaging with the people under study. If anthropological knowledge is created through relations (Strathern 1993 in Hastrup 2005: 141), then a better understanding of the intimate 'moral worlds' (Kleinman 1997: 95)[1] of specific individuals requires the researcher's profound involvement with these worlds, which means that the methodological choice of being a detached observer might not be adequate. Even the attempt to establish informal, everyday interactions with refugees as a way of being- with them[2] might not suffice. The profound involvement in other people's moral worlds may necessitate a different stance, one of commitment and concern, informed by 'ethics of care' (Held 2006: 130). Such a stance of 'being- for' the other (Bauman 1995: 51) implies the assumption of moral responsibility for the other.[3] According to Levinas, as cited by Bauman (1995: 64–65), this assumption also includes the 'responsibility for determining what needs to be done to exercise that responsibility'. Guided by those premises, fieldworking can be a process of intentional acts that confront the needs of the other and promote meaningful relationships of support, assistance and care. An alternative politics of research may, thus, mean fieldwork with 'therapeutic' qualities that can trigger 'a re-envisioning of the everyday' (Castaneda 2006: 94). In the project of re-envisioning the everyday, researcher and refugees can journey together.

Within this frame of analytic positioning and engaging with the subjects of inquiry, the present chapter immerses in the particulars of two persons' daily worlds and attempts to create a representation of human beings, instead of creating a representation of 'victims of forced migration'. The specific persons whose lives are chosen to be represented are Afghans and refugees in Greece but these traits are not highlighted as categories of differentiation from 'us' (Europeans, prosperous natives, academics or whatever 'us' might imply). Rather, they are used as auxiliary elements that help to elucidate the ways in which those individuals construct and experience their everyday worlds. The two person's daily lives are described as continua within time and space, carrying all kinds of possibilities for hope and disappointment, dream and disillusionment, passive sufferance and radical action. This perspective does not imply that the two individuals are represented as omnipotent beings that flow freely in a universe of eventuality. The fabric of their daily worlds is woven within specific historical and socio-political contexts that render for them some possibilities more 'possible' than others and put constraints on their dreams and desires. But, where observation from a macro-lever would only perceive lay-figures defeated by vast supra-local forces, a close inquiry of personal life-worlds brings visibility to humans facing familiar and unfamiliar challenges and striving, within given circumstances, to create viable worlds according to their personal visions about well-being. This point of view is supported by a model of everyday life that has its origins in the writings of Lefebvre and de Certeau. Each, from a different perspective, contributed during the last half of the twentieth century in the emergence of an alternative paradigm for the apprehension of the quotidian (Highmore 2002b: 14, Sheringham 2006: 7). Lefebvre bequeathed us the notion of the dialectics of everyday life, the fecund intertwining of habitual with transcendental moments (Highmore 2002: 13, Gardiner 2004: 228) while de Certeau spoke about the potentialities for creativity and resistance hidden in the details of mundane life (de Certeau 1984: xiv).

It is argued in this chapter that humans are cocreators[4] of their lives and where this fact becomes most obvious is in interrupted lives that have to restart in unknown places, among unknown people. The creation of familiar worlds (creation from scratch, in the context of exile) presupposes the quality of creativity as a process channelling and materializing individual dynamics embedded in specific subjectivities. Creativity is thus examined in the paper, in terms of its forms, its attributes and the prerequisites for its emergence not as exceptional condition or state of being destined for the 'chosen few', but as constituent element of human everydayness, that stems from subjectivities animated by the desire for a fulfilling life. The term 'subjectivity' is chosen as a means for the approach and exploration of the two persons' intimate selves and their potential for creation because it connects subjective experience, emotional states, motives and dreams with the socio-political and cultural environments within which subjects circulate (Good et al. 2008: 2–3) and also suggests 'what really matters' for the subjects,[5] what is considered important, what they would strive for, what they would fear and try to eliminate from their everyday worlds. Moreover, subjectivity carries the past into the present, for past experience is the material from which subjective selves are formed. Memories that the persons recollect and narrate provide a window for the comprehension of their experience in the present and the choices they make in order to proceed in life. The understanding of people's past, of the way in which the past has been integrated in their subjectivity, gives the clues for the understanding of their present choices and their aspirations for the future.

The Context: Greece as Receiving Country of Migrants and Refugees. The Place of Afghan Refugees in Greek Society

As is often mentioned in studies of migration, until the 1970s Greece used to be a country of emigration. It was only after the 1990s that Greece gradually became a receiving country.[6] Nowadays, in a population of 11 million inhabitants it is estimated that the foreign nationals amount up to one million (Committee of Civil Liberties, Justice and Home Affairs 2007: 119), of whom about half a million are legal migrants (Ministry of Home Affairs 2007), 29,000 are asylum seekers (UNHCR 2008) and the rest are undocumented migrants. The majority of migrants (more than half of the people) are of Albanian origin (Ministry of Home Affairs 2007) and a great percentage of the rest come from the post-communist countries of Eastern Europe (Bulgaria, Rumania and Ukraine). Concerning asylum seekers, until 2004 the majority came from Iraq while during the last four years people from Pakistan, Bangladesh, Georgia and Afghanistan have submitted most applications (UNHCR 2008).

Afghan asylum seekers have been recorded in Greece since 1980 but the number of their asylum applications was less than fifteen per year until 1996 (MPI 2004). Since 1996 there has been an annual rise of Afghan people applying for asylum in Greece, with the number of applications reaching its peak in 2008 (more than 1820 applications). In 2005 the Greek government implemented a regularization project for the undocumented migrants that led many asylum seekers (including a number of Afghans) to resign from the asylum procedure and apply for a permit of residence (green card). Though lots of Afghans applied, only three hundred of them were finally given a green card (Ministry of Home Affairs 2007) and they are now legally considered as 'economic migrants'.[7]

A large percentage (maybe about eighty per cent) of the Afghan refugees living in Greece come from Iran (some of them were born and raised there) while a smaller percentage come from Pakistan. They or their parents had fled from Afghanistan during the 1980s, after the Communist coup in 1978 and the ensuing war between Soviet troops and mujahidin insurgents. A second wave of people fled during the 1990s, at the time of the civil war between rival mujahidin parties while a third wave fled later, when the Taliban regime came into power. Most Afghan refugees (estimated at over two million) that have settled in Iran met with a hospitable reception and became well integrated in Iranian society (Shahrani 1995). After the American invasion of Afghanistan in 2001 and the fall of the Taliban regime, though, Iranian policy towards Afghan refugees changed and life became difficult for them in Iran. The following years thousands of Afghans repatriated to Afghanistan voluntarily or by coercion, as deportees (Strand et al. 2004). As insecurity and poverty persist in Afghanistan, the returnees see no future in their country. They cannot go back to Iran so, in a way, they are forced by circumstances to seek refuge in Europe. That is why Afghanistan remained the sixth most important source country of asylum seekers in the European Union in 2008 (UNHCR 2008).

Seeking asylum in Europe is not an easy solution. European asylum and migration policies become stricter every year and new inhibiting measures are introduced and applied: increased control of the external borders of the European Union, biometric registration of aliens entering the borders, restrictions on the procedures of granting refugee status to the applicants. Greece, as a member of the EU, is supposed to conform to the common European legislative agenda regarding asylum and migration. Situated at the periphery of European Union and being part of the Union's southeast borderline, Greece constitutes a major gateway to Europe, especially for people originating from Asia. Coming from Turkey, people use two main routes to enter Greece. One route passes across the Evros River, at the northeast land borders of Greece with Turkey. The other way to get to Greece is by crossing the narrow maritime zone that divides the Eastern Aegean Islands from the Turkish coasts. The fact that the country is situated at the Union's external borders and that Greece's state apparatus and social welfare system are friendly only to the native upper social strata (Sotiropoulos 2004: 17) and very hostile to everybody else, make Greece a difficult place for asylum seekers to live. Afghans who escape the frontier-security special forces[8] and manage to enter the country are usually arrested, detained and maltreated by the police. Arrested newcomers are detained in police stations or detention centres near the border, in penal prisons or in the Athens airport transit zone (Committee on Civil Liberties, Justice and Home Affairs 2007: 119). The duration of the detention varies from a few days to several months and the conditions of detention are poor and degrading. Submitting an asylum application in Athens is an extremely difficult and arduous procedure. The majority (ninety-five per cent) of asylum applications are lodged with one single agency, the Attica Police Asylum Department in Athens (NOAS et al. 2008: 14). The number of officers occupied with receiving the applications is disproportionately low compared to the number of people they serve, so thousands of asylum seekers have to queue up for weeks in order to lodge their applications and some never succeed. As a result of the asylum agencies' dysfunction (which to some extend might be deliberate in order to discourage asylum seekers from applying), a large percentage of people arriving in Greece remain undocumented, in a limbo state with respect to their social rights (especially health services and education) and in constant risk of being arrested by the police and detained once more.

Social assistance is minimal or absent even for the ones who succeed in their applications for asylum. Although the 'asylum seeker' status provides legal protection against detention and deportation and free access to medical care and education, it guarantees little social assistance in terms of accommodation and employment. Reception facilities are few with approximately 750 places available around the country (NOAS et al. 2008: 32). People have to survive on their own. Unless they have relatives or friends able to offer hospitality, they may end up sleeping in parks until they find some low paid job in the black labour market (usually in the agricultural or construction sector) and manage to afford a room in cheap hotels or in crowded apartments of poor neighbourhoods.

Because of the absence of legal and social rights people are stuck in a vicious circle of poverty and exclusion. Their outward image of indigence and destitution amplifies the xenophobic feelings of the Greek population,[9] further perpetuating social exclusion. These conditions make Greece an undesirable country for Afghan asylum seekers. Almost all of them would like to go to Great Britain or some other country in Northern Europe. However, after 2003, people who are arrested upon entering the borders are fingerprinted so even if they make it to another European country they are sent back to Greece (for, according to the Dublin Regulation, asylum applications can be submitted only in the 'first safe country' one arrives in after entering the European Union). That is why Afghans living in Greece feel stuck and imprisoned. They cannot proceed to the rest of Europe and they cannot go back to Afghanistan because their country is devastated and they are not welcome in the states where they grew up. In Greece they cannot proceed with their lives because of the impediments created by the Greek institutional and social environment. 'We were in a small prison and now we have come to a big one' is a comment I have heard more than once by Afghan refugees that have been imprisoned in Afghanistan before coming to Greece.

Two Young Afghan Men, Living in Athens

My journey with the small group of Afghans who finally became the subjects of my research started four years ago, when I moved to Athens in order to conduct fieldwork for my dissertation. My interests by that time concerned refugees' ways of coping with institutional violence in exile. I began volunteering in a couple of NGOs that provided social service to refugees and I made the first contacts with young Afghan asylum seekers. Later I asked some of the Afghans I knew for permission to interview them in order to record their life histories. Our regular meetings for the interviews resulted in the establishment of friendly relations between us, relations that last up to the present day.

Friendship between researchers and their subjects is a topic treated with scepticism by anthropologists. Counter arguments against the possibility of friendship are synopsized in two main theoretical positions: according to the first, friendship cannot exist but is rather a romantic illusion of the researcher. The unbridgeable gaps between him/her and the subjects and the utilitarian motives of the researcher make pure friendship unattainable.[10] This stance is connected with the modern Western ideal about friendship which, according to Carrier (1999: 35), lays stress on 'involuntary sentiment unclouded by calculation or interest'. Drawing on Parry (1986), Carrier (1999: 23) relates the modern ideal of friendship between autonomous and spontaneous selves that are not motivated by interest, with the modern 'ideology of the pure gift' and the concomitant distrust of interested exchange.[11] In actual and not ideal terms, friendship might contain interest and affectionate bonds at the same time. Wolf (1966: 13–15) describes 'instrumental friendship' as a kind of friendship thriving in relatively open and fluid social situations (like in the case of refugee populations), where people strive for access to natural and social resources and may, for this purpose, use their friends as sponsors. My friendship with the Afghan men was built on exchange: they offered me information and in return I offered them some assistance with their contacts with NGOs and Greek bureaucracy. This fact did not prevent our interaction from being one of kindness, respect and mutual care.

Another element that could generate distrust on the possibility of friendship between my informants and me is the cultural and social gap that separated us, them being Muslims and me being a married European woman. According to Giddens (1999 in Bell and Coleman 1999: 1), 'there is a global revolution going on in how we think of ourselves and how we form ties and connections with others. . . New forms of intimacy are replacing older connections'. New forms of relations are not conduced in a cultural vacuum, but they instead arise as a result of the recombination and use of familiar cultural models (Papataxiarchis 1996: 205). For us, a familiar idiom was that of kinship, for we could create intimate relations 'as if' they were my younger brothers.[12] Moreover, the specific men, as refugees shifting from one cultural environment to the other, had become cosmopolitans in their own way, making use of diverse cultural elements in the process of their self-formation and transformation. They were flexible and versatile in the way in which they related to new people. Social and cultural differences existed between them and me but they were not unbridgeable. Rabinow (1977: 162) gives a balanced account of his friendship with his basic informant, which negates neither their differences nor their relationship: 'Our Otherness was not an ineffable essence, but rather the sum of different historical experiences . . .

But a dialogue was only possible when we recognized our differences . . . By so doing, we began a process of change'.

The second group of arguments questioning the idea of friendship between researcher and informants supports the fact that friendship is possible but holds that whenever it occurs it distorts the research process and the research findings. Distortion on the part of the researcher means that deep involvement and familiarity with the informants can obscure his/her perception and judgement, make him/her biased and partial and when it comes to refugees 'more likely to accept a particular "imagined" history, or become incorporated into refugees' survival strategies' (Jacobsen and Landau 2003: 192). On the part of the informants, distortion occurs as 'reactivity': a close relationship with the researcher transmutes their behaviour and spontaneous responses. As friend, the researcher can only get access to an artificial reality produced by his/her interaction with the informants. The assumption that close, caring or even interested relations between people distort their perception and judgement is, in my opinion, a false one. Relating and judging are two different processes that should be evaluated separately. Moreover, as Hastrup (2004: 456) indicates, anthropological knowledge is not object-knowledge but relational knowledge emerging within a dialogical field. Thus a decent ethnographic account will not be the outcome of aseptic laboratory conditions but of the proper use of anthropological tools (reflexivity being one of them). When it comes to refugees, a warm and trusting relationship might be the condition par excellence[13] for the apprehension of their intimate worlds and consequently of the larger socio-political context that influences their lives, as Lammers (2007: 76) and Rodgers (2004: 21–22) suggest.

Being friends with my informants, I habitually shared common activities with them and our local worlds intersected, giving birth to a mutual interest in exploring the world of the other. Through this exploration I had the opportunity to grasp the moving picture of their everyday life, as it evolved over time and I often asked myself about the hidden powers that actuated this evolution. Below, I try to sketch the lives of two of my Afghan informants. Their stories are unique and exceptional, being their own, but at the same time they are common. They are stories like those of many other people under similar conditions who strive to run their daily lives, heal their wounds and actualize their visions for the future.

Zhia

I first met Zhia[14] in 2004. He was born in Kabul in 1978 and belongs to the Afghan tribe of Tajiks. He was raised in a well off, middle-class family. His father was a civil servant and he has a younger brother and two younger sisters, still living in Kabul. He recalls that when he was a child, many educated men used to visit their house. They talked about poetry and recited poems and stories that little Zhia absorbed and kept in his mind. He admired his father's brother, who moved to Moscow to study civil engineering. Zhia chose to study the same subject at the University of Kabul but a year after he began his studies, the Taliban occupied Kabul and shut down the university. He joined a guerrilla group, fighting against the Taliban under the command of a Tajik warlord. He did not participate in active combat but remained behind the lines, working on the planning of war operations. In 2001 he left Afghanistan in a military helicopter that took him to neighbouring Tajikistan. Two years later (in 2003) Zhia arrived in Greece from Turkey. He was arrested and detained for three months on the island of Rhodes. After he was released he came to Athens. He found a job in a small industry, sewing belts for ten hours a day. He took Greek language courses at the University of Athens and two years later he spoke fluent Greek.

Zhia is full of vitality and restless energy. From the beginning of his stay in Athens he contacted many NGOs that ran programmes for refugees and participated in their activities. He became involved in an NGO named Mosaic, which had a special agenda to encourage refugees and migrants to organize activities and programmes under their own initiative. Through this NGO, Zhia taught Greek in classes for migrants, became a radio producer, wrote a scenario and directed a small theatrical play. He took part in exhibitions for amateur photographers and had the leading role in a short movie. Every time he participated in yet a new activity he announced his achievements with the enthusiasm of a little child. He perceived all these artistic activities not as an attempt to achieve 'high art' but rather as a game and as an essential way of expressing himself and communicating with people. He often mentioned that the Tajiks had always been the most cultivated of all the Afghan tribes. His speech was embellished with fables and verses of poems he had brought with him from Afghanistan. Once I asked him if he had a bad time in Greece and he answered:

> You point at me and you say: 'Here is an unhappy man, with all those problems that he has'. If you ask me, I will tell you that I'm not unhappy. I will point at my friends and say: 'Here are some unhappy people with so many problems'. But if you ask them, they will, in turn, say that they are not unhappy. You have to understand people from the East. They have hope and faith in God. They have in mind the things they want to do, and they hope.

Zhia lives in a four-room apartment on the ground floor of an old block of flats, in a neighbourhood inhabited mostly by immigrants. Every morning he rides his motorcycle to work and he stays there until late in the afternoon. He lives with three other Afghan friends. During the evenings they gather in their living room that is covered with carpets and loaded with couches. Many other friends come to visit them and they chat, watch Afghan satellite channels on the television and eat Afghan dishes prepared every time by the least tired housemate. Some evenings Zhia is not with them because he is involved in many other activities. They also spend many hours in Internet cafes, communicating with family and friends all over the world. In the summer they spend less time at home. They either go swimming at beaches near the city or they ramble in squares and open spaces. In their summer holidays they arrange trips to the Greek islands, like most of the natives do. After the legalization project, Zhia and several of his friends acquired 'green cards' that permit them to travel back to Afghanistan or to other European countries, something they could not do under the asylum seeker's status. Since then, their everyday routine in Greece has been interrupted by long journeys to Afghanistan (usually in August) and shorter ones in European cities (usually during Christmas holidays) where they are hosted in friends' houses.

The ideal life that Zhia is dreaming of would include constant movement within different social environments, an abundance of social interactions, frequent travels in different countries and financial prosperity. After a journey to Finland where his uncle lives, he is seriously thinking about moving to Northern Europe in order to start a new life, once more. This plan challenges and condenses the contents of his dreams, generating chances for new experiences in unknown places and possible opportunities for financial success. He knows that his legal status does not allow him to live in another country but he is very self-confident and he knows that someday soon he will succeed in relocating to the North.

Ismat

Ismat is a gentle and melancholy person, with great inner strength who I met in 2004. He was born in 1980, in Ghazni, a province at the centre of Afghanistan. He belongs to the tribe of the Hazaras, a poor and unprivileged tribe of Afghanistan. His family – his parents, two older brothers and three younger sisters – was one of the poorest in their village. Both his parents were sick and Ismat remembers hard winters with no food for the family. He was tearful as he narrated this period of his life to me. When he turned twelve years old, his brothers decided to send him to Pakistan, so that he could work and send money to the family. He worked for a shoemaker and during the nights, he slept at the shop. He began attending a school in Pakistan, in secret because his brothers would not agree with his choice. It was a secular school, sponsored by the Japanese government. At the beginning his classmates laughed at him and called him 'the donkey' because of his poor clothes but because he was a very good student, he gradually gained their respect.

He came upon some books about Marxism in a bookshop window, and he started studying political philosophy. Later he was accepted in medical school. He says that those years in medical school were his happiest years. He and his fellow students formed groups of a political and cultural character and, undertaking several projects, they felt, as he said, 'free and alive'. Their activities were considered by the dictatorial regime of Pakistan to be provocative and one of their comrades was murdered while the rest were badly beaten. They asked for protection from the UNCHR. According to

Ismat's narrative, the local department of an influential NGO[15] issued him with a fake membership card, with the help of which he managed to get into Iran. From there he went to Turkey and in 2003 he entered Greece from Turkey.

During the first year of his stay in Greece he was deeply depressed. He had been informed that his beloved young woman, whom he had left in Pakistan, was forced by her family to marry someone else. Later, his mood improved so he started to make contacts with Afghans and Greeks, through NGOs and political parties of the left. He is currently trying hard to offer assistance to his compatriots concerning practical matters such as informing them and sensitizing them about their rights.

For the last three years he has been employed as a building worker by a contractor; they are friends and Ismat calls him 'my communist boss'. Recently, Ismat devoted his political activities to the problems of the Afghans who are stuck at the port of Patras, living in slums they made themselves and waiting to find a way to get to Italy. He managed to gain the trust of his fellow Afghans in the slums and they asked him to be their representative and negotiator with the Greek authorities. Two years ago, he received certification in the Greek language and in the summer of 2008 he applied to the University of Athens in order to study social anthropology.

Ismat lives alone in a small apartment with one room. He enjoys privacy because, as he says, he never had it in Afghanistan. Their house was always crowded, with the big family living together in one room and people passing by all the time. Now his friends visit him whenever he decides. They are numerous and he is rarely without company. He is too busy to cook, so he lives on fast food. His cell phone rings all the time with calls from Afghan people or Greeks working with refugees. They ask for his help as advisor, negotiator, mediator or just translator. He makes himself available to everybody so every other afternoon he is in a different place (police stations, hospitals, NGOs) mediating for some compatriot and trying to offer solutions. He declares that it is not religiosity that motivates him, as is usual for many of his compatriots, but his longing for justice and his solidarity for people in difficult situations like those he once experienced. During his spare time he reads books and he writes poems and papers of protest that he distributes to other people. He would like to have his writings published in a book and he is dreaming of a career as a teacher of young children, for he feels great affection and can be very caring towards children.

Creating Familiar, Everyday Worlds in Exile

The lives of Zhia and Ismat in exile are indicative of their attempt to create local worlds, familiar and at the same time 'utopian', in the sense of worlds bearing the elements which Zhia and Ismat each imagine or envision as representing the ideal world. According to Barry Sandywell (2004: passim), the realm of everyday life has historically been devalued by philosophical and later by sociological discourse as a 'non place' where nothing exceptional happens. The writer points out that this attitude towards the ordinary has recently started to change and a kind of 'paradigm shift' has occurred in its conceptualization. The sphere of the quotidian is being reassessed as a locus of transformation of the self and of the world, as a domain of 'hitherto uninvestigated processes through which people make sense of their lives given the material and cultural resources available to them' (Sandywell 2004: 175). Such an approach towards the everyday is apt as an alternative way of representing life in exile. But a question arises: what exactly are we referring to when we talk of everyday life?

Several writers indicate problems and gaps in the theoretical production of the everyday partially due to its breadth, pervasiveness, and self-evidence. Sandywell (2004: 160) notes that 'the everyday' holds 'uncertain ontological status' within the human sciences, while Highmore (2002b: 1) describes it as a 'problematic, contested and opaque terrain'. As Ries observes, although the 'minutiae of daily life' stand at the core of the anthropological investigation, 'reflection on the singularity of the everyday as a spatial, temporal, and philosophical category is relatively rare' (Ries 2002: 725).

Given the analytical indeterminacy of the category, it is expedient to put forward one definition (or description) of everyday life that would seem most appropriate for the study of refuges. Lefebvre formulates a broad but articulate definition. According to him:

> everyday life is profoundly related to *all* activities, and encompasses them with all their differences and their conflicts; it is their meeting place, their bond, their common ground. And it is in everyday life that the sum total of relations which make the human – and every human being – a whole takes its shape and its form. In it are expressed and fulfilled those relations which bring into play the totality of the real. (Lefebvre 1991a in Gardiner 2004: 242)

Starting from this definition, we can conceive the everyday as 'intermediary and mediatory level' (Lefebvre 1961 in Sheringham 2000: 190), as field conjoining institutional structures with subjective experience and official with unofficial forms of social practice[16] (Burkitt 2004: 214). Moreover, in the realm of the quotidian, 'routinized, static and unreflexive' moments alternate with moments of 'surprising dynamism' and 'penetrating insight' (Gardiner 2000: 6) and routine intertwines dialectically with creativity (Gardiner 2004: 244).

Zhia's regular participation in the programmes of an NGO becomes part of his everyday routine. It is on the ground of this regularity that Zhia meets the opportunity to create tiny works of art like a collection of photographs or the direction of an amateur theatrical play. Similarly, Ismat makes part of his everydayness activities such as meetings with political groups or the advocacy of his compatriots' rights. Both men engage in regular everyday activities whose outcome is either art, in the case of Zhia, or a transformation of the social relations that surround him, in the case of Ismat. By their choices while attempting to reconstruct their lives, the two men become agents of 'creative practice' as Lefebvre defined the concept.[17]

At the same time Ismat and Zhia keep going to work, return home to rest, share lazy hours with friends or spend time keeping their houses tidy and clean. These habitual, repetitive activities are the sustaining ground and the cohesive material for their creativity. The idea of 'dialectical intertwining' of habit with creativity can be useful for the investigation of the 'redemptive elements' and the 'emancipatory possibilities' (Seigworth and Gardiner 2004: 153) that reside in refugees' everyday lives and vitalize refugees' efforts towards resilience.[18] Habit and creativity, dwelling in the minutiae of the quotidian, function through different paths as remedies for the wounds and the ruptures caused by flight.

Habits are 'protective cushions' (Felski 2002: 615) when uncertainty and instability prevail. Often in the afternoon Zhia meets with friends for some rounds of *carrom,* a board game they used to play in Afghanistan. They constructed the game's wooden board themselves and use a hall provided by an NGO for their meetings. I attended some of their games and I was struck by their childlike enthusiasm, no matter what their current problems were. They gave an impression of 'being at home' within this game that connected them to their childhood. Ismat keeps a small collection of books in his library, written in *dari*. Every once in a while he returns to these books, which are dear and precious to him. He leafs through them and rereads few abstracts. This habit is a shelter in moments of fatigue and disappointment. According to Harrison (2000 in Gardiner 2004: 246), habits and embodied routines are built up 'through a process of "enfolding" memory, in a manner that helps to "filter out" the background noise of the everyday life and provides us with a degree of shared ontological security a la Giddens'. In the case of refugees, the so-called 'background noise of everyday life' caused by the fatigue of long-lasting insecurity might sometimes be deafening, but still habits can provide a healing element, a sense of the world as 'reasonably predictable' (Gardiner 2004: 234).

Friends keep gathering every evening in the houses of Ismat and Zhia. They chat about what happened during the day, drink tea, share Afghan dishes and watch Afghan satellite channels. This routine goes on day after day, even if the participants are jobless, without legal papers or in the worst of moods. Their life may be ruptured in multiple ways but they can find refuge (being refugees once more) on a daily basis in these peaceful, trivial moments. Enfolded memories that will become the material for the production of embodied routines have to be selective and focused on small details connected with the preservation of life (such as the preparation of a lunch, the way it used to be done by one's parent). For Ries (2002: 732–74) this kind of quotidian productiveness of 'gardening, nurturing, covered dishes and casseroles', simultaneously habitual and creative, imposes order on the social/physical world, fosters growth and contradicts mortality.

Concerning the creative aspects of everyday life, one might wonder first about the modalities and then about the origins of creativity in the context of exile. The former can be better understood through Sandywell's (2004: 172–76) model of everyday life as a zone of transformation of the self and of the world. Arriving in a new environment, refugees have to accommodate themselves to it and simultaneously adjust the environment to their own needs. The first part of this process implies that the newcomers must, voluntarily or not, experiment with different 'forms of selfhood' (Sandywell 2004: 176) displaying creativity through self-formation. Ismat, as well as being a refugee, becomes an informal leader for a group of his compatriots, a hard worker for his boss and a student in Greece. Zhia, once a warrior in his country, becomes an artist and playful youth, enjoying his time in Athens. By experimenting with and undertaking different roles, the two men influence their microcosms – the people they know, the small audience of Zhia's artistic creations or the group of compatriots that Ismat assists through his political activities. The two men's daily activities either convey an alternative image of being in the world or have a direct impact on the existing social relations of their close environment. Zhia collaborates with other refugees during his involvement in artistic projects. His ideas are inspiring and motivate more people to get involved. Ismat strives to share his visions for the just treatment of refugees with compatriots and Greeks with whom he interacts in various activities. His arguments and actions have a subtle influence on some people's beliefs about the refugee condition. In almost invisible ways, the two men's experimentation with different forms of selfhood brings about a small-scale transformation of their local worlds.

The process of adjusting the environment to one's needs falls into de Certeau's (1997b in Highmore 2002a: 148) notion of creativity as 'the act of reusing and recombining heterogeneous materials' already existing in a given socio-cultural space which is 'constructed and spread by others'. Zhia and Ismat create their envisioned worlds in a borrowed, unprivileged and insecure social space – as refugees in Greek society – combining 'scarce resources' in an inventive way. They use the social space provided by NGOs or political parties, applying it to their own needs and visions.[19] This process of inventive recombination aims at the reconstruction of a familiar world in the place of the one that was lost.

The idea of loss brings us to the question of the origins of creativity in exile. A prevailing feature in the lives of refugees is the violent loss of a familiar way of life,[20] of a familiar world. How does loss generate creativity? Ismat's and Zhia's recollection of moments of fulfilment (childhood among family friends reciting stories or student years characterized by political activism) indicates what is absent from their present. They strive in a creative way to restore those missing parts. Zhia was raised in an intellectual family environment. Now, as a refugee working in a small factory for the greater part of his day, he tries to create a field of activities which respond to his intellectual and aesthetic needs, strongly connected to his family memories.

He finds this field available in an NGO and elaborates it in an imaginative way, undertaking several initiatives. Ismat regards the way in which he and his fellow students organized their struggle in Pakistan as a focal point in his life. Living in Greece he tries to reproduce the same model of interaction with the people he relates to.

Scarry denotes that 'pain and the imagination are each other's missing intentional counterpart, and they together provide a framing identity of man-as-creator' (Scarry 1985: 169). Pain and absence motivate imagination, which, in turn, motivates intentionality to create anew what is absent. Ismat often spoke of the pain and sorrow he felt because of the sudden and violent interruption of his student struggles. Might the remedy for his pain be his daily similar struggles to help compatriots claim their rights in Greece? According to Scarry, when the world fails to provide the object (of stability, of affection, etc.), 'imagination is there, almost on an emergency stand-by basis, as a last resource for the generation of objects. Missing, they will be made-up' (Scarry 1985: 166). Absence 'will motivate either a search (an alteration in the ground of the world) or an act of material invention (an introduction of a new object onto the ground of the world)' (Scarry 1985: 167).

Rapport, from a similar viewpoint, associates creativity with the state of being displaced: 'Becoming a refugee or exile from a social milieu or a relationship or a worldview, becoming someone else, individuals assure themselves of a distance from which to look askance and consciously create anew' (Rapport 2003: 51). For Rapport (2003: 75) the inner source of creativity is 'existential power', the kind of power that 'compasses the force, the will, the energy, in a word the agency, whereby individuals produce effects in their worlds'. Creativity occurs within particular combinations of possibilities and intentionalities embedded in the everyday. Lefebvre (2002: 341) introduced the term 'moments' to describe those combinations. According to him, 'moment' is 'the attempt to achieve the total realization of a possibility'; 'it creates a time and a space' and it can be situated 'as a function of a history, the history of the individual' (Lefebvre 2002: 344–48). Resilience can be approached through Lefebvre's 'theory of moments' as a succession of insights, decisions and acts originating in moments within everyday life. Ismat and Zhia transform their selves and clear their paths in exile through moments when they look back and reinterpret their past, envision the future they desire to have, and make small decisions based on their desires. A succession of moments renders them different from their initial selves in a subtle, untraceable way.

The idea of succession implies the deep connection between temporality and processes of resilience and healing, for these processes cannot be conceived as being separate from time. On the ground of everyday life, habitual behaviour alleviating different pains and fears alternates with moments of transcendence and creativity that contribute to the transformation of the self and of the world. Lefebvre (2002: 340) speaks of the 'newness which springs from repetition'[21] and names this newness 'difference'. For him 'difference' is a product of the 'new and unforeseen that introduces itself into the repetitive' (Lefebvre 2004: 6). Within this model, resilience can be understood as the difference that emerges when moments introduce themselves into the repetitive rhythm of daily life.

Everyday Life and Subjectivity

It is obvious from the discussion above that the everyday cannot be treated as an abstract and transcendental entity. It is rather approached as a canvas whereon individuals inscribe their personal trajectories. There exists no everyday without an author and each everyday life is a unique synthesis, according to the symbolic and material resources available to each one of us. As Lavie, Rosaldo and Narayan note (1993: 6), 'creative processes emerge from specific people, set in their social, cultural and historical circumstances'. The same can be said for the familiar worlds composed of clusters of habits. These worlds are inhabited by specific individuals who adopt (sometimes involuntarily) or recombine the available cultural practices to compose their own habitual environment.

Thus, any attempt to understand everyday life should take into account the actors, together with the past and present influences on them that come from their inner and social environments. Investigations of daily worlds should simultaneously be investigations of subjectivity. Ortner and Biehl et al. give two distinct definitions of subjectivity, both based on the idea that subjectivity is the outcome of the interplay between an inner and an external world. As Ortner notes: 'By subjectivity I will mean the ensemble of modes of perception, affect, thought, desire, fear, and so forth that animate acting subjects. But I always mean as well the cultural and social formations that shape, organize, and provoke those modes of affect, thought and so on' (Ortner 2005: 31).

For Biehl et al. (2007: 5) subjectivity is 'the agonistic and practical activity of engaging identity and fate, patterned and felt in historically contingent settings and mediated by institutional processes and cultural forms'. Everyday life and subjectivity can be thought of as communicating vessels, each nourishing and sustaining the other and, subsequently, each mirroring the other.[22] The same forces (historical, social, cultural, political) that shape subjectivities set the scenery for the everyday to unfold. Similarly, the existential power that animates subjectivity is expressed through the multiple nuances of individual daily worlds.

Ismat's and Zhia's subjectivities (and so their visions for the making of their 'ideal world') are composed from heterogeneous elements such as cherished memories, traumatic events, or influential relationships that originate in a very different socio-cultural environment from the one they presently inhabit. Both young refugees find a way to express their subjectivity in the circumstances they face while in exile, through the shape of creative practice, art and politics embedded in the everyday. The quest for knowledge and cultivation of the spirit is an important element in the life of Zhia, as a result of the way he was raised by his family. If it had not been interrupted by the war, his life trajectory in Afghanistan might have been carved in a way that conforms to this quest. It is characteristic of his intellectual inclination that he participated in the civil war not as a fighter but as 'organizing mind' behind the lines. When he came to Greece and started a life from the beginning, Zhia was oriented towards activities that could fulfil this quest that he had inherited from home. He participated in theatre, photography, teaching and what is perhaps more creative than the activities themselves is the fact that he inventively carried them out in a hostile and deficient social environment, as a refugee living in Greece. A recurring theme in Ismat's discussions with me was the poverty and injustice he had experienced throughout his life, as a child growing up in a poor family and later as an adolescent struggling alone to complete his education in Pakistan. This strong sense of injustice and exclusion influenced his worldview. He strongly believes that people facing social injustice should join together and cooperate in order to claim their rights and find their own solutions to their problems. This ideal directs his actions and the way in which he relates to other people. Whether in Pakistan as a student, or in Greece as a refugee, he incites people around him to undertake initiatives and devotes his time to collective activities of a political character.

The life trajectories of the two men and the elements they insistently pursue as vital for their well-being imply the existence of a 'guiding model' for the construction of their everyday worlds within various contexts, whether they live near their family or in exile. This model, unique for each man, reflects his unique subjectivity. It is their subjectivity that channels their existential power and gives it its unique expressions as they are manifested in each man's everyday life.

Conclusion

The everyday life of the Afghan people I met in Athens unfolds in time on 'peculiar' sites[23] like borderlands, refugee camps, prisons, public urban spaces, and shifting dwellings in unprivileged neighbourhoods and places of work. Under these conditions, there are times when the habitual occurs less often than the unusual and the extraordinary. Throughout those times everything at stake (the needs, the desires and aspirations, the day-to-day existence) has to be negotiated anew. Negotiation needs strength which springs from people's existential power, their sense of pride and dignity and the obligation they feel to their loved ones who stayed behind. The lives of these refugees are also products of bio-political operations orchestrated by asylum policies that restrict and inhibit individual potentialities. In this context, negotiating means struggling to achieve one's goals against institutional structures and disciplinary technologies that set the boundaries between legality and illegality.

The social researcher's uncomfortable and ambivalent position in confronting individual lives that stand 'at the margins' (of legality, of the state, of the society) entails a moral responsibility as far as those lives are conceived as 'radical alterity' and treated with fear and hostility. According to Highmore (2002b: 2) 'the everyday (as a theoretical and practical arena) has the potential ability of producing, not difference, but commonality'. So, by approaching and describing from a near distance the intimate worlds of people constituting Otherness in Western societies, social science can undermine the divisive forces generated by ideas of alterity. By attempting to comprehend the dreams, hopes and desires that motivate these 'marginal' lives, social research can proceed and ponder upon the fields of human experience that might be common and shared, even among people from the most heterogeneous backgrounds. Moreover, accounts of people's daily strivings and achievements under adverse conditions may generate a reflexive stance towards the fact that adversity and suffering are inescapable attributes of human worlds and constitute 'the moral core of experience' (Biehl et al. 2007: 11). The widening of our understanding of human potentialities and the small steps towards reconciliation with aspects of life that cause fear and pain, can in this context represent the modest contribution of anthropological writing to the enhancement of hope and faith in humankind.

Notes

1 'Moral world' is for Kleinman a local world where each one of us conducts a 'moral life'. Here the term 'moral' is used with its broader meaning, referring to values (Kleinman 2006: 1). According to the writer, 'Life, in this sense is inevitably moral, because for each and every one of us, life is about the things that matter most to us. Just carrying on our existence, negotiating important relations with others, doing work that means something to us, and living in some particular local place where others are also passionately engaged in these same existential activities- all this is, by definition, moral experience' (Kleinman 2006: 2).

2 Bauman (1995: 50) uses the term 'being- with' in order to describe a form of togetherness in which 'no more of the self tends to be deployed in the encounter than the topic- at- hand demands; and no more of the other is highlighted than the topic- at- hand permits. Being- with is a meeting of incomplete beings, of deficient selves'.

3 'Taking moral responsibility means not to consider the Other any more as a specimen of a species or a category, but as unique, and by so doing elevate oneself (making oneself chosen) to the dignity of uniqueness' (Bauman 1995: 60).

4 Cocreators both in the sense that humans have to deal with life's contingency that might present them with unexpected opportunities or tragedies and losses and in the sense that creation never occurs in a vacuum but is the result of our interaction with the environment, the environment that we inhabit and the one we have internalized.

5 The phrase is borrowed from the title of Kleinman's book (2006).

6 This argument is contested by recent historical research showing that the Balkan Peninsula was an area of constant movement of people in the context of the Ottoman Empire (Psimmenos and Georgoulas 1999: 39).

7 It happened that most of the 'subjects' of my research finally succeeded in changing their legal status from 'asylum seekers' to 'economic migrants'. This fact led me to a temporary 'classificatory' confusion extending to the theoretical frame I should use to describe those people whose qualities, after all, had remained the same. This shift from 'refugees' to 'migrants' being more than a categorical reordering entailed considerable changes at the level of the individuals' everyday life, because of the differentiation of civil rights assigned to them through each legal category. The change of status that happened during my research proved very illuminating; it made clear to me the association of legal status with the quality of everyday life as another example of bio-political intervention.

8 The Greek coast guard's special units literally commit headhunting in an attempt to prevent foreigners from entering Greek waters. Small boats approaching the Aegean islands are being pushed back and shot and their passengers are thrown in the sea or arrested and maltreated (Pro-Asyl 2007: 12–14).

9 For a period of several months, the Greek residents of a neighbourhood situated near the city centre protested against the 'degradation' of their district that, according to them, has been 'invaded' by migrants, mostly Afghans. Afghan people choose to stay in this neighbourhood because of the low rents so the neighbourhood gradually evolved into the main district of accommodation for the Afghan community.

10 It is within this scope that Crick (1992: 176) denotes: 'With the substantial inequalities of wealth and power which normally separate anthropologist and informant, combined with the researcher's professional reasons for being in the field, speaking of "friendship", as we often do, is somewhat odd'.

11 He concludes that this ideal of friendship is a cultural element and can only be realized 'among people who can pursue political and economic survival and success through relatively impersonal mechanisms' (Carrier 1999: 36).

12 A possible objection here is that my informants and I did not even share a common idiom of kinship, having been raised in different societies. Yet, in the 'as if' condition mentioned above, affection and care towards relatives gave us enough common ground to use as a model for our friendship.

13 Trust is a sensitive issue for people who have been forced to flee from their familiar worlds. As Daniel and Knudsen (1995: 2) observe: 'Unlike life under "ordinary" circumstances, or more correctly, under circumstances over which one exercises a certain measure of control, in the life of a refugee, trust is overwhelmed by mistrust, besieged by suspicion, and relentlessly undermined by caprice'. During fieldwork trust might be gained if the researcher offers time, devotion and constancy to his/her relationship with refugees.

14 In order to protect the privacy of my informants I have used pseudonyms.

15 While the act of issuing a fake document may constitute malpractice or illegal activity on the part of a reliable NGO (which is why I decided not to disclose the name of the NGO), it was essentially compatible with the objectives of the NGO, that is, the assistance of refugees and in this case saving Ismat's life. We may recall here the term 'tactics', by which de Certeau described '"ways of operating": victories of the "weak" over the "strong" (weather the strength be that of powerful people or the violence of things or of an imposed order, etc.), clever

tricks, knowing how to get away with things, "hunter's cunning"' (de Certeau 1984: xix).

16 For Burkitt (2004: 214), following Bourdieu (1998), official forms of social practice refer to legitimate and articulate behaviour which is normalized and codified by the state and its institutions and also by the social fields of science, art, religion and ethics. In contrast, relations of love, intimacy and friendship, being less systematized and codified, are considered as unofficial forms of social practice.

17 Lefebvre (2002: 232) used the term 'praxis' or 'social practice' to refer to activities that 'produce the human world'. His classification of human activities contains the category of 'creative practice' as 'practice which creates material works and practice which creates practice, that is, which modifies human relations (including their ethical dimension)' (Lefebvre 2002: 242).

18 The underlying question for such an investigation is expressed insightfully by Veena Das (1997 in Ries 2002: 739): 'How can terror be transformed into a world in which one can dwell again, in full awareness of a life that has to be lived in a loss?'

19 Their social manoeuvres refer to de Certeau's (1984: xiv) location of everyday creativity in 'the innumerable practices by means of which users reappropriate the space organized by techniques of sociocultural production'. De Certeau (1984 in Mitchell 2007: 100) uses the paradigm of a North African migrant living in Paris to show how he appropriates not only housing facilities but also the French language in his own singular way. The migrant creates his own system within the larger system imposed on him, thus establishing 'a degree of plurality and creativity'.

20 Familiar does not always mean peaceful or stable and secure. Many refugees, like the Afghan people I met, were born and raised in war and conflict, their local, familiar worlds having been pervaded by violence. This is a point made by Ries (2002: 737) when she observes: 'The fundamental strategy of terror-war wherever it occurs is to undermine the rhythms and small securities of everyday practice . . . by deliberately employing the objects and rituals of daily life as tools of terror'. When people who were raised in conditions like these become refugees, they have to reinvent intimate worlds where the familiar can also be protective and sheltering.

21 Lefebvre (2002: 340) uses the example of music: '[T]he repetition of sounds and rhythms in music offers a perpetual movement which is perpetually reinvented'.

22 Subjectivities and everyday worlds have undergone analogous transformations in the wake of postmodernity. A need for reconceptualization has been expressed for both, so that their present fluidity and multiplicity of states can be comprehended and analysed. Such an endeavour presupposes a focus on the particular.

23 It should be noted that the use here of the term 'peculiar' bears the problem of comparison, since we cannot construe the existence of an 'average' site for the everyday, compared to which any other site seems peculiar.

References

Abu-Lughod, L. 1993. *Writing Women's Worlds.* Berkeley, Los Angeles and London: University of California Press.

_____. 2006. 'Writing against Culture', in H. Moore and T. Sanders (eds), *Anthropology in Theory. Issues in Epistemology.* Malden, Oxford and Victoria: Blackwell Publishing, pp. 466–79.

Bauman, Z. 1995. *Life in Fragments. Essays in Postmodern Morality.* Oxford and Malden: Blackwell Publishing.

Biehl, J. 2007. 'Transformations in Social Experience and Subjectivity', in J. Biehl, B. Good and A. Kleinman (eds), *Subjectivity.* Berkeley, Los Angeles and London: University of California Press, pp. 27–33.

Biehl, J., B. Good and A. Kleinman. 2007. 'Introduction: Rethinking Subjectivity', in J. Biehl, B. Good and A. Kleinman (eds), *Subjectivity.* Berkeley, Los Angeles and London: University of California Press, pp. 1–23.

Bourdieu, P. 1998. *Practical Reason.* Cambridge: Polity Press.

Burkitt, I. 2004. 'The Time and Space of Everyday Life', *Cultural Studies* 18(2/3): 211–27.

Carrier, J. 1999. 'People Who Can Be Friends: Selves and Social Relationships', in S. Bell and S. Coleman (eds), *The Anthropology of Friendship.* Oxford and New York: Berg, pp. 21–38.

Castaneda, Q. 2006. 'The Invisible Theatre of Ethnography: Performative Principles of Fieldwork', *Anthropological Quarterly* 79(1): 75–104.

Committee on Civil Liberties, Justice and Home Affairs. 2007. 'The conditions in centres for third country national (detention camps, open centres as well as transit centres and transit zones) with a particular focus on provisions and facilities for persons with special needs in the 25 EU member states'. Brussels, European Parliament: DG Ipol publication. Retrieved 20 October 2010 from http://www.aedh.eu/plugins/fckeditor/userfiles/file/Asile%20et%20immigration/Study_of_European_Parliament_about_detention_and_enferment_in_Europe.pdf

Crick, M. 1992. 'Ali and Me. An Essay in Street-corner Anthropology', in J. Okely and H. Callaway (eds), *Anthropology and Autobiography.* London and New York: Routledge, pp. 175–92.

Daniel, V. 2002. 'The Refugee: A Discourse on Displacement', in J. MacClancy (ed.), *Exotic No More. Anthropology on the Front Lines.* Chicago and London: The University of Chicago Press, pp. 270–86.

Daniel, V. and J. Knudsen. 1995. 'Introduction', in V. Daniel and J. Knudsen (eds), *Mistrusting Refugees.* Berkeley, Los Angeles and London: University of California Press, pp. 1–13.

de Certeau, M. 1984. *The Practice of Everyday Life.* Berkeley, Los Angeles and London: University of California Press.

Denzin, N. 1997. *Interpretive Ethnography. Ethnographic Practices for the 21st Century.* Thousand Oaks, London and New Delhi: Sage Publications.

Felski, R. 2002. 'Introduction', *New Literary History* 33: 607–22.

Gardiner, M. 2000. *Critiques of Everyday Life.* London and New York: Routledge.

———. 2004. 'Everyday Utopianism. Lefebvre and His Critics', *Cultural Studies* 18(2/3): 228–54.

Good, B., et al. 2008. 'Postcolonial Disorders: Reflections on Subjectivity in the Contemporary World', in M.J. DelVecchio Good et al. (eds), *Postcolonial Disorders.* Berkeley, Los Angeles and London: University of California Press, pp. 1–40.

Greek Ministry of Home Affairs. 2007. 'Statistical data concerning the number of aliens' permits of residence per nationality'. Athens. Retrieved 1 May 2009 from http://www.antigone.gr/stats/default.php

Hastrup, K. 2004. 'Getting it Right. Knowledge and Evidence in Anthropology', *Anthropological Theory* 4(4): 455–72.

_____. 2005. 'Social Anthropology. Towards a Pragmatic Enlightenment?', *Social Anthropology* 13(2): 133–49.

Held, V. 2006. *The Ethics of Care.* Oxford and New York: Oxford University Press.

Highmore, B. 2002a. *Everyday Life and Cultural Theory. An Introduction.* London and New York: Routledge.

_____. 2002b. 'Introduction: Questioning Everyday Life', in B. Highmore (ed.), *The Everyday Life Reader.* London and New York: Routledge, pp. 1–34.

Jacobsen, K. and L. Landau. 2003. 'The Dual Imperative in Refugee Research: Some Methodological and Ethical Considerations in Social Science Research on Forced Migration', *Disasters* 27(3): 185–206.

Kleinman, A. 1997. *Writing at the Margin. Discourse between Anthropology and Medicine.* Berkeley, Los Angeles and London: University of California Press.

_____. 2006. *What Really Matters.* Oxford and New York: Oxford University Press.

Kleinman, A. and J. Kleinman. 1997. 'The Appeal of Experience; The Dismay of Images: Cultural Appropriations of Suffering in Our Times', in A. Kleinman, V. Das and M. Lock (eds), *Social Suffering.* Berkeley, Los Angeles and London: University of California Press, pp. 1–23.

Lammers, E. 2007. 'Researching Refugees: Preoccupations with Power and Questions of Giving', *Refugee Survey Quarterly* 26(3): 72–82.

Lefebvre, H. 2002. *Critique of Everyday Life.* London and New York: Verso.

_____. 2004. 'The Critique of the Thing', in H. Lefebvre, S. Elden and G. Moore (eds), *Rhythmanalysis: Space, Time and Everyday Life.* London, New York and Harrisburg: Continuum International Publishing Group, pp. 5–18.

Malkki, L. 1997. 'Speechless Emissaries. Refugees, Humanitarianism, and Dehistoricization', in K. Hastrup and K. Fog Olwig (eds), *Sitting Culture: The Shifting Anthropological Object.* London and New York: Routledge, pp. 223–54.

Marcus, G. 1998. *Ethnography through Thick and Thin.* Princeton: Princeton University Press.

Migration Policy Institute. 2004. 'Greece: Annual number of asylum applications by nationality, 1980 to 2004'. Washington. Retrieved 26 October 2008 from http://www.migrationinformation.org/DataHub/countrydata/data.cfm

Mitchel, J. 2007. 'A Fourth Critic of the Enlightenment: Michel de Certeau and the Ethnography of Subjectivity', *Social Anthropology* 15(1): 89–106.

Norwegian Organization for Asylum Seekers, Norwegian Helsinki Committee and Greek Helsinki Monitor. 2008. 'A gamble with the right to asylum in Europe. Greek Asylum Policy and the Dublin II Regulation'. Oslo and Athens. Retrieved 2 November 2010 from http://www.noas.no/wp-content/uploads/2012/10/Greece_DublinII_report.pdf

Ortner, S. 2005. 'Subjectivity and Cultural Critique', *Anthropological Theory* 5(1): 31–52.

Papataxiarchis, E. 1996. 'The Cultural Construction of Identity', *Topika B*: 197–216 (in Greek).

Parry, J. 1986. 'The Gift, The Indian Gift and the "Indian Gift"', *Man* 21: 453–73.

PRO-ASYL and Group of Lawyers for the Rights of Refugees and Migrants. 2007. 'The truth may be bitter, but it must be told. The situation of Refugees in the Aegean and the Practices of the Greek Coast Guard'. Frankfurt/Main and Athens. Retrieved 29 October 2008 from http://www.proasyl.de/fileadmin/proasyl/fm_redakteure/Englisch/Griechenlandbericht_Engl.pdf

Psimmenos I. and S. Georgoulas. 1999. 'Migration Pathways: A Historic, Demographic and Policy Review of the Greek Case', in A. Triandafyllidou (ed.), *Migration Pathways: A Historic, Demographic and Policy Review of Four European Countries*, pp. 38–62. Retrieved 16 March 2006 from http://www.eui. eu/RSCAS/Research/IAPASIS/IAPASISfinal.pdf

Rabinow, P. 1977. *Reflections on Fieldwork in Morocco*. Berkeley, Los Angeles and London: University of California Press.

Rapport, N. 2003. *I'm a Dynamite: An Alternative Anthropology of Power*. London and New York: Routledge.

Ries, N. 2002. 'Anthropology and the Everyday, from Comfort to Terror', *New Literary History* 33: 725–42.

Rodgers, G. 2004. '"Hanging Out" with Forced Migrants: Methodological and Ethical Challenges', *Forced Migration Review* 21: 48–49.

Rosaldo R., S. Lavie and K. Narayan. 1993. 'Introduction: Creativity in Anthropology', in S. Lavie, K. Narayan and R. Rosaldo (eds), *Creativity/Anthropology*. Ithaca and London: Cornell University Press, pp. 1–8.

Sandywell, B. 2004. 'The Myth of Everyday Life. Toward a Heterology of the Ordinary', *Cultural Studies* 18(2/3): 160–80.

Scarry, E. 1985. *The Body in Pain: The Making and Unmaking of the World*. Oxford: Oxford University Press.

Seigworth, G. and M. Gardiner. 2004. 'Rethinking Everyday Life', *Cultural Studies* 18(2/3): 139–59.

Shahrani, N. 1995. 'Afghanistan's Muhajirin (Muslim "Refugee-Warriors"): Politics of Mistrust and Distrust of Politics', in V. Daniel and J. Knudsen (eds), *Mistrusting Refugees*. Berkeley, Los Angeles and London: University of California Press, pp. 187–207.

Sheringham, M. 2000. 'Attending to the Everyday: Blanchot, Lefebvre, Certeau, Perec', *French Studies* 54(2): 187–99.

———. 2006. *Everyday Life. Theories and Practices from Surrealism to the Present*. Oxford: Oxford University Press.

Sotiropoulos, D. 2004. 'Democratization, Administrative Reform and the State in Greece, Italy, Portugal and Spain: Is There a "Model" of South European Bureaucracy?'. Discussion Paper. Hellenic Observatory, London School of Economics and Political Science. London. Retrieved 19 March 2008 from http:// eprints.lse.ac.uk/5682/1/Sotiropoulos17.pdf

Strand A., A. Suhrke and K. Harpviken. 2004. 'Afghan Refugees in Iran: From Refugee Emergency to Migration Management'. Retrieved 20 October 2009 from http://www.cmi.no/afghanistan/peacebuilding/docs/CMI-PRIO-Afghan RefugeesInIran.pdf

Trouillot, M.R. 2003. *Global Transformations. Anthropology and the Modern World*. New York and Hampshire: Palgrave Macmillan.

United Nations High Commissioner for Refugees. 2008. 'Asylum Levels and Trends in Industrialized Countries, First Half 2008'. Geneva. Retrieved 15 June 2009 from http://www.unhcr.org/statistics.html

Wolf, E. 1966. 'Kinship, Friendship, and Patron-Client Relations in Complex Societies', in M. Banton (ed.), *The Social Anthropology of Complex Societies*. London: Taviston Publications, pp. 1–22.

Chapter 6

Behind the Iron Fence

(Dis)placing Boundaries, Initiating Silences

Maša Mikola

As owner of the burrow I had hoped to be in a stronger position than any enemy who might chance to appear. But simply by virtue of being owner of this great vulnerable edifice I am obviously defenceless against any serious attack. The joy of possessing it has spoilt me, the vulnerability of the burrow has made me vulnerable; any wound to it hurts me as if I myself were hit.

Franz Kafka[1]

Introduction

Ljubljana Asylum Home, or Azilni dom as it is officially called, is operated by the Slovenian Interior Ministry, and asylum seekers who ask for international protection in Slovenia are required to live there while their applications are being processed. This Home was moved from an inner suburb of Ljubljana to the very fringe of the city in 2004. With this move, basic living conditions for asylum seekers improved, but the sense of distance and displacement increased.

This chapter discusses 'otherizing' as a spatial process and examines the contradictory nature of the concept of home. I talk about the body of an asylum seeker as a border-zone where interactions between the political and individual are enacted. I examine acts of self-harm as acts of resistance, which disrupt trajectories of fear and power and go against the dominant narrative of seeking asylum as an entirely powerless state. The aim of the chapter is to offer a more complex way of seeing such spaces as holding a web of intersecting individual narratives. In-betweeness, injustice, pain and uncertainty give birth to extraordinary events, such as acts of self-harm, which impact on everyday narratives constructed around the politicized issue of seeking asylum. I conclude by looking at the concept of silence as a space where commonality is negotiated; as both a space of boundary and discourse that can act as a bridge or barrier between the concepts of self, the other and home.

The relevance of the issues presented in this chapter goes beyond the Slovenian case. The criminalization of asylum procedures and the extension of the sphere of illegality around asylum seekers and refugees have been expanding in the Western world over the last few decades. The atmosphere that gives rise to the politics of exclusion has not only been cultivated in Slovenia, but has spread to include many actors and has global dimensions. This atmosphere cannot be adequately challenged without the inclusion of individual voices, personal stories and singular events. Asylum seekers and other forced migrants narrate these stories with their own voices and their own bodies, which are products and subjects of the increasingly inhumane political climate. This chapter is based on a single event, but one that reveals dozens of individual actors and other stories within the boundaries of that particular Asylum Home as well as many other transient 'homes' of millions of people who fled their actual or real homes.[2]

Background to the Slovenian Case

With respect to the housing available for asylum seekers, after Slovenia became independent from Yugoslavia in 1991, former military barracks located around the country became available when the members of the Yugoslav army were removed. They were first occupied by the members of Teritorialna obramba or Territorial Defence, a newly formed Slovenian army established to protect the territory of the infant state, who were then replaced by social or cultural youth initiatives, which created squats, some of which were appropriated to accommodate refugees from former Yugoslav republics. After these refugees left, many to settle in other countries, asylum seekers were placed there. In this way the former military barracks, which were initially symbols of protection, became places which members of the old Yugoslav People's Army, now viewed as enemies, were required to leave, repositioning the barracks as a symbol of the newly obtained Slovenian independence and, finally, as a symbol of a 'constant threat'; that of the refugees who came to inhabit these sites (Milohnič 2001: 131–34).

This illustrates well how unreasonable, or even impossible, it is to determine and define absolutely 'outside' and 'inside' as two completely separate entities, since the members of the Yugoslav People's Army, as well as refugees in Slovenia during the 1990s, were from other parts of the former Yugoslavia, which only shortly before had been a common state – once counterparts in the 'brotherhood and unity' project, now newly proclaimed adversaries. One accommodation centre that underwent such a transformation in Veliki otok, near Postojna in western Slovenia, was first a military barrack, then a refugee centre, and finally became reinstituted as the Centre for the removal of Aliens,[3] which was subsequently required to omit the contentious 'removal' from of its title, becoming, somewhat humorously, the Centre for Aliens in 2005. The Centre for Aliens in Veliki otok, which – ironically – translates as 'Big Island', still exists, housing people who do not posses the required documents, who entered Slovenia without such documents, and/or those who are waiting there for deportation.

Before the 'Big Island' refugee centre near Postojna was transformed into the Centre for (the Removal of) Aliens, asylum seekers – those with or without documents – were housed in an inner suburb of Ljubljana, close to the city centre. When Slovenia joined the European Union in 2004, people with documents were physically separated from those without, and both groups were relocated to more secluded sites: those without documents to the aforementioned Centre for (the Removal of) Aliens, those with documents to the Asylum Home on the fringes of the capital. New anxieties came about, part and parcel with the oft-mentioned advantages of being a member of the European Union, and this was certainly the case with Slovenia. New fears were invoked, of strangers waiting in the shadows of the newly affirmed borders. The Asylum Home accommodated these new strangers and provided a location where broader European politics could be enacted.

Before the Asylum Home moved, the building was overcrowded and ill equipped. It was not in compliance with international regulations and had attracted criticism from the local residents who formed a civil initiative, which strived for the removal of the Home from the neighbourhood. The unofficial president (Oblak 2001) of the initiative said:

> They [asylum seekers] congregated at certain points – at children's playgrounds, certain green areas, around the closest shop, in some neighbouring bars. There were piles of rubbish, clothes and food left behind after they had gone. Ecological and health problems arose because there was excrement and needles among the rubbish, and there were dogs and children prying around while on walks with their parents. Some foreigners have not slept in the centre at all (probably because it was overcrowded), but on the benches, patches of grass, staircases and cellars of the nearby apartment blocks. They lit bonfires and grilled provisional dinners on the green areas below balconies of surprised residents, and they debated and sang late into the night.

Soon after these comments were made, the Asylum Home was physically relocated to the outskirts of Ljubljana, further dislocating the residents from the life of the city. Now on the fringe of the city, the Asylum Home no longer posed any serious threat to the residents, as there were practically no permanent residents around the new area, only transitory workers and commuters.

Anthropologist Ghassan Hage (2002) talks about otherizing as not only a mental process, but also a spatial process. By examining the fear of the refugee, Nikos Papastergiadis (2006) also argues that the whole political imagery is both unconscious and spatial. The concept of the 'abject other' links both sameness and otherness to the moment of separation between self and other.

'Abjection' can mark the moment of location as the 'Other'. The fact that the new location of the Asylum Home occurred in 2004 was significant. Refugees and asylum seekers in the European Union, to which Slovenia was admitted that year, already held a certain status and a certain location – a certain designation – before Slovenia joined the Union. It was already determined who they were, what they were like and where they belonged. Along with the EU economic-political order, Slovenia accepted a certain socio-ideological order, which already had an established system, and which included a spatial logistics of exclusion.

At a press conference held in the Asylum Home in 2008, one of the asylum seekers whose right to stay in the country had been granted said that whilst she had arrived in the country legally, with her passport and a tourist visa, and whilst she wanted to seek asylum without the interference of the police, it was shocking to her that the first thing that the Asylum Home employees did was call the police and take her to the police station in a police car as if she was a criminal. They held her there for six hours, confined at the police station regardless of the fact that she had given them her passport and told them who she was, the reason for her arrival, described the journey she had made and had breached no laws. As she said, the only thing she asked for was protection (Azilni dom Vič: Ruska prosilca za azil sta si zaradi kratenja pravic prerezala žile [Vič Asylum Home: Russian asylum seekers slit their wrists due to a breach of rights], 2008). The reasons for her arrival were straightforward and legitimate; nevertheless, the degrading ritual initiated by the Asylum Home and carried out by the police inadvertently re-enforced the mythology of outsiders that was necessary in the process of internal exclusion and criminalization in the context of the European Union.

The Asylum Home

Like other accommodation centres for asylum seekers around Europe, the Asylum Home was designed to provide all the basic services required by asylum seekers in one location. It was built as a controlled space removed from the social networks of the city (Isin and Rygiel 2007). With the reloca-tion of the Centre for the Removal of Aliens to 'Big Island', and the Asylum Home to the fringes of Ljubljana (although these were officially separate entities, they had been located in the same building in the city centre), the Asylum Home built its own detention facility now that it was physically separated from the Centre for the Removal of Aliens. Apart from the deten-tion facility, the building was arranged in a manner that was in compliance with international requirements; separate departments were built for single women, families and unaccompanied minors. A new kitchen and a dining room were created, as well as a room for religious activities, a couple of common rooms and offices for representatives of NGOs, an interrogation room, and an outside area.

Jelka Zorn (2007a, 2007b), a Slovenian social scientist, argues that the Asylum Home is a 'total institution': she is referring to the concept as it is defined by Erving Goffman in his work on 'Asylums' (1961), in which he writes that a total institution is 'a place of residence and work in which a large number of like-situated individuals, cut off from the wider society for an appreciable period of time, together lead an enclosed, formally administered round of life. There is a barrier placed between the person inside (inmate) and the wider world outside' (Goffman 1961: xiii). The Interior Ministry and its co-workers (the police, security services, and lawyers assigned by the Interior Ministry) all contribute to maintain this barrier, and the detention facility constantly reminds the inhabitants of its totality. The detention facility is located close to the middle of the building. It is surrounded by other parts of the building where people move freely, where children play and engage in sporting activities. Those living behind the barred windows are therefore constantly reminded of what it means to have their right of freedom of movement taken away from you. To those who move 'freely' around the detention facility, this is a reminder of the temporary nature of their current state, which can be changed at any time.

People living in the Ljubljana Asylum Home have to abide by the house rules, their rooms are supervised and the level of cleanliness is monitored every day at 7.30 A.M. They have to return back 'home' by 10 P.M., unless they are permitted to stay out late by the administration of the Home. Children are present at decision-making sessions, including negative evaluations, and live with the other residents among warehouses and factories (Zorn 2007a).

The Asylum Home employees carry out all interviews with the asylum seekers, including first contact interviews, at the Asylum Home. The decisions are announced there. The Asylum Home is a state institution with no sense of the public left within it; it acts more like a corporate entity in which relationships and also legal outcomes often depend on sympathies and relationships between administrators and asylum seekers. As the asylum seekers living in the Asylum Home, together with the activists of the Rog Social Centre (Statement of asylum seekers in the Republic of Slovenia 2008), pointed out in their public statement on 22 March 2008:

> An asylum seeker lives in a house that imprisons and many of the freedoms of the asylum seeker are only apparent . . . We believe that, when examining our asylum applications, the Interior Ministry, or the Asylum Home it represents, acts outside jurisdictions. Namely, negative decisions do not comply with valid legal acts and regulations, but are rather based on emotions, 'logical references', suppositions and assumptions denying dangers imposed on asylum seekers, as well as on the basis of the 'I believe or I do not believe' criteria.

International regulations enable inherently violent relationships between 'landlords' and 'tenants' in the Asylum Home which renders it a home that can never really be a home, that is in fact designed to be oppressive and transitory – a sort of anti-home. The concept of home, which is often seen only in positive terms, as a binding or unifying force, is, by this same principle, an exclusionary force, which can be channelled towards violence and hatred. We could argue that at home, actions are often based on emotions and that outsiders can be harshly separated from insiders. Angelika Bammer (1992) argues that home, like the nation, is a fictional construct. She says that home is a 'mythic narrative', through which the power of distinction between 'us' and 'them' is consolidated. There is 'the power to create not only an identity for ourselves as members of a community ... but also the discursive right to a space (a country, a neighbourhood, a place to live)' (Bammer 1992: ix–x). Mitzi Goldman links imaginings of home with mechanisms of exclusion (which is linked back to hatred) in so far as 'a unified sense of self and nation depends on the exclusion or "othering" of any foreign element that disrupts that image of unity' (Goldman in Morley 2008: 31). Benjamin Disraeli even declared that 'home is a barbarous idea; the method of a rude age; home is isolation; therefore anti-social' (Disraeli in Morley 2008: 17). So, in this regard, there is an ironic tension between the exclusion of asylum seekers in the apparent defence of the Slovenian homeland, and those who are then left yearning for the very security that is also the basis of their exclusion.

Nevertheless, even in theory, there is an important distinction between a home and the Asylum Home. Time spent at the Asylum Home is a time of instability and flux that people experience when they lose connections and networks that are as physical as they are symbolic: when they lose their home in search of another place to call a home. The Asylum Home is a place to stay while on this journey; it is neither fixed nor stable. 'The narrative of leaving home produces too many homes and hence no Home', claims Sara Ahmed (Ahmed 2000: 78). Movement between homes in fact allows 'the home' to become a 'fetish'; home is thus somewhere one travels to, at once a destination and 'the impossibility and necessity of the subject's future (one never gets there, but is always getting there)' (ibid.). The Asylum Home presents a rite of passage toward this impossibility. It presents us with a paradox, because the stories of people inhabiting the Home are fundamentally oriented towards the future – bound in movement and transition – but they are contained in an inflexible, static structure that prevents them from moving.

Trajectories of Resistance

Asylum and immigration law are conditioned by political claims concerning security and the protection of territories and the borders surrounding those territories, which are driven by (and feed into) the logic and the politics of fear. Sara Ahmed argues that 'the economy of fear works to contain the bodies of others. This is a containment whose "success" relies on its failure, as it must keep open the very grounds of fear. In this sense, fear works as an affective economy' (Ahmed 2004: 127). The plan and organization of contained places, such as the Asylum Home, stem from the fear of the impossibility of containment (ibid.: 124).

In a sense, the walls of the Asylum Home replace the bodies' porous limits, a person's fluid relationship to the world, with a hard edge. In the West today, Jean-Luc Nancy argues, the shores or banks – which are points of departure and arrival and are always uncertain; not belonging to anyone specifically – have been displaced. In this world 'the edge hardens and the limit closes' (ibid.: 52). It could therefore be argued that the limits of the Asylum Home reflect the edges of the European Union.

In 2008, two young Russian men who arrived in Slovenia without identification documents, and who were found likely to exploit the asylum procedure, were detained in the closed department of the Ljubljana Asylum Home. During their lunch break one afternoon they slashed their wrists and were rushed to hospital. They were subsequently returned to the detention facility. They opposed their return to the closed department, and after their demands to be transferred to the 'open' part of the Home were not met, they embarked upon a hunger strike. Soon after they escaped from the Asylum Home.

Even though there was little public debate following these events, their acts brought some journalists to the Asylum Home. Activists intensified their opposition, claiming that the Asylum Home was not a place for the protection of people that lived in it, but a place of their endangerment. In their opinion, the human rights of asylum seekers were not being upheld and the procedures used by the staff and officials working with asylum seekers were inhumane (Azilanta odklanjata hrano 2008). Some asylum seekers also voiced their opinions, but the two men who provoked this attention mostly stayed silent. Only one of the news reports at the time broadcasted a short interview with one of the men, in which he said that he was seeking protection for the first time and instead of help, got detention (ibid.).

How can we understand the acts of self-harm by asylum seekers? Can we in any sensible way insert them into the logic of the operation of such institutions? Who or what do they respond to? Michel Foucault argued that 'the liberty of men is never assured by the institutions and laws intended to guarantee them. This is why almost all of these laws and institutions are quite capable of being turned around – not because they are ambiguous, but simply because "liberty" is what must be exercised' (Foucault 2000: 354–55). So in this way we can understand acts of self-harm such as cutting one's wrists or embarking on a hunger strike as acts of resistance. Acts such as these can be seen as a response to the logic of the system. By violently transgressing their bodies in reaction to incarceration, they challenge the attempt made to control their bodies and identities. We can say that it is a part of the process or of the possibility of becoming free, emerging from the condition of un-freeness, which always entails the chance of staying un-free in the future. Because the asylum seekers' accommodation centres, similar to detention centres, can be seen as 'abject spaces' (Agamben 1998) where people are treated as 'those without presence', a decision to harm one's own body is a way of creating 'spaces of resistance' (Isin and Rygiel 2007: 185). Spaces of resistance are attached to every subjectivity, as a means of influencing the whole system.

In order to understand the event at the Asylum Home in Ljubljana as a way of 'setting the edge to the limit' (following Nancy's narrative), we can argue that resorting to harming one's own body represents a way of re-possessing it. It is a way of dismissing the 'zones of indistinction' (Diken 2004), non-places (Augé 1995) or empty spaces (Agamben 2005) which a refugee is forced to inhabit, in order to retain their own identity and agency of self. In this sense, harming one's body is a way of challenging the fear that leads to the containment of bodies of those considered as the Other. The silent act at the Asylum Home, which is reminiscent of numerous similar acts which have occurred in detention centres around the world, is a way of making oneself present, of disturbing the trajectory of fear initiated and controlled by the asylum.[4] In Nancy's words, edges are there to disclose the limit.

The subject is defined by its limits. This enables a dialogical encounter (Bakhtin 1990) between the internal and the external, which renders this limit porous, a space of breath, of exchange (Irigaray 2002). The inside has become the outside, even though it is exactly its interiority that makes expressions of distrust, unhappiness and disobedience possible.

In the Light of Silence

We could describe living at the Asylum Home as like living in a tight, demanding burrow[5] where 'one is supposed to be safe, neatly tucked inside', but as Kafka's story shows, 'in the most intimate place of shelter one is thoroughly exposed; the inside is inherently fused to the outside' (Dolar 2006: 167). What we may forget, however, is that the same goes for the world outside the Asylum Home; the one deemed to set the rules. There is a constant process of exchange happening between these two worlds. The dichotomy of inside and outside and their connectedness not only relate to the organizational structure, but also to 'something which exists in the most intimate of organisms' (Dolar 2006: 167). From such a perspective the paradoxes of official governmental rhetoric becomes evident. It is a paradox to say, as the Head of the Sector for Asylum has said, that residents of the Asylum Home can enjoy an 'absolute freedom if they abide by the House rules and ask for the permission to leave the Home at certain times' (Azilanta odklanjata hrano 2008). Such a conditional 'freedom' is and cannot be 'absolute'; it is only provisional. Similarly, the status that adheres to that 'freedom' – the status of a seeker of international protection – is only provisional and conditional. The politics of exclusion adopts a contradictory attitude whereby the decisions concerning who is and who is not permitted to participate in the wider political and social sphere is never entirely clear, and is administered in an arbitrary fashion, even though it works through the protection of the law.

We could say that acts of self-harm in such an environment still work in accordance with the state discourse that objectifies subjects by denying them the language with which to speak and in this way stripping them of their origin, since, according to Giorgio Agamben (1998), it is only in language that the subject has its site and origin.[6] We could see the manifestations mentioned as a 'proclamation of [the] inhumane', of one without language merely producing sounds (according to Agamben), not language which serves to declare what is just and unjust. No conversation, no negotiation follows the moment of denying someone the ability to speak. For many theorists discussion would stop at this point. However, we can and should be able to go beyond this juxtaposition of power. Being dispossessed of language, of the ability to speak, does not necessarily lead to muteness; it does not withdraw all agency from the dispossessed. What this dispossession rather reveals is a complex temporal and spatial web of encounter between the two worlds of the subject and the subjected (Ahmed 2000: 8) or, as the philosopher Mladen Dolar would say, reveals silence itself. It is in this space of silence, where the dialectics dissolve, that the two worlds meet one another.

Conversations, dialogues and outflows accompany relationships of struggle and power. This is what 'acts of resistance' can teach us. We should not forget that any system or politics carries people and stories with it. Writing about the former Australian detention facility at Woomera, Nikos Papastergiadis (2006: 438) remarks that:

> No human interaction can remain devoid of meaning and value. Although the camp is designed as the place in which such distinctions are suspended, it also produces its own counter responses. It inspires resistance and it leaks. Not only will the refugee eventually leave the camp, but the administrators must also go home with their own stories.

The silence that surrounds the accommodation, reception and detention centres is not serene and peaceful. One would not want a silence of this kind creeping into one's own home. The 'home' of the Asylum Home or a detention centre is not quiet even though it might be silent. As Papastergiadis notes, we can distinguish the home from the 'anti-home' by the status of silence: 'In the home silence signifies tranquillity ... whereas in the anti-home silence is filled with a deafening anguish' (Papastergiadis in Morley 2008: 48). Silence is there 'to provide space for voice' (Dolar 2006: 152). The acts of self-harm provide one of these voices.

Conclusion

As Luce Irigaray remarks, '[s]ilence is the speaking of the threshold', and 'relations between two different subjectivities cannot be set up starting from a shared common meaning, but rather from a silence, which each one agrees to respect in order to let the other be' (Irigaray 2008: 5). It would not be justifiable to say that in the case presented, the silence produced received silence in return because there was an understanding and respect existing between the men and asylum officials. But if the silence is met by silence, because it does not demand anything (Dolar 2006: 172), then the silence actually announces a law, some kind of human law, or law of humanity, 'the zero-point of voice, its pure embodiment' (Dolar 2006: 172). Referring to the act of stitching the lips together, performed by asylum seekers in the Villawood detention centre in Western Sydney in 2002, Sara Wills notes that by this act of self harm, asylum seekers are not only saying 'you refuse to let me be in this space, you refuse to let me see, you refuse to let me speak', but also 'you refuse to see, you refuse to speak' (Wills 2004: 65).[7]

The silence across the iron fence or razor wire therefore marks our common existence and questions our understanding of home, because the suspicion and fear that is inherent to the experience of the unknown and the other means that our economy of fear also permeates places we should feel intimately connected to, secure at, places which we may call home. Feeling at home means also 'feeling at home with oneself', and as Martin Heidegger (2001) once said, homeliness is about reaching what is on the one hand closest to us but is, on the other hand, the most remote from us. It is about reaching the Other. However, this reaching never takes an actual form, but is in fact an ideal, an abstraction. And the Other is not just the other that stands on the opposite side to us. We may at least feel our bellies touching, and possibly our lips too, and if there is not much affection between us naturally, there is still a breath that brings us together. In this sense, there is always an intimate connection between the designations of 'me' and 'the Other', with the possibility of change arising from the differences, oppositions and tensions between the two.

It was only after two men cut their wrists at the Ljubljana Asylum Home that people 'on the outside' were able to see the Asylum Home and hear the people living there. Indeed, it was almost the first time that a debate around the issues of asylum had been initiated in Slovenia. Following this incident, a group of asylum seekers and former asylum seekers, together with the activists of the Rog Social Centre, formed the movement 'The World for Everyone', through which they attempted to make their voices heard, talk to the media, and proclaim their rights. Once a month, the voice of an asylum seeker could be heard at one of the radio stations in Ljubljana. A silent dissent embodied as self-harm created a threshold, through which people with names, faces and voices emerged.

Subsequently, not much has changed in Slovenia. The new International Protection Bill, which in general introduced more restrictive procedures (not all of which were in compliance with international law), began to operate despite the sustained opposition of NGOs, social movements and asylum seekers. In 2011 the new Aliens Act came into force. Seekers of international protection can still be kept in the closed department of their new 'Home', which is bounded by razor wire. The Asylum Home is still (dis)located in the industrial zone on the brinks of the city with poor public transport, which asylum seekers can hardly afford due to their employment restrictions. Nevertheless, it is encouraging to read and hear the opinions of people in Ljubljana saying that living next to the Asylum Home is not problematic or scary, that 'people are kind and they greet you on the street (in contrast to other Slovenians) and passing it [the Home] at whichever hour of the day is fine' (Azilni dom Vič: Ruska prosilca za azil sta si zaradi kratenja pravic prerezala žile 2008).

However, as long as people's presence and their rights are not acknowledged, and they continue to self-harm in order to gain 'recognition', a dialogue concerning the concepts of hospitality toward the Other will be inhibited. In order for such a dialogue to occur and be framed in a constructive manner, we need to recognize places that we call home as contradictory, complex and full of boundless limits.

Notes

1 From the short story of Franz Kafka, 'The Burrow' (1931).
2 The material sources that contributed to this chapter were gathered in published debates around the issue of asylum in Slovenia over the last decade; they include newspaper articles and readers' comments, radio broadcasts and television reports, statements of asylum seekers published in the media, public statements by social movements and civil initiatives, as well as the opinions of some Slovenian academics researching the topic.
3 The Centre for the Removal of Aliens housed the so called 'illegal immigrants' and was formally set up as a detention facility. However, because it was joined by the Asylum Home in Ljubljana prior to 2004, the employees did not fully distinguish between the two categories. People housed in the Centre were therefore often able to leave the Centre, pass through the Asylum Home and move around more or less freely.
4 In her ethnographic examination of the role of emotions in constituting the power relations within one of the UK removal centres, Alexandra Hall argues that '[u]nderstanding the immigration removal centre as a place of politics, resistance and emotion supplements notions of "the camp" as an empty, anomic space' (Hall 2010: 887).
5 I refer to one of Kafka's short stories titled 'The Burrow' (first published in 1931) which deals with the question of passing from the interior to the exterior.
6 Following Agamben's (1998) argument, infancy conceptualizes an experience of being without language, not in a temporal or developmental sense of preceding the acquisition of language in childhood, but rather as a condition of experience that precedes and continues to reside in any appropriation of language.
7 Sara Wills (2004) refers to an incident which occurred in the Villawood detention centre in Western Sydney in 2002, during which a teenage male, together with a couple of other young men, 'numbed his lip with an ice cube, then punched the

needle through, cross stitching his mouth, back and forth, six times. The right side of his mouth was drawn tight; the left not so much, leaving space to slip in a cigarette' (Levett 2008).

References

Agamben, G. 1998. *Homo Sacer: Sovereign Power and Bare Life*. Stanford: Stanford University Press.
_____. 2005. *State of Exception*. Chicago/London: The University of Chicago Press.
Ahmed, S. 2000. *Strange Encounters: Embodied Others in Post-Coloniality*. London/ New York: Routledge.
_____. 2004. 'Affective Economies', *Social Text 79* 22(2): 117–39.
Augé, M. 1995. *Non-places: Introduction to an Anthropology of Supermodernity*. London/New York: Verso.
'Azilanta odklanjata hrano [Asylum seekers rejecting food]'. *24 ur*, 20 February 2008. Retrieved 25 October 2010 from http://24ur.com/novice/slovenija/azilanta-odklanjata-hrano.html.
'Azilni dom Vič: Ruska prosilca za azil sta si zaradi kratenja pravic prerezala žile [Vič Asylum Home: Russian asylum seekers slit their wrists due to a breach of rights]'. *Dnevnik*, 20 February 2008. Retrieved 1 April 2013 from http://www.dnevnik.si/kronika/300228.
Bakhtin, M.M. 1990. *Art and Answerability*. Austin: University of Texas Press.
Bammer, A. 1992. 'Editorial', *New Formations* 17: ix–x.
Diken, B. 2004. 'From Refugee Camps to Gated Communities, Biopolitics and the End of the City', *Citizenship Studies* 8(1): 83–106.
Dolar, M. 2006. *A Voice and Nothing More*. Cambridge/London: MIT Press.
Foucault, M. 2000. *Power: Essential Works of Foucault 1954–1984, vol. 3*. London: Penguin Press.
Goffman, E. 1961. *Asylums: Essays on the Social Situation of Mental Patients and Other Inmates*. Garden City, NY: Anchor Books, Doubleday and Company, Inc.
Hage, G. 2002. Speech presented at 'Let's Talk about Race – Culture, Privilege and Prejudice' public forum, University of Western Australia, 12 September 2002. Retrieved 1 April 2013 from http://www.docstoc.com/docs/44370797/Let-s-Talk-About-Race-C-Culture-Privilege-and-Prejudice-concentrate.
Hall, A. 2010. 'These People Could be Anyone: Fear, Contempt (and Empathy) in a British Immigration Removal Centre', *Journal of Ethnic and Migration Studies* 36(6): 881–98.
Heidegger, M. 2001. *Poetry, Language, Thought*. New York: Harper and Row.
Irigaray, L. 2002. *Between East and West: From Singularity to Community*. New York: Columbia University Press.
_____. 2008. *Sharing the World*. London: Continuum.
Isin, E. and K. Rygiel. 2007. 'Of Other Global Cities: Frontiers, Zones, Camps', in B. Drieskens et al. (eds), *Cities of the South: Citizenship and Exclusion in the 21st Century*. London: Saqi, pp. 170–209.
Kafka, F. 1961. *Metamorphosis and Other Stories*. Victoria: Penguin Books.

Levett, C. 2008. 'The Other Side of the Fence', *Sydney Morning Herald*, 19 July 2008. Retrieved 25 October from http://www.smh.com.au/news/national/the-other-side-of-the-fence/2008/07/18/1216163156854.html?page=fullpage#conten tSwap1.

Milohnič, A. 2001. *Evropski vratarji: migracijske in azilne politike v vzhodni Evropi* [European Goalkeepers: Migration and Asylum Policies in Eastern Europe]. Ljubljana: Mirovni Inštitut.

Morley, D. 2008. *Home Territories: Media, Mobility and Identity*. London/New York: Routledge.

Oblak, B. 2001. 'Ilegalne migracije v Sloveniji ali Kako so Šiškarji postali "kseno-fobi"' [Illegal Migration in Slovenia or How the Residents of Šiška Became the 'Xenophobes'], Speech at the Faculty of Social Sciences roundtable Ilegalne migracije, Slovenija in EU – pro et contra, Ljubljana, 15 May. Retrieved 1 September 2010 from http://wega3.tripod.com/nastopFDV.html.

Papastergiadis, N. 2006. 'The Invasion Complex: The Abject Other and Spaces of Violence', *Geografiska Annaler* 88B(4): 429–42.

'Statement of asylum seekers in the Republic of Slovenia currently situated in the Asylum Home of Ljubljana, who, together with activists of the Social Centre Rog, formed the movement World for Everyone'. 2008. Retrieved 5 September 2010 from http://www.njetwork.org/Statement-of-asylum-seekers-in-the.

Wills, S. 2004. 'Losing the Right to Country: The Memory of Loss and the Loss of Memory in Claiming the Nation as Space (Or Being Cruel to be Kind in the "Multicultural" Asylum)', *New Formations* 51: 50–65.

Zorn, J. 2007a. 'The Right to Stay: Challenging the Policy of Detention and Deportation', *European Journal of Social Work* 12(2): 247–60.

———. 2007b. 'Izbrisani, migracije, EU [The Erased, Migration, EU]', *Terminal*, Radio Študent, Ljubljana, 1 March. Retrieved 1 October 2012 from http://old.radiostudent.si/article.php?sid=11251.

Epilogue

A Migrant or Circuitous Sensibility

Nigel Rapport

The tensions in migrant experience which the chapters in this collection evince are ones commonly noted: between opportunity and exclusion; between senses of becoming and achievement on the one hand, and loss and regret on the other. The tensions appear to be a constant of the contemporary world. As John Berger (1984: 55) has phrased it, market forces, ideological conflicts and environmental change now uproot such a large number of people that migration can more and more be portrayed as 'the quintessential experience' of the age. Exile, emigration, banishment, labour migrancy, tourism, urbanization and counter-urbanization are the central motifs of modern culture, Lewis Nkosi (1994: 5) suggests, and being rootless, displaced between worlds, living between a lost past and a fluid present, are 'typical symptoms of a modern condition at once local and universal'.

There is an image, one I often recall, from W.G. Sebald (2005: 211) which he intended as a kind of nightmarish motif and was something which he personally found it difficult to remove from the mind: 'Columns of trucks, with a cargo of refugees, move along dusty roads without stopping in zones of devastation around the world endlessly'. But then the trucks and their constant passing need not only presage a downward spiral. There is also the 'return to humanness', as Imre Kertesz (2010) described the release from Nazi death camps; and there is the ascent, the progress, personal and collective, from poverty, nescience and despotism to the openness of a liberal modernity. To migrate, in the imagery of the editor of this volume, Anne Sigfrid Grønseth, is to enter a zone of ambivalence; of memory and nostalgia but also of hope in new beginnings; of visions and life-projects that create a future as well as being impregnated by the past. There is a contrariety here, at least, which can be fruitful: fantasy and creativity existing alongside vulnerability and alienation, in the mind of the migrant. The journeying consciousness may open up spaces within which it comes into its own.

It is a privilege to have the final word. I do not abuse that privilege, I hope, in contributing a final chapter to this collection whose character is not ethnographic so much as inter-textual and referential, circuitous and citational. I find my own voice in migrating between the imagery and words of others (Kertesz, Sebald, Berger. . .).

In titling his book, *Migrancy Culture Identity* (without the use of any further syntax), Iain Chambers drew attention to the way in which migrancy, movement and travel describe not only a physical displacement, possibly unwanted, but also a more intrinsic aspect of the human condition. Selfhood, urbanity, translation, imagination, modernity were equally aspects of the nature of movement in human life. The act of writing, similarly, was 'everywhere characterized by movement: the passage of words, the caravan of thought, the flux of the imaginary, the slippage of the metaphor' (Chambers (1994: 10). There is, furthermore, a 'paradox in the belly of writing: like the ambiguity of travel, it starts from known materials – a language, a lexicon, a discourse, a series of archives – and yet seeks to extract from the limits of its movement, from the experience of transition, a surplus, an excess, leading to an unforeseen and unknown possibility' (Chambers 1994: 10).

Writing a circuitous essay in a citational style, I would hope to end at a point that reveals something new, excessive, of 'being human, being migrant' which makes the journey worthwhile.

Or is such a hope merely flippant? Is the image of writing – and of selfhood, translation, imagination, modernity, urbanity, whatever – as being intrinsically movemental – and therefore discerning movement as part of the nature of things and thus acceptable, even positive – a flippancy when placed next to Sebald's image of columns of trucks and their constant human cargo?

Sebald himself struggled with this in his own writing. Was it a moral act to write in spite of the columns of trucks? Even to write about the column of trucks? Was it moral merely to write? Sebald's conclusion was that it is inappropriate, ethically as well as epistemologically, to seek to approach the tragic experience of nightmarish displacements directly. Portrayals of terrible events that are, for instance, too sentimental in style (such as often seems the official culture that remembers and mourns the Holocaust) claim a false intimacy with the dead and embody a 'compromis[ing] moral position' (Sebald, cited in Homberger 2001). Sebald's own style of composing his texts of remembrance and testimony was famously circuitous.

Being Human, Being Migrant contains two very different notions. The comma between the two phrases can suggest equivalency or opposition. The comma, in other words, can connect (as if a colon or a hyphen) and equally it can differentiate (as if a dash or an oblique). Is it human to be migrant or is it human not to be migrant? The issue is both ontological and political. Ontologically the chapters in this book argue that is a human capacity, practice, need, history and right to migrate. Politically, they attest, it is often the case that the migrant is forced to move because his or her humanity is not accorded proper respect in an erstwhile location; and also, his or her humanity may not be accorded sufficient recognition, either, at the point where the column of trucks sheds its cargo.

In the remainder of this chapter I shall explore the notion that migration can be said to compass a way of being human that is particularly representative, particularly 'humane': I mean being migrant between cultural worlds, or customary frameworks of self and society. The image I have in mind comes from the novelist Sherwood Anderson and what he sees as the 'grotesque' way in which cultural difference and personal distance occurs through the process of exclusiveness and partisanship. Truth becomes falsehood, he suggests (1992: 23), when people try to live exclusively by fetichizing one component of the complexity of the human condition and by excluding others. There are a great many human truths, concerning virginity, passion, poverty, acquisition, carelessness, concentration, etc., and the humane option is to accord respect to them all, even to try to live by them all. But so often, instead, the human practice is to define me and mine through limitation: 'This is my cultural community and tradition: I do not believe or belong in what lies beyond the border'. The difficult but morally uplifting, humane stance is, in the earlier words of Robert Louis Stevenson (1892), to recognize that in the realm of culture: 'Everything is true; only the opposite is true too: you must believe both equally or be damned'.

The theme is given a more extended treatment in the novel by Stevie Smith, *Over the Frontier*, which she published in 1938. In her uniquely poetic style – in which autobiography is given merely a thin veneer of characterization – Smith tells the story of her alter ego, Pompey Casmilus, taking a journey from England to a Germany preparing for war. Pompey makes the journey in flight from a failed love affair and in search of a space for recuperation. She travels with a female friend to a spa, in the converted Schloss Tilssen, on the edge of the Baltic Sea. As the weeks of her rest-stay turn to months, she finds herself increasingly involved with other inmates of the spa regime, and the strange array of personalities and conditions they represent. She is led to imagine their pasts, and the true intentions behind their present idiosyncratic habits and peccadilloes. But do her flights of imaginative fancy come to include Pompey herself? We do not know. Pompey's reliability as narrator is never assured to the reader, never finally confirmed nor denied. What do we understand by her accounts of nights spent sailing the Baltic towards Lapland, of her forays into the local town and her befriending of the urbane and international 'Jew Aaronsen', and of the fellow inmates of the Schloss (Mrs Pouncer, Colonel Peck) who may only be pretending short-sightedness and absent-mindedness?

Pompey finds herself amorously falling for a young Englishman, Tom Satterthwaite, who gradually reveals to her that his mission is espionage. He makes regular forays away from the Schloss, over different borders, and relays to Britain information concerning military realities: plans, arms and troop-movements. Slowly he introduces Pompey herself into this world, enlisting her help. She dons a uniform and rides with him through the night;

she observes, she sleeps in safe houses, she fires on the enemy to escape safely with her information. But having stepped 'over the frontier' – from England to the Continent, from a nervous recuperation to a belligerent activity, from detachment to enlistment – she realizes at the sudden conclusion of the novel that she is not convinced by her role but also that there is now no return. She is not a good soldier, but equally she is no longer the innocent non-combatant that she was in London before her journey. She sees through the world of espionage, the mutual acts of distrust between warring enemies who are equally disreputable and inhuman in their military machinations; but she also sees through the framework of truths she took for granted in her previous London life. She finds herself 'over the frontier' of frontiers. Her recuperation gives way to a new, and difficult, but morally authentic restlessness.

There are two particular moral conclusions at which Pompey arrives which I would elaborate upon here. The first, as with Sherwood Anderson, concerns an impatience with partiality and partisanship. 'No, I am not interested to concentrate upon politics, fascism or communism, or upon any *groupismus* whatever', Pompey comes to assert (Smith 1985: 256), because all are variations upon a theme whose exaggerated exclusivity and sectarianism is blatantly false, boring and banal. Instead, 'C'est la vie entière que c'est mon métier', Pompey cites (without further attribution): the human speciality should be an interest in giving recognition to, and providing testimony of, the tantalizing nature of the complex complete human condition, and not in fetichizing any one particular projection. 'England' and 'Germany', 'masculine' and 'feminine', 'separating' and 'engaging', 'resting' and 'achieving' – such cultural classes arrive at a true comprehension of human nature only together, not by way of the sectarian exclusiveness that fixates upon and essentializes and privileges one over another.

Second, Pompey considers the fate of 'Jew Aaronsen'. He is the most intelligent and cultured person whom she has met on her journey, and she feels a desire to protect the civilitude he represents by wiping out his barbaric German enemies utterly. But is not such a desire itself a sign of intolerance? And is not the 'idealismus' of the Jews, the proud and stubborn differentiation, a provocation and presage to martyrdom? Is there not a 'too willing martyrarchy' in setting up and maintaining against all the odds, through the centuries and geographies of oppression, a sociality that makes exclusivity an end in itself? The Jew inspires persecution, Pompey fears —and feels that immorality in her own (English) entrails.

What, then, would be the moral intentionality? This is, Pompey concludes, to cross the frontier of formal, behavioural, collective exclusivity by taking all persecuting and persecuted idealism with 'a pinch of salt', overcoming the German-Jewish stand-off, believing in both cultural worlds, and in neither. In practical terms, one must perhaps pay lip-service to the frameworks of cultural convention, to the established hierarchy of cultural truths, but one retains an ironizing practice with regard to such fetichization. Paying lip-service may seem an act of political-moral quietue but the ironic is actually a proud and 'mighty spear thrust of derision' which cuts to the heart (Smith 1985: 198–99). This is how civilization is preserved for more enlightened times: through the pinch of salt that guarantees one's independent, migrant consciousness:

> Scatter the salt before the Roman gods, acquiesce in the uttermost fantastic formularies of the inquisition, ratify the amendments, sign the protocols, scatter, acquiesce, ratify and sign, but keep your heart to yourself for a space to laugh in, for not the most searching pang can strip naked the inmost core of laughter within a secret heart, that holds fierce and close within itself the power to dispel the dream, the dream that persecutes and is persecuted. [. . .] [Idealismus and groupismus are] slain, slain and finally slain by the laughter behind an acquiescence that mocks and kills.

Strategic essentialism, or, indeed, any form of cultural fundamentalism (Smith's 'idealismus' and 'groupismus'), is the target my Epilogue would hit. To prescribe *a migrant or circuitous sensibility* is to urge that claims to fixed identities, classes and categories, to closed communities, cultures and traditions, should be deemed ontologically and morally illegitimate. In the words of Ernest Gellner (1993: 3–4): 'We are all human [. . .] Don't take more specific classifications seriously. [. . .] Don't freeze people in their social categories. In the end we are all human'.

To say we are all – and only – human is also to say that we are all individuals. For it is in individuality, individual embodiment, that humanity manifests itself. As F.R. Leavis (1972: 53) observed, it is always and only as 'a man' that 'humanity' appears before us: 'only in living individuals is life there, and individual lives cannot be aggregated or equated or dealt with quantitatively in any way'. What, then, is the 'social condition' that has nothing to do with the 'individual condition', and 'what is the "social hope" that transcends, cancels or makes indifferent the inescapable tragic condition of each individual?' (Leavis 1972: 53).

This is, indeed, a conclusion of venerable descent, taking us back to the humanistic revolutions in knowledge and justice that began with the European Renaissance: 'Chaque homme porte la forme entière de l'humaîne condition' (1965: 782), concluded Michel de Montaigne, one of its representative figures. Each individual human being carried the history of humanity within himself or herself and each life was an exemplar of human life; since, to be human was to be individual. The paradox that linked particular and general in this way – the way in which individual particularity could be an exemplification of the generality of the human, and the way in which the individual, 'Everyman', should be accorded the respect, integrity and dignity that one would grant to Humanity – provided Montaigne with the subject matter of his famous *Essais*. Published in 1580, these amounted to a number of short subjective treatments of a diversity of topics (experience, solitude, physiognomy, monstrous children, cholera, cannibalism, the verse of Virgil, virtue, vanity, repentance). Montaigne's aim was that his honest self-portrayal might be read as a mirror of the human whole; by being true to himself he would be expressing human truths. But more than this, his self-expressions did not necessarily comprise a system. Indeed, the individual was a complex entity and self-contradictory, internally inconsistent. Nevertheless, all the individual's (contradictory) truths remained his or her own, since they were the product of the same individual body; bodily integrity guaranteed individual authenticity. Here, then, were *Montaigne's Essais, Montaigne's* interpretations: together they espoused no single point of view but in moving among the variety, owning up to it all, he, Montaigne, came to recognize, and could begin to comprehend, the true complex nature of the human.

'What do I know?', Montaigne prescribed as a personal motto, and yet he also ascribed dignity to the human in attempting to know, however much the non-rational and random might exist alongside rationality in human cognition. Montaigne's *proscriptions*, meanwhile, concerned the arrogance, pride, fearfulness and narrowness which gave rise to closed worlds of custom and tradition, and the intolerance and fanaticism that accompanied a doctrinaire or fundamentalistic practice.

Since each human being bore the stamp of the species whole, Montaigne was particularly concerned with individual well-being. How might the essentially human, inconsistent and migrant sensibility accrue happiness? Self-knowledge was key, Montaigne felt (hence the 'therapy' of writing autobiographical essays). Equally important was the space to move. One moved between varieties of experience and varieties of interpretation of experience; between past, present and future awarenesses; and between experience and the experience of experience, the meta-experience that represented self-knowledge. And how did one achieve this space? Writing at a time of religious warring in Europe, between Roman Catholic and Protestant absolutisms, Montaigne urged detachment. The individual should find his or her freedom and happiness through an inner tranquility, detaching his or her sensibility from the repressive practice of cultural classification and social structuration. One achieved space by effecting a distance between public convention and exchange and one's independent, unfettered consciousness. In other words, Montaigne would appear to agree with what Stevie Smith described as taking repressive forms of life where possible with a 'pinch of salt'. One practices a freedom of individual conscience and consciousness, and lives one's difference amid political and behavioural quietude, because once one engages absolutism with an opposite desire – utterly to destroy it – however moral, one delivers oneself up to a situation of violence and anarchy.

But then the inquisitions of Spain, of Nazi Germany, now of the mullahs' Iran, threaten self-expression even at these depths. A cynical fitting-in would not have saved the Jew Aaronsen in Stevie Smith's narrative, as it did not save the countless victims of religious oppression following the Protestant Reformation in Montaigne's Europe. It has not been always possible to escape martyrdom, ostracism, banishment or forcible 'resocialization' through practising irony in one's heart. There is a human right to demand more: a space for the free migrant consciousness which is publicly anticipated and sanctioned.

This demand might be briefly stated: the individual migrant sensibility claims a space in which to come into its own. The self is an individual's rightful life-project, and the future is the self's paradigmatic domain (Rapport 2003). Whatever may be the cultural traditions of the past and the social structures of the present, the future is the individual's birthright: here he or she puts into effect the lineaments of his or her perfectly original and unique vision. It would be a definition of a universal liberal society – a 'cosmopolis' – that it recognized its individual citizens in terms of their capacities and their 'rights to become' in ways and shapes that cannot be known (defined, classified, limited, apportioned) in advance (Rapport 2010b).

One of the key insights of Gregory Bateson's work on cybernetics was that repetitive movement can become part of a process: the repetition can give rise to something new, can deliver change and need not represent merely more of the same. In other words, to inhabit a migrant consciousness, always moving between positions, can be truly insightful. Bateson's most famous application of this was in the concept of schismogenesis: 'a process of differentiation in the norms of individual behaviour resulting from cumulative interaction between individuals' (1936: 175). If a relationship takes the form of two individuals or groups who always react to the behaviour of the other, then an exponential differentiation can develop, following simple mathematical laws. Rather than a mere to-ing and fro-ing, the movement between participants in the relationship gives rise to a qualitative change. 'Complementary schismogenesis' describes the progression of a relationship wherein the behaviour of the partners becomes increasingly polarized: the more sadistic, for instance, the one partner becomes, the more masochistic the other becomes. 'Symmetrical schismogenesis' describes a progressive change in a relationship where the behaviour of partners becomes increasingly similar: the more generous or indignant or warlike the one partner becomes, the more so the other.

The more general application of the insight, Bateson felt (1980: 141), was that 'recursion' or repetitive movement lay behind all kinds of communicative processes, and was key, too, to an understanding of consciousness and self-knowledge. The human mind was characterized by circular (and more complex) recursive chains of determination. This recursiveness gave rise to the organism's autonomy and individuality, also its self-control. It was through an awareness of repetition, an experiencing of experience, that the human mind came to know itself, became able to correct itself, able to experiment and make choices, and to apprehend order.

My point, and the end-point of this essay (which it is to be hoped makes the circuitous journey worthwhile), is that the repetitive (possibly forced) migration across cultural boundaries, between cultural worlds and closed communities, such as Sebald despaired of forgetting, can be party to a processual knowledge. The migrant comes to see beyond cultural closure: to know that no 'idealismus' and 'groupismus' is sufficient. The migrant comes to apprehend that it is in a migrant or circuitous consciousness as such that the human is to be essentially found, and that the humane or moral stance is to dwell in and to dwell upon that movement.

Growing up in the Gorbals is the autobiographical and novelistic account, by Ralph Glasser, of Jewish migrants who left Baltic ports such as Riga, and the pogroms of the Russian empire in the late nineteenth century, to find the Golden Land, in America. En route some found themselves in the slums of Glasgow and stayed. It would not be true to say that they established a 'community' in the Gorbals, however, Glasser observes (1986: 21), because the strongest bond among the collection of exiles was a negative one: to 'close the door firmly on the past'. They sought an 'ultimate escape' from poverty and oppression, and saw this not in a sentimental fixation upon the past, and not in roseate vignettes of *stetl* life and semi-rural Judaism. 'For many exiles, and even more so for their children, the best solution for the Jewish Problem was to cease to be Jews' (Glasser 1986: 21).

In analytical terms, a migrant sensibility encourages, nurtures, the human potential for emancipation from what John Stuart Mill (1963: 194) famously dubbed the 'despotism of custom', from the closures and limitations of cultural fundamentalism and all fashions of communitarian essentialism: religiosity, ethnicity, nationalism, localism (cf. Rapport 2010a). Instead, one embraces a human inheritance of diversity and wholeness, and espouses an ethos of openness, movement and the recursive process of true knowledge in an individual life.

References

Anderson, S. 1992. *Winesberg, Ohio*. Harmondsworth: Penguin.

Bateson, G. 1936. *Naven: A Survey of the Problems Suggested by a Composite Picture of a New Guinea Tribe Drawn from Three Points of View*. Cambridge: Cambridge University Press.

———. 1980. *Mind and Nature: A Necessary Unity*. Glasgow: Fontana.

Berger, J. 1984. *And Our Faces, My Heart, Brief as Photos*. London: Writers & Readers.

Chambers, I. 1994. *Migrancy Culture Identity*. London: Routledge.

Gellner, E. 1993. 'The Mightier Pen? Edward Said and the Double Standards of Inside-out Colonialism', *Times Literary Supplement*, 19 February, pp. 3–4.

Glasser, R. 1986. *Growing up in the Gorbals*. London: Pan.

Homberger, E. 2001. 'Obituary: W. G. Sebald', *The Guardian Newspaper*, 17 December. Retrieved 1 December 2009 from http://www.guardian.co.uk/news/2001/dec/17/guardianobituaries.books1.

Kertesz, I. 2010. 'Dossier K', talk presented at the Deutsch-Amerikanisches Institut, Heidelberg, 14 October.

Leavis, F.R. 1972. *Nor Shall My Sword: Discourses on Pluralism, Compassion and Social Hope*. London: Chatto & Windus.

Mill, J.S. 1963. *The Six Great Humanistic Essays of John Stuart Mill*. New York: Washington Square.

Montaigne, M. 1965. *Essais (Livre III)*. Paris: Bibliotheque de la Pleiade.

Nkosi, L. 1994. 'Ironies of Exile: Post-colonial Homelessness and the Anticlimax of Return', *Times Literary Supplement*, 1 April, p. 5.

Rapport, N. 2003. *I am Dynamite: An Alternative Anthropology of Power*. London: Routledge.

———. 2010a. 'Cosmopolitanism and Liberty', *Social Anthropology* 18(4) : 464–70.

———. 2010b. 'Human Capacity as an Exceeding, a Going Beyond', in N. Rapport (ed.), *Human Nature as Capacity: Transcending Discourse and Classification*. Oxford: Berghahn, pp. 1–26.

Sebald, W.G. 2005. *Campo Santo*. Harmondsworth: Penguin.

Smith, S. 1985. *Over the Frontier*. London: Virago.

Stevenson, R.L. 1892. *Across the Plains*. London: Scribner's.

Notes on Contributors

Christina Georgiadou is a PhD candidate in Social Anthropology at the Aegean University. She is conducting research on Afghan refugees living in Greece. Her fields of interest are research ethics, activist anthropology, everyday life, and refugee and migration policies. She studied medicine and is currently specializing in psychiatry while also volunteering in NGO refugee services in Athens.

Anne Sigfrid Grønseth is an Associate Professor in Social Anthropology at the Department of Pedagogy and Social Science at University College of Lillehammer, Norway, where she directs the Research Unit of Health, Culture and Identity. Until recently she held an additional one-year position as Senior Researcher at the Norwegian Centre for Minority Health Research. Recent publication are *Lost Selves and Lonely Persons: Experiences of Illness and Well-Being among Tamil Refugees in Norway* (Carolina Academic Press, 2010) and *Mutuality and Empathy. Self and Other in the Ethnographic Encounter* (ed. with D.L. Davis) (Sean Kingston Publishing, 2010).

Naoko Maehara is a doctoral student in Social Anthropology at Queen's University Belfast. Her thesis focused on the emotional dynamics of cross-border married life, and was conducted with Japanese migrant women in Ireland. Her interests range from transnationalism to globalization and from psychological anthropology to emotion and memory studies.

Maša Mikola is a Research Fellow at the Centre for Citizenship and Globalisation at Deakin University in Melbourne, Australia. She completed her PhD at the University of Nova Gorica, Slovenia in 2009, with a dissertation focusing on migration and the issues of space, place and belonging in Melbourne. She researches in the fields of migration, citizenship, youth issues and urban anthropology.

Barbara Pinelli is a lecturer in Anthropology of Migration at the University of Milano-Bicocca. She is currently researching female forced migration to Italy along the Libya-Mediterranean Sea route and conducts her research in the refugee camps. In particular, her research interests are focused on the camp as a structure of power, control and discipline, on multiple and overlapping forms of violence and abuse that shape the lives of women asylum seekers, and on the formation and reconstruction of subjectivity in conditions of suffering and vulnerability.

Nigel Rapport (FRSE) is Professor of Anthropological and Philosophical Studies at the University of St. Andrews, Scotland, where he directs the Centre for Cosmopolitan Studies. He has also held the Canada Research Chair in Globalization, Citizenship and Justice at Concordia University of Montreal. His research interests include social theory, identity and individuality, and links between anthropology and literature and philosophy. His most recent book is *Anyone, the Cosmopolitan Subject of Anthropology* (Berghahn, 2012).

Maruška Svašek is Reader in Social Anthropology at Queen's University Belfast and Co-Director of the Cultural Dynamics and Emotions Network. Her main research interests include migration, emotions and material culture. Recent books include *Emotions and Human Mobility. Ethnographies of Movement* (Routledge, 2012) and *Moving Subjects, Moving Objects. Transnationalism, Cultural Production and Emotions* (Berghahn, 2012). She is also co-editor (with Birgit Meyer) of the book series *Material Mediations: People and Things in a World of Movement* (Berghahn).

Index